For dear Jurij,

—with the respect of a student
and the love of a devoted friend.

Love X
April 28, 1992

POST-CONTEMPORARY

INTERVENTIONS

Series Editors: Stanley Fish & Fredric Jameson

THE TAO

AND THE LOGOS

Literary Hermeneutics, East and West

ZHANG LONGXI

DUKE UNIVERSITY PRESS Durham & London 1992

Grateful acknowledgment is made for the
following permissions:
T. S. Eliot: Excerpts from "Little Gidding,"
"Burnt Norton," "East Coker," and "The Dry
Salvages" in Four Quartets. Copyright 1943 by
T. S. Eliot and renewed 1971 by Esme Valerie
Eliot. Reprinted by permission of Harcourt
Brace Jovanovich, Inc., and Faber and Faber Ltd.
Stéphane Mallarmé. Excerpts from "L'Après-
midi d'un faune," in French Symbolist Poetry,
trans. C. F. MacIntyre. Copyright © 1958 by
The Regents of the University of California.
Reprinted by permission.
Rainer Maria Rilke: Excerpts from The Selected
Poetry of Rainer Maria Rilke by Rainer Maria
Rilke, edited by Stephen Mitchell. Copyright
© 1982 by Stephen Mitchell. Reprinted by per-
mission of Random House, Inc. Excerpts from
The Sonnets to Orpheus by Rainer Maria Rilke,
translated by Stephen Mitchell. Copyright ©
1985 by Stephen Mitchell. Reprinted by permis-
sion of Simon & Schuster, Inc.
© 1992 Duke University Press
All rights reserved
Printed in the United States of America
on acid-free paper ∞
Library of Congress Cataloging-in-Publication
Data appear on the last page of this book.

To Weilin

Contents

Preface

The present study of the nature of language and its implications for both the making of literature and its reading has grown out of my sustained interest in hermeneutics—the art of understanding and interpretation—considered in the perspective of East-West comparative poetics. Not very long ago, hermeneutics as a term was known only to a limited number of specialists in some special fields, but in recent years it has increasingly become a household word in the discussion of various branches of human studies, particularly in theology, law, and literary theory. Most of these discussions, however, are not just informed by philosophical hermeneutics but are also circumscribed by it and are confined within limits of the Western tradition alone. This seems to me quite unsatisfactory because understanding and interpretation are not just philosophical categories designed for a purely theoretical interest; they are rather the immanent facts of life: they are, so to speak, part and parcel of human existence. "*Understanding*," says Hans-Georg Gadamer in reference to Heidegger's existential analysis of Being, is "the *original form of the realization of Dasein*, which is being-in-the-world. Before any differentiation of understanding into the various directions of pragmatic or theoretical interest, understanding is *Dasein*'s mode of being, insofar as it is potentiality-for-being and 'possibility.'"[1] That is to say, instead of being a theoretical construct, the hermeneutic phenomenon is ontologically constitutive of human life, for human beings can exist and develop only to the extent that they can adequately understand and work out the relationship between their being and the world in which they find themselves. The relationship of the Self with regard to the Other, which manifests itself everywhere in life, already forms the context in which the hermeneutic problem necessarily arises. Obviously, then, hermeneutics has implications that are truly universal; it is not and cannot be limited to one particular realm of study, to one culture or one tradition.

It is against the background of Western philosophical hermeneutics that I have come to think about language and interpretation from a perspective that incorporates the non-Western. There is no need for me to dwell on the importance of language, since the problem of language has so often come to occupy the center of twentieth-century theoretical discussions—in analytical philosophy as well as phenomenology, in structuralism as well as poststructuralism—and since the understanding of speech and written texts has always been the hermeneutic problem par excellence. My discussion of the nature of language, however, though grounded in philosophical hermeneutics, eventually departs from it by concentrating on a particular set of problems in understanding literature. In other words, the focus of attention in my study is a specifically *literary* hermeneutics based on an examination of the language poets use, and an inquiry into the implications of such language for the reading and interpretation of literature. Of course, much has been written on literary hermeneutics, notably by Hans Robert Jauss in relation to his theory of an aesthetics of reception. According to Jauss, the hermeneutic process may be profitably separated into a triad of "an initial, aesthetically perceptive reading," "a second, retrospectively exegetical reading," and "a third, historical reading," of which the different horizons, "the hermeneutic difference between the former and the current understanding of a work," constitute the basis for a new way of looking at literary history, a "method of historical reception."[2] In my study of literary hermeneutics, however, I am not concerned with dividing the reading experience into different phases to set up the hermeneutic distance between past and present understanding of a literary work. Indeed, I suspect that the reconstruction of a past horizon of expectations, which for Jauss is a prerequisite for reception theory, can at best be considered as methodologically useful in the study of literary history—especially in delineating changes of aesthetic taste and social norms—but we cannot take such historical reconstruction for granted without being critically aware of its premises and its tentative, hypothetical nature. Without in any way denying the significance of literary hermeneutics for the aesthetics of reception, I am nevertheless more interested in rethinking the metaphorical nature of language, the inherent inadequacy and suggestiveness involved in the use of words as signs and symbols, and the implications of all these for the writing and reading of literature. Such questions are undoubtedly at the center of much debate in contemporary literary theory, which has to a large extent shaped my discussion of hermeneutic problems in this book.

It is perhaps on the basis of its scope of observation that the present study may ask to be distinguished from what has already been written in the study of philosophical or literary hermeneutics, for my discussion of language and interpretation goes beyond the boundaries of the Western critical tradition to include a more extensive view from the vantage point of *East-West* comparative studies. So far virtually no work has been done in literary hermeneutics that attempts to bring the East and the West to a fruitful mutual illumination, while many journal articles and essays under the rubric of East-West comparative literature seem to me deficient either because they juxtapose texts from different cultural traditions without justifying the choice of those texts for comparison or because they mechanically apply terms, concepts, and approaches of Western criticism to non-Western works.[3] The ground or justification for comparison has been a vexed question for comparative literature from the very beginning, but the validity of comparative literature never comes so close to a real crisis as when the comparison involves the East and the West, between which there is little *rapports de faits* and for which the only appropriate discourse of critical commentary, many would argue, is the discourse of difference. But comparative literature by now should have outgrown the search for actual contacts between writers of different nations and the influence of one upon the other—the tracing of sources, borrowings, and indebtedness René Wellek once sarcastically called the "foreign trade" of literature.[4] If direct contacts and relations no longer constitute the only legitimate ground for comparison, it is then possible to see that comparative poetics —that is, the study of critical and theoretical issues shared by the East and the West—may yield much more interesting and valuable results than the traditional kind of influence study.

Literary theory, which by definition transcends national and linguistic boundaries, provides a truly fertile ground for comparison and promises a great deal of insight into the art of literature by examining a variety of culturally heterogeneous and historically unrelated works. Theory opens a new vista for comparative studies, but a theoretically informed study must put different cultural traditions on an equal footing. In other words, a study in comparative poetics must not merely apply Western concepts and approaches to non-Western texts, but must consider and examine theoretical issues from a critical perspective that incorporates both the East and the West. If literary theory is thinking critically of literature and interpretation, the study of theory must also think critically of theory itself—and not least of the very differentiation of the East and the West.

Perhaps I should make it clear at this point that the word "East" used in this book refers mainly to the cultural and literary tradition of China, though there is also some discussion of the philosophy of the great Indian Buddhist thinker Nagarjuna. Such an arbitrarily synecdochic use of the word *East* is not meant to deny the distinctions among the various cultures of the East, but the arbitrariness of the word serves to call in question the very name of the East as opposed to the West. Once the usually unquestioned meaning of the word is brought to conscious reflection, it becomes possible to dismantle the fixation of a cultural dichotomy we call the East and the West—and especially to avoid the pitfall of ethnocentrism in cultural studies, the bad practice of imposing the values and conceptual apparatus of the one on the other. What I have attempted to do in this book, then, is not to apply Western hermeneutic theory to the reading of Chinese literature but to look into the very concept of hermeneutics—that is, the relationship between language and interpretation as it has been conceived in the Western critical tradition and in classical Chinese poetics. This may on the one hand introduce to readers and literary scholars in the West a dimension of hermeneutic theory from a very different cultural context, while on the other hand help systematize our understanding of the Chinese critical tradition by piecing together insights and utterances that are scattered over the voluminous writings of Chinese philosophy, poetry, and criticism. In this sense, the present study is also an attempt to suggest a consistent line of hermeneutic thinking in Chinese poetics.

Such a study is theoretical only in the sense that it is an investigation of the extent to which the inadequacy and suggestiveness of verbal expressions influence both the writing of a literary work and its reading, that it considers both writing and reading in the framework of a communicative process mediated by aesthetic experience. But it is not theoretical in the sense of providing a model, a criterion, or a paradigm for practical criticism. Literary hermeneutics to my mind is not a set of prescriptive rules or a methodology with which the interpreter is able to solve problems of textual criticism once he has grasped the technicalities and applied them to a particular text. The use of literary hermeneutics lies rather in deepening our perception of the workings of language and our experience of the art of literature; it helps describe more correctly and perceptively what happens when words and sentences are woven into a literary text, and when they are subsequently reactivated in the process of reading. In the light of such a hermeneutics, we may bring to our conscious reflection those principles that underlie the composition and performance of a literary text, and may thus understand the work of literature better than its author or the uninformed reader does.

Throughout this book, I shall refer to both Western and Chinese sources and put them in a sort of critical dialogue. The justification for such an intercultural dialogue, as I already mentioned, lies in the universality of the hermeneutic phenomenon—that is, the ever-present problems of language and interpretation. Although hermeneutics as a theory evolves out of the German philosophical tradition, it is indeed possible to characterize the Chinese cultural tradition as a hermeneutic one, for it has a long exegetical tradition evolving around a set of canonical texts and a wealth of commentaries, comparable to the tradition of biblical exegesis which furnishes the cornerstone of Western hermeneutic theory. Many theoretical issues in reading and commenting on the canon are common to both Chinese commentators and biblical exegetes, and bear directly on literary criticism in both traditions. In China as in the West, the nature of language and its correlation with literary interpretation are gradually understood in a historical process, but a study of such correlations in cultures as drastically different as the Chinese and the Western precludes comparisons in a chronological order. Many comparable ideas and concepts do not emerge at the same time in China and the West; thus comparisons and parallels in this book are not historically oriented but aim to identify some common themes in the critical understanding that have emerged at various moments in the East and the West. By "themes" I mean certain problems of understanding common to both Chinese and Western traditions, certain crucial ideas and concepts about the nature of language—its inherent metaphoricity, ambiguity, and suggestiveness; its implications for the author and the reader of a literary work; and so forth. Of course, each of these themes develops in its own tradition and has its own history, which must not be overlooked when a point of convergence is located; but what contributes to the thematic coherence of this study as well as to an extensive view of literary hermeneutics is not the self-enclosed particularity of each theme but its broad theoretical implications beyond the enclosure.

My interest in such common themes also justifies my disengagement from certain technical problems, like that of authorship, which can be a pretty thorny one especially on the Chinese side. Almost all the ancient

Chinese works—such as the Confucian *Analects* and the books named after Laozi or Zhuangzi—are either compiled by the philosopher's disciples or contain some interpolations or spurious chapters, so much so that it seems always questionable whether one can speak, say, of the different chapters of the book called *Zhuangzi* as if they come from the same author and represent the ideas and thoughts of the same philosopher. In my discussion, however, I do not distinguish what are generally accepted as the authentic chapters from the spurious ones, since it is not the authenticity of authorship but the ideas in the book and the actual influence they have exerted in the Chinese tradition that are of concern and relevance here. As the philosopher Zhuangzi himself might argue, the name Zhuangzi is just a convenient denominator that has its meaning or meanings only within certain historically and arbitrarily defined limits.

In bringing together historically unrelated texts and ideas, I attempt to find a common ground on which Chinese and Western literatures can be understood as commensurable, even though their cultural and historical contexts are different. The ultimate goal of such thematic comparisons is to transcend the limitation of a narrowly defined perspective and to expand our horizon by assimilating as much as possible what appears to be alien and belonging to the Other. If the encounter with something alien and unfamiliar is where hermeneutics starts, the enrichment of experience and knowledge in a mutual engagement of the Self and the Other, or what Gadamer calls the "fusion of horizons," is the final destination it will lead us to. The process of understanding is a process of learning or self-cultivation (*Bildung*), in which the unfamiliar becomes familiar, adding to the repertory of our knowledge, and the alien is absorbed till it becomes part of ourselves. As Gadamer reminds us: "It is the task of philosophy to discover what is common even in what is different. According to Plato, the task of the philosophical dialectician is 'to learn to see things together in respect of the one.'"[5] This seems to me an extremely apposite formulation not only of the task of philosophy but also of literary hermeneutics in a truly comparative outlook. Indeed, philosophy and literary hermeneutics are closely related, for the specific problems of literary interpretation are grounded in the nature of language and can be best understood in the larger framework of philosophical hermeneutics. Accordingly, my discussion of literary interpretation is preceded by an examination of philosophers' concepts of language, and my comments on the works of poets and writers—those of Rilke, Mallarmé, and Tao Qian, for example—are not intended to be interpretations of individual works as such, but to bring out the implications of those works for the theoretical point I try to make. The comparison of their seemingly unrelated and very different works aims precisely to "see things together in respect of the one."

But what is the nature of the "one"? How do we come to recognize the shared, the common, or the same in cultures and literatures that are definitely different? In an essay on Friedrich Hölderlin, Heidegger makes a fine distinction between the same and the equal or identical: "The equal or identical always moves toward the absence of difference, so that everything may be reduced to a common denominator. The same, by contrast, is the belonging together of what differs, through a gathering by way of the difference."[6] For anyone who tries to bring the literary traditions of the East and the West into comparison and find the sameness that underlies different cultural manifestations, it is very important to bear this distinction in mind. As Heidegger says, it is "in the carrying out and settling of differences that the gathering nature of sameness comes to light." The same "gathers what is distinct into an original being-at-one," but it does not level everything into "the dull unity of mere uniformity."[7] In other words, to find out the sameness is not to make disparate things equal or identical, or to erase the differences that inhabit the various cultural and literary manifestations. At the same time, however, to recognize the distinction Heidegger specifies is also to accept the very possibility of sameness and not to dismiss the same as merely equal or identical. This is of special importance at the present because the goal of this East-West comparative study is unabashedly the finding of the sameness despite profound cultural differences, while so many contemporary or postmodern Western theories are predicated on the assumption of cultural, ethnic, gender, or some other difference. In fact, it is against the background of an overemphasis on difference in contemporary Western theory that the present study has concentrated on the sameness that gathers different literary traditions together and makes intercultural dialogues possible.

The postmodern world, according to Jean-François Lyotard in his influential study of the postmodern condition, is a world of difference and heterogeneity in postindustrial Western societies, and his book on the postmodern condition ends with a virtual call to arms—to "wage a war on totality," to "activate the differences and save the honor of the name."[8] With their eyes focusing on a world of cultural and critical differences, many critics and theorists in the West may view with suspicion any effort to find the same, as if it is merely an attempt to level everything into the dull uniformity of the equal or identical. With the increasing departmentalization of knowledge and the specialization of academic expertise, the "original being-at-one" and the "aesthetic non-differentiation" seem to have broken into small pieces, and it is difficult to see what may bring the fragments of the splintered oneness again together. What we find as the same may appear especially suspicious when the intercultural comparison involves the Chinese tradition, for is not China the very symbol of cultural difference for the Western theoretical discourse? For example, when Foucault wants to emphasize the insurmountable gap between the East and the West as mutually incomprehensible cultural systems, it is precisely a passage from a "certain Chinese encyclopaedia" that represents such total and irreducible difference. In that hilarious passage, an absurd "Chinese" method of classification, which puts strangely categorized animals in one locale in spite of their radical incommensurability, reveals the fundamental difference in ways of thinking and naming in language. The juxtaposition of things in such an unthinkable order, or rather disorder, Foucault remarks, is conceivable only in *heterotopia*—the inconceivable space that undermines the very possibility of description in language, a space that repels and attracts at the same time, displaying the "exotic charm of another system of thought," while showing "the limitation of our own, the stark impossibility of thinking *that*."[9]

In an excellent study of postmodernist theories, Steven Conner observes that in this concept of heterotopia, the postmodern world of "pure difference" finds its "most famous image," "a name for the whole centreless universe of the postmodern."[10] As I have argued elsewhere, however, the hilarious passage from the so-called Chinese encyclopaedia, which Foucault quotes from an essay by Borges, is in fact a Western fiction; and by citing that fiction as a representation of the Chinese mind, Foucault does not disengage from the tradition of creating cultural myths of the Other —myths which have always presented the Other as pure difference, a foil to the West, either as an alluring and exotic dreamland, a utopia where the West has its ideals imaginatively realized, or the land of stagnation, spiritual purblindness, and ignorance, against which the higher values of Western progress and civilization stand out for everyone to see.[11] But "once such a heterotopia has been named, and, more especially, once it has been cited and re-cited," Conner contends, "it is no longer the conceptual monstrosity which it once was, for its incommensurability has been in some sense bound, controlled, and predictively interpreted, given a centre and illustrative function."[12] The point is, however, that the heterotopia was never really the conceptual monstrosity Foucault claims it to be, for the different Other is evoked by and for the West to facilitate its self-knowledge or self-critique, and the heterotopia is created only to be metaphorically colonized from the very start. Therefore, difference or heterogeneity, insofar as it inscribes a contemporary Western desire for cultural critique, does not carry the power of universal legitimation and should not be the definitive last word which critical discourse invariably endeavors to reach as if it were the only and final goal of intercultural comparative studies. Indeed, insofar as Western theory dictates the ways and terms in which critical discourse invariably speaks of the non-Western Other as pure difference, understanding of truly different, non-Western cultures and literatures is virtually impossible. Speaking in the voice of and for the Other, I would reject the designated role of pure difference and attempt to go beyond the Self and the Other in an effort to attain to an expanded horizon of experience and knowledge. And in that effort, hermeneutics with its claim to universality, if only paradoxically the universality of the finiteness of all understanding, may promise to give us the best support.

Given the scope of my project to deal with hermeneutic problems in philosophy and literature, in China and the West, I am constantly aware of the inadequacy of my own knowledge for the task I have willingly undertaken to accomplish. I know that I have often stepped out of familiar grounds and trespassed upon the turf of others who have the right to claim familiarity and solidity of scholarship in those fields. The comparatist may indeed often appear to the specialist as such an unwelcome trespasser, an overreaching anomaly in an academic world that has branched out into such a labyrinth of specialization. But to go beyond the usual boundaries of academic field, to step out of one's familiar bush in order to see the forest, though inevitably a risky undertaking in a highly specialized world, seems to me always worth trying. I remain unconvinced of the claim to uniqueness of any literary or cultural tradition—namely, the view that the East and the West are so distinctly different that ways of thinking and expression cannot be made intelligible from one to the other, and therefore the knowledge of one must be kept apart from that of the other. One of the things I have decided to do in the present study is precisely to pull down the usual barriers between scholarly colonies known as fields or disciplines, surrounded by academic hedgerows and marked out by departmental lines. I would challenge the departmentalization of knowledge and try to show some basic hermeneutic concerns and strategies shared by the East and the West. This is undoubtedly a difficult task that I am ill-equipped to fulfil, but I feel encouraged by the example of Mr. Qian Zhongshu, whose work always gives me guidance in bringing the East and the West together, though his formidable knowledge and scholarly accomplishment I cannot emulate. Many of the ideas developed here were first generated in my conversations with him in Beijing several years ago and inspired by his masterly comments on Chinese and Western works in his magnum opus, modestly entitled *Guan zhui bian*.[13]

An embryonic form of the argument in this book was first sketched out in a short article I published in Chinese in 1983.[14] Since then, I have been encouraged by many of my friends and colleagues on this side of the Pacific, who generously supported my effort to develop the ideas I had in mind. I want first of all to thank Professor Jurij Striedter for sharpening my mind in thinking about literary theory and for insistently demanding clarity and consistency. My thanks also go to Professor Stephen Owen, with whom I had many enjoyable conversations about Chinese as well as Western poetry. I would like to express my gratitude to Professor Daniel Aaron for his warm friendship and for commenting on a draft of the first two chapters. An old friend, Professor Donald Stone, deserves credit for giving me much encouragement. I am grateful to Professor Haskell Block and would also like to thank Linda Haverty, Marina van Zuylen, and Irene Kacandes for reading portions of an earlier draft of this book. I want to thank Professor Eugene Chen Eoyang and Professor Kang-I Sun Chang for offering constructive criticism and suggestions that helped me bring the book to its final form. I also want to thank Reynolds Smith and Pam Morrison at Duke University Press for their assistance and Stephanie Sugioka for her careful editing. And last but not least, I want to thank my wife Weilin for her unfailing support and for her almost blind confidence in me. To her this book is dedicated with gratitude and love.

In chapter 1 I have incorporated, with necessary changes and revisions, an essay first published in *Critical Inquiry* 11 (March 1985). The later part of chapter 2 was published in the inaugural issue of *Critical Studies* (vol. 1, no. 1, 1989). I want to thank Professor W. J. T. Mitchell and Editions Rodopi respectively for giving me permission to reuse the two published essays.

Zhang Longxi
Moreno Valley, California
September, 1991

A Note on Translation
and Transliteration

have translated all the passages quoted from Chinese sources mainly to make the translation part stylistically consistent with the rest of my writing. In the bibliography, however, I have listed, under the heading of a Chinese work, the title of its English version if a reasonably good translation is available. For works originally in German or French, I have tried to use existent English translations where possible, sometimes silently amended for accuracy. When no English version seems to exist or when I feel unsatisfied with the ones I find, I have supplied my own translation. Lines of French and German poems are always cited in the original followed by their English rendition.

For the transliteration of Chinese names and words, I have generally followed the pinyin system, which has a few letters pronounced quite differently from the way they sound in English, but the reader will be able to pronounce them by remembering the following approximate equivalents: c = ts, q = ch, x = sh, z = dz, and zh = j. The name of Tao Qian, for example, is pronounced like Tao Chian, and Zhu Ziqing sounds something like Ju Dzi-ching. There are a few exceptions, however. The names of Confucius and Mencius are already familiar enough to many Western readers, and a changed spelling according to the rules of pinyin orthography may only lead to unnecessary confusion. For the same reason, the term *tao* and its derivatives (*taoism*, *taoist*) are not spelled as "dao," "daoism," and "daoist." A problem may arise when we put the poet Tao Qian and the philosophical notion of *tao* together, because, in addition to being pronounced differently, Tao and *tao* in the Chinese original are two completely different characters. Throughout this book, the philosophical notion of *tao* is kept in lowercase and italicized, and the reader is advised not to relate it to the name of the poet Tao Qian, even though he was himself very much interested in the philosophical ramifications of the *tao*.

1

The

Debasement

of Writing

Polonius. What do you read, my lord?
Hamlet. Words, words, words.
—Shakespeare, *Hamlet*, act 2

Duke Huan is reading in the hall, while
Pian the wheelwright is hewing a wheel
at the steps in front of it. Having put
down his auger and chisel, he goes up
and says to the Duke: "May I dare to
ask, my lord, what kind of words are
you reading?" "The words of the
sages," says the Duke. Again he asks:
"Are the sages still alive?" "No, they
are dead," the Duke replies. The wheelwright says: "Then, what you are reading, my lord, is nothing but the dregs of
the ancients!"
—Zhuangzi, *The Tao of Heaven*

The Unconscious Creation of Genius

Socrates, according to Plato, once showed his contemporary poets some of their most perfect writings and found, upon inquiring about the meaning of their works, that "any of the bystanders could have explained those poems better than their actual authors."[1] In the original context of Socrates' defense, the point of this passage is to prove that no one is wise, especially with regard to knowing oneself, while its argumentative cogency depends on the strength of the ancient Greek idea of poetic inspiration—the idea that when the poets are singing, they are possessed and not quite in their right mind, and are therefore unable to understand the meaning of their own works. Such an idea is presented with a certain degree of humor and irony in Plato's *Ion*, where Socrates states politely but unambiguously that poetry is not an art guided by rules and that it originates not from knowledge but from inspiration. The making of poetry is a miracle, for just like the frenzied bacchanals who, when possessed, draw milk and honey from the rivers, the poets sing when they are divinely inspired, when "the deity has bereft them of their senses, and uses them as ministers, along with soothsayers and godly seers."[2] Ultimately, it is to these memorable passages in Plato that we may trace the romantic idea of poetry as unpremeditated, spontaneous, and irrational—a kind of natural cry not executed according to the poet's intention and reflective consciousness.

Since Plato, the idea of unconscious creation of poetry has provided an answer to the question of why literature is in constant need of comment and interpretation and, even more important, of why literary interpretation cannot be judged by the criterion of authorial intention.[3] To be sure, the fact that Socrates asked the poets to explain their own works seems to suggest that the need of interpretation was prior to the discovery of the poets' inability to explain, but in a way Socrates already anticipated that inability, for he had first interviewed the politicians before questioning the poets and had come to the conclusion that most people were likely to be ignorant of their own ignorance. Therefore, when he asked the poets for self-interpretation, he was somehow prepared to discover them no less blind to their own ignorance than the politicians, a finding that would then confirm his observation. Indeed, of all men, poets were perhaps the least able to achieve self-consciousness, since their work depended on divine inspiration rather than on their conscious knowledge. For Socrates, the inspirational origination of poetry could best account for the poets' hermeneutic inability, because "it was not wisdom that enabled them to write their poetry, but a kind of instinct or inspiration, such as you find in seers and prophets who deliver all their sublime messages without knowing in the least what they mean."[4] From this notion of divine inspiration, the conclusion is almost inevitable that poets serve as the mere mouthpiece of gods and that when they sing of the great deeds of gods and heroes in the frenzy of divine madness, they talk deliriously and do not know what they are talking about. It is therefore up to the interpreter to give an explanation of "what the poets mean" in what they literally say in their poetic works.

In the nineteenth century, these seminal ideas were fully developed in European romanticism, above all in the transcendental idealism of German philosophy. The ancient idea of the unconscious creation of art, now integrated with the notion of genius, became an essential concept in romantic aesthetics. Of the numerous reflections on genius and creativity, we may take those of Friedrich von Schelling as representative, since his contribution to romantic literary theory probably made the most noticeable impact. Although not the first to introduce the concept of the unconscious into aesthetics, Schelling, as M. H. Abrams observes, was "more than anyone, responsible for making that Protean term an ineluctable part of the psychology of art."[5] For Schelling, the origin of poetry is mysterious, inexplicable. He ascribes poetic inspiration to "an obscure unknown power," an "incomprehensible principle which adds the objective to the conscious without the cooperation of freedom and in a certain way in opposition to freedom."[6] As a force uncontrolled and uncontrollable, like the force of destiny, inspiration pushes the poet to the perfection of art without his conscious effort. According to Schelling, the writing of poetry seems an involuntary act, and the poet, no matter how specifically purposeful he may be, seems to be compelled "to express or represent things he does not himself fully see through and whose meaning is infinite."[7] The similarity to Plato's argument is obvious, but the Socratic irony and playfulness in the dialogue of *Ion* disappear in the romantic idea of the unconscious genius, where the poet's unawareness of his own effort is understood as an attribute of the inspired genius. The contradiction between conscious effort and unconscious creation is a central issue in romantic aesthetics. Schelling maintains that every aesthetic production begins with such an intrinsic contradiction because a work of art is certainly completed with deliberation and consciousness, and yet it is not and cannot be made at will or according to a specific intention. Whatever is completed with deliberation can be learned and taught, but that which makes a poem truly poetic and constitutes the very essence of poetry can neither be learned from others nor taught to them, nor can it be accomplished by a conscious effort. "The work of art," says Schelling, "reflects for us the identity of conscious and unconscious activity. But the opposition of the two is infinite, and it is overcome [*aufgehoben*] without any contribution of freedom. The basic character of the work of art is thus an *unconscious infinity* (synthesis of nature and freedom)."[8] To reconcile successfully the opposition between nature and freedom, or rather nature and culture, is the prerequisite for achieving artistic perfection, and for Schelling genius is that transcendental spirit which alone can resolve the contradiction in a perfect synthesis of the two opposites.

This and virtually all other references to genius in German aesthetics can be traced back to their fountainhead in Immanuel Kant, as Schelling's argument follows a line Kant first formulated in his *Critique of Judgment*. The contradiction Schelling sees in aesthetic production is also the one Kant tries to solve in the third critique: a contradiction which takes shape in the matrix of a set of antinomies and which, for Kant, involves not only the production of art but also its reception—namely, the antinomy of aesthetic judgment. For Kant, however, art, unlike Schelling's concept, at least begins as a rational and conscious act—"a production through freedom, i. e., through a power of choice that bases its acts on reason"— and the recognition of a work of art must be based on the perception of its intended purpose, "since art always presupposes a purpose in the cause (and its causality)."[9] In other words, the production of a work of art is purposive and intentional, not an unconscious infinity as Schelling argues. However, Kant also acknowledges that art as distinguished from science is not something that "we *can* do the moment we *know* what is to be done, i.e., the moment we are sufficiently acquainted with what the desired effect is."[10] Thus the distinctive feature of an artistic work is its uniqueness or unrepeatability, its being "purposive on its own."[11] Here again we find a contradiction of aesthetic production in that on the one hand art is conceived as being produced by a conscious effort, by following norms and rules, while on the other hand it is considered as impossible to be reproduced by mechanically following rules.

In Kant's third critique, which is concerned with the problem of aesthetic judgment, this contradiction is closely related with the antinomy of artistic reception. An aesthetic judgment is faced with the contradiction between its private, individual nature and its implied universality; for an aesthetic judgment, though not without reasonable ground, is a judgment based on personal taste and therefore unlikely to be universally applicable. When I say that something is beautiful, this statement is not meant to be valid just for myself but carries an implied sense of general agreement. Nevertheless, it is a statement based on my individual taste and perception. For that individual statement to lay any claim to universal validity, it must be based on a concept shared and accepted by others, representing something beyond the limited range of individual subjectivity; and yet it cannot be based on a logical concept in order to be sufficiently distinguished from a logical judgment, which does not make any statement about aesthetic value or evaluation. To find a way out of that dilemma, one must base a judgment of taste on something that is not a concept but that can validate aesthetic judgment, and one must find someone who has the special capacity of going beyond the two sides of the opposition. Both of these are proposed by Kant as solution to the antinomy, and both are found in his idea of genius; for genius, says Kant, has the special talent to represent "aesthetic ideas" which transcend all concepts while still providing necessary grounds for the validation of aesthetic judgment. Without going into all the details of how "aesthetic ideas" are differentiated from logical concepts and how they are represented in the creative works of genius, we may notice that Kant's idea of genius as a solution to the dilemma of aesthetic judgment bears on both the creative and the receptive aspects of aesthetic experience. The capacity to represent ideas that are not logical concepts, or the "irrationality of genius," as Gadamer observes, "brings out one element in the creative production of rules evident both in creator and recipient, namely that there is no other way of grasping the content of a work of art than through the unique form of the work and in the mystery of its impression, which can never be fully expressed by any language." That is to say, genius is not only the capacity of creation but also that of judgment. "Genius in understanding corresponds to genius in creation," says Gadamer. Though Kant himself did not develop this idea, his concept of genius already provides the basis on which "more must be built later."[12] For Kant, genius is first and foremost the spirit of creativity; and poetry, which demands the highest degree of spontaneous creativity and holds the highest rank among all the arts, "owes its origin almost entirely to genius and is least open to guidance by precept or examples."[13] In creating a work of art, genius is not only above the rule but is itself the rule. It "gives the rule to art," thereby solving the contradiction between conformity and inventiveness.[14] It produces things for which there can be no determinate rule, hence its *originality*; and it gives art the rule that it may be followed but not reproduced by others, hence its *exemplariness*.

Kant, however, never emphasizes the role of the unconscious in the creation of art. The idea is only implied when he maintains that genius as natural gift is not acquired but spontaneous and unintentional, that though it is capable of great achievement, genius does not know where its own capability comes from, that it "cannot describe or indicate scientifically how it brings about its products." "No *Homer* or *Wieland* can show how his ideas, rich in fancy and yet also in thought, arise and meet in his mind," says Kant; "the reason is that he himself does not know, and hence also cannot teach it to anyone else."[15] What Kant merely implied was taken up by Schelling and developed into a psychology of artistic production, where the concept of genius became inseparable from that of the unconscious. For Kant, as Gadamer notes, genius was "only a complement" to what was essential in aesthetic judgment, but with his successors it soon became the predominant concept in aesthetics.[16] Concerned with the validity of aesthetic judgment, Kant puts more emphasis on taste than genius, insisting that genius needs to be guided and curbed by good taste, which "clips its wings, and makes it civilized, or polished," and that in case of a conflict which calls for sacrificing one of the two, then the sacrifice "should rather be on the side of genius."[17] As a kind of *sensus communis*, aesthetic taste is the power that makes the work of genius accessible to others, that allows it to be shared by the community. In the romantic apotheosis, however, genius becomes an isolated Byronic hero, a rebel fighting not just against the classicist rules in art but against the entire value system of society. Schopenhauer speaks eloquently of the "lonely existence [*ein einsames Dasein*]" of genius in an alien and hostile world, arguing that the great works of a genius can be accomplished "only insofar as he ignores the ways and means, the thoughts and opinions of his contemporaries, quietly creates what they dislike, and scorns what they praise."[18] It is true that Schopenhauer's philosophy did not have a notable impact until the 1850s and that he disliked Fichte, Schelling, and Hegel; but despite the delayed effect, as René Wellek observes, "Schopenhauer definitely belongs to the early decades of the nineteenth century," and "his aesthetics is actually quite similar to Schelling's."[19] Gadamer also remarks that it was "through Schopenhauer and the philosophy of the unconscious" that genius as a "universal concept of value . . . achieved a true apotheosis" and "acquired enormous popular influence."[20] The ideas of inspiration and divine madness are quite evident in Schopenhauer's concept of genius, as he detects a close relation, a kind of kinship, between genius and madness, both of which are sublimely unconscious. Genius, Schopenhauer argues, does not work with abstract concepts but with the Idea, and "just because the Idea is and remains perceptual, the artist is not conscious *in abstracto* of the intention and aim of his work. Not a concept but an Idea is present in his mind; hence he cannot give an account of his actions. He works, as people say, from mere feeling and unconsciously, indeed instinctively."[21] Thus, first developed by Fichte and Schelling, the idea of the unconscious genius was then immensely popularized by Schopenhauer and quickly became a critical commonplace not only in Germany but everywhere in Europe.

Art as the unconscious creation of genius had important implications for the rise of hermeneutics in the nineteenth century and its emphasis on the receptive side of aesthetic experience. When the creative activity was understood as an unconscious process, interpretation became absolutely indispensable, since art by its very nature addresses an audience who needs to know the meaning of a work of art through the mediation of interpretation. An unconsciously created work could not be complete unless it was completed by conscious understanding, but, with its focus put on the creative genius, the romantic theory of unconscious creation could not adequately deal with the problem of reception and interpretation. For how could poets offer guidance in the understanding of poetry if they themselves did not know what they meant? How could they ever be entrusted with the task of interpretation if they themselves could not yet answer the question Socrates once put to them? Understanding is always a conscious activity, and unconscious creation must be understood consciously. In due time, therefore, the question of how to bring the unconscious creation of genius to the level of conscious understanding would necessarily arise, and the focus of attention would shift from the creative process to the interpretive activity. It is inevitable that in romantic literary theory, hermeneutics should complement aesthetics. Considering that, since Kant, German philosophy of art had largely concerned itself with the question of unconscious genius, it should not at all be surprising that the first systematic theory of general hermeneutics came out of the German tradition.

The Task of Hermeneutics

To understand the unconscious creation of genius is certainly an important goal for Friedrich Schleiermacher's project of general hermeneutics. Some scholars have argued that Schleiermacher, despite his affinity to Friedrich Schlegel and other romantic poets, was not a romantic himself. Martin Redeker, for example, maintains that Schleiermacher joined his romantic friends in their cultural activities and made use of their language, "but in the end he did not yield to the temptation of romantic fantasy and sentimentality, of their fabrication and mawkishness [*Erfindsamkeit und Empfindsamkeit*], since his crucial religious and theological concepts were not rooted in romanticism."[22] Redeker concedes, however, that not only did Schleiermacher learn from the romantics how to understand poetry and art in general, but "his hermeneutics, his interpretation of Plato, and his philosophical development also received an impetus from the romantic outlook on life."[23] There is no question that the romantic theory of unconscious creation and the ensuing need for interpretation formed a perfect background for the rise of Schleiermacher's hermeneutics.

Long before Schleiermacher formulated his hermeneutic theory, readers and critics had of course often wrestled with the problems of understanding and interpretation. There had been a philological approach to classical literature and a long tradition of biblical exegesis, but it is Schleiermacher who first shaped a general hermeneutics out of such specialized applications. "At present," Schleiermacher wrote in 1819, "there is no general hermeneutics as the art of understanding but only a variety of specialized hermeneutics."[24] In his project to establish hermeneutics as a general theory beyond the particularity of local theories of interpretation, there is evidently something like a Kantian critique, for just as the critical philosophy inquires into the very capacity of knowing before it is concerned with any concrete knowledge, Schleiermacher's hermeneutics demands that we investigate the nature of understanding itself before we understand particular texts or rules of textual criticism. For him, hermeneutics is not a mere bundle of exegetical rules but an art, a *Kunstlehre*: the art of methodical understanding that probes and articulates what the author is unaware of in the act of writing. If to understand means to bring into consciousness what the author has accomplished unconsciously, the task of hermeneutics must then be defined in terms of the relationship between the author and the interpreter. Schleiermacher declares:

> The task is to be formulated as follows: "To understand the [speech] at first as well as and then even better than its author." Since we have no direct knowledge of what was in the author's mind, we must try to become aware of many things of which he himself may have been unconscious, except insofar as he reflects on his own work and becomes his own reader. Moreover, with respect to the objective aspects, the author had no data other than we have.[25]

Evidently, Schleiermacher tries to seek support for his hermeneutic theory from the romantic aesthetics of genius, to which the concept of unconscious production is essential. The focus of attention in Schleiermacher's formulation, however, is not the creative artist but the critic, not the author but the interpreter. By bringing into conscious reflection many things that may have remained unreflective and involuntary for the author, the interpreter is able to reach a higher degree of knowledge than the author himself. This audacious manifesto of hermeneutics was justly famous and influential in the nineteenth century and was repeated by Boeckh, Steinthal, Dilthey, and others. Indeed, this formulation of the hermeneutic task as to understand a text better than its author is so revolutionary and has such far-reaching implications for dealing with the tension between author and interpreter with regard to the text that it has become a widely accepted principle. In so defining the goal of all interpretation, as Gadamer comments, it "contains the whole problem of hermeneutics."[26]

It is nevertheless important to note that Schleiermacher had his reservations about the romantic obsession with the unconscious. When he began to lecture on hermeneutics at the University of Halle in the summer of 1805, he had been translating Plato for years. This was not only a project to put the Platonic dialogues in German but also an attempt to discover the inner coherence of Plato's thought through the fragmentary form of dialogues so that the philosopher could be understood in his unique individuality. Before that inner context was fully reconstructed, Schleiermacher warned his reader, it would be "premature" to claim that "we might now be able to understand Plato better than he understood himself," for such a claim would indeed be unworthy of the spirit of Plato, considering that the philosopher himself "puts so high a value upon the consciousness of ignorance."[27] It is the interpreter who must first of all be made aware of his own ignorance in relation to the author and the text, for he can fully understand the author only insofar as he understands the language of the text after careful examination. Schleiermacher tried to understand Plato by working out the interrelationship of the dialogues in a hermeneutic circle. In that circle, "every dialogue is taken not only as a whole in itself, but also in its connection with the rest," and out of that circle, Plato's thought ideally emerges as a complete and coherent structure so that "he may himself be at last understood as a Philosopher and a perfect Artist."[28] In his Plato translations, therefore, Schleiermacher had already applied the hermeneutic principles that he came to formulate later theoretically and more systematically. It is quite clear that for his hermeneutics the inner coherence of the language and the individuality of the author, the text and its historical context, are equally important, and that the meaning of the text is worked out in a circular process that goes from parts to the whole and from whole to the parts.

For Schleiermacher, the author is not only an unconscious being but also a linguistic being, and one must attend to two moments—the psychological and the grammatical—in order to understand an author's speech. It is Schleiermacher's great contribution that he adds to the psychology of art a linguistic dimension and thereby seeks to ground hermeneutics in the analysis of language. Speaking is conceived both as a moment in the development of the person and a moment in relation to language as a system. The interpreter can understand the text better than its author not just because the author is unconscious of what he says, but because the meaning of the text, far from being determined once and for all by the author as an individual, has to be negotiated in a hermeneutic process in relation to the total structure of a given language: "Language is the only presupposition in hermeneutics, and everything that is to be found, including the other objective and subjective presuppositions, must be discovered in language."[29] Since Dilthey later emphasizes the psychological moment in Schleiermacher's hermeneutics, which is a one-sided picture formed in the perspective of Dilthey's own *Lebensphilosophie*, it is particularly important not to overlook the linguistic side of Schleiermacher's theory in which the author is understood as a person only insofar as he is understood in his language.[30] As Schleiermacher remarks, "One must already know a man in order to understand what he says, and yet one first becomes acquainted with him by what he says." Language speaks through the individual author as much as the author speaks the language, for "each person represents one locus where a given language takes shape in a particular way, and his speech can be understood only in the context of the totality of the language."[31] Therefore, to understand a speech means to comprehend the language and what it says about the thinking of the speaker: the two sides are complementary to each other. As Schleiermacher points out, the art of speaking and that of understanding are closely related: "Rhetoric and hermeneutics belong together and both are related to dialectics." It is therefore extremely important to keep in mind the relationship of understanding with thinking and speaking. "Speaking is the medium for the communality of thought [*die Gemeinschaftlichkeit des Denkens*]": "Indeed, a person thinks by means of speaking. Thinking matures by means of internal speech, and to that extent speaking is only developed thought. But whenever the thinker finds it necessary to fix what he has thought, there arises the art of speaking, that is, the transformation of original internal speaking, and interpretation becomes necessary."[32]

Of great significance here is Schleiermacher's statement that interpretation arises, of necessity, in the process of transformation when thinking takes the material form of fixed, external speech. Internal speech does not call for interpretation because it is transparent and self-sufficient, nothing but "developed thought [*der gewordene Gedanke*]," and can understand itself as such. But as soon as the thinker tries to "fix what he has thought," the moment he wants to formulate and communicate in language as external speech, his thought must depend on words for conveyance. Internal speech is thus transformed into something very different from itself and becomes inadequate for the very purpose of communication. It seems, then, that language always frustrates itself in its role as the medium for communication; it has such inherent deficiency and its operation is so problematic that no one should take understanding for granted. Instead, as Schleiermacher argues, we must take as the basic assumption for hermeneutics "that misunderstanding occurs as a matter of course, and so understanding must be willed and sought at every point."[33]

When we come back to the initial question of understanding literature, it becomes quite clear that poetry needs to be interpreted not only because the poet is unconscious of his creation but because the language of poetry seems either defective for its purpose or incapable of making the meaning of poetry self-evident. We can think of literary interpretation as an effort to make poetry speak, and the basic assumption of literary criticism, as

Northrop Frye puts it, is "not that the poet does not know what he is talking about, but that he cannot talk about what he knows."[34] We must understand this not in terms of the poet's decision not to talk but in terms of the very nature of poetic language, the meaning of which is quite beyond the control of the individual poet and his decisions. The alienation of thinking in language—the transformation of internal speech into linguistic signs, especially in the fixed, external form of writing—makes interpretation indispensable. The poet who should be the most skillful in the use of words is ironically the one who has difficulty in speaking, and the interpreter is called on to speak for him. It is this ironic inarticulation of poetry that constitutes the area in which the whole project of literary hermeneutics must begin its investigation. However, the more specific problems in literary hermeneutics have their roots in the larger problems dealt with in general hermeneutics, and our discussion of literary interpretation must therefore start on a more general level, with questions posed by philosophers, before we turn to those raised by poets.

The Necessity of Commentary

Comment and interpretation are necessary, of course, not just for poetic texts but for texts of all kinds, and the overabundance of books is not merely an outcome of modern mass printing. In the late sixteenth century, Michel Montaigne already felt amazed and even repelled at the teeming munificence of commentaries when he complained that "there is more trouble in interpreting interpretations than in interpreting the things themselves, and there are more books on books than on any other subjects. We do nothing but write comments on one another."[35] Yet the multiplicity of commentaries is a common phenomenon in cultural traditions where we find a set of canonical texts and a host of exegetical works that help to hand down the canon in the ebb and flow of cultural continuity. This is true of the classical Greco-Roman tradition, the Bible with its imposing array of exegeses, the Buddhist sacred literature, and the Chinese heritage of learning with its emphasis on accumulative wisdom rather than individual originality. "I transmit but do not innovate," says Confucius; "I trust and devote myself to the study of the ancients."[36] This unpretentious statement may have captured the true meaning of the word *tradition* because the handing over of a cultural heritage depends on a present conscious effort to preserve and enact what was valuable in the past, on our appreciation of what the ancients have achieved and bequeathed to us, and on the shared nature of language, which is the instrument of transmission par excellence.

Confucius meant transmission in speaking, and in one of his more metaphysical moments, he realized that speaking had its limitations. "I will not speak," declares Confucius. His disciple Zigong anxiously asks: "What do we, the youngsters, have to transmit, if you should give up speaking?" The Master replies by posing a rhetorical question: "Does Heaven ever speak? Yet the four seasons run their course, and a hundred things rise and grow. Does Heaven ever speak?"[37] The ideal way of teaching (for here Confucius is mainly concerned with the transmission of virtue and knowledge to his disciples) would be teaching by concrete examples in life rather than by precepts couched in words: a way of teaching that is effortless and wordless, totally absorbed and quietly implemented, just like the way Heaven regulates all things to perfection without saying a single word. By pointing to the cyclical course of the seasons and the generative process which seem to follow the unspoken laws of nature, Confucius discloses his desire to have the moral order in society shaped on the model of the heavenly order in the universe, allowing virtue and knowledge to come to the world naturally and become our spontaneous behavior, our intuitive second nature. This was of course the dream of a teacher-philosopher, the dream that knowledge and virtue could be taught in their purity, without ever being filtered through words or trickling down through interpretations and reinterpretations, that the transmission of culture could totally dispense with language and, indeed, that nothing would ever come between thinking and its realization in life: a dream, as we shall see, that appears to have been at the heart of philosophy in both the East and the West.

As a great pedagogue, however, Confucius knew only too well that teaching was impossible without the employment of words, even though words might confuse and mislead those who were being taught. While reluctantly granting words the value of usefulness, he nevertheless remained suspicious of the value of language per se and of any extravagant use of it. "A virtuous man is certainly capable of making valuable speech," he says, "but a man of valuable speech is not necessarily a man of virtue."[38] Having recognized the possible discrepancy between the profession of virtue in words and the speaker's moral qualities, Confucius gave his warning against naive credulity in the face value of verbal excellence. His attitude toward language at times came close to a completely utilitarian one, as he insisted, "So far as words can get to the point, that is enough."[39] In this pragmatic view, language serves a strictly communicative purpose, but difficulties immediately arise when we turn to real situations in linguistic communication where words hardly ever get to the point in exactly the way Confucius would have approved, for very often there is either more or less in language than is sufficient to get to the point. But language surely serves more purposes than Confucius here allows it, and in the artistic use of language its function is not just to get to a point. Even if the function of language is to send a message to its destination, it would still take more than the plainness of homespun words for an effective delivery. After all, Confucius himself acknowledges that some kind of rhetorical embellishment (*wen*) is necessary for effective verbal communication. "Intention has its destination," he is quoted as saying. "Speech complements intention, and embellishment complements speech. If you do not speak, who will know your intention? If you speak without any embellishment, your words will not go far enough."[40] Here, Confucius is certainly not endorsing the use of language from a purely rhetorical or literary point of view, since all his teachings invariably point to a single direction—namely, the perfection of morality in society as well as in individual life. It is therefore simply impossible to consider the nature and function of language as separated from moral and political issues in the framework of Confucian ideology.

In any case, the tension between being and saying, intention and expression, is evident enough when Confucius warns that the man of virtue and the man of speech may not exactly correspond. In that brief dialogue between Confucius and Zigong, such tension is dramatized in the Master's desire for silence and the disciple's anxiety for transmission. Language is here at work on two different levels: On the one hand is Zigong waiting to transmit what Confucius has to say, and on the other is the Master who professes to say nothing or, on still another level (as we know from an earlier quote), to transmit what was already made and said in antiquity. In spite of his claim of being a mere vehicle of ancient virtue and wisdom, however, Confucius is in fact one of the most influential thinkers in ancient China, and the *Analects* becomes one of the source-books in the Chinese cultural tradition, an original work that has itself elicited numerous annotations and commentaries. Thus, books are written which interpret the *Analects*, which interprets Confucius, who interprets the ancients. Within this chain of interpretations and reinterpretations, the locus of origin seems always receding, and Confucius' desire for silence remains at the center of a whirl of words incessantly dancing around it. The commentaries are complementary to one another in endless reiterations and explanations, and the possibility of interpretation proves to be truly inexhaustible.

If all commentaries ultimately come from the desire to reclaim that which has been lost in the transformation of thinking into language or to reveal that which is hidden or obscured in verbal expression, they must belong, as Michel Foucault would say, to the archaeology of knowledge. They dig into the layer of literal sense of the text and attempt to retrieve what was the primal discourse in its pretextual condition, but they never really get to the origin of discourse, only to an endless self-proliferation. Commentaries invite and produce more commentaries. "The task of commentary can never, by definition, be completed," says Foucault:

> Language sets itself the task of restoring an absolutely primal discourse, but it can express that discourse only by trying to approximate to it, by attempting to say things about it that are similar to it, thereby bringing into existence the infinity of adjacent and similar fidelities of interpretation. The commentary resembles endlessly that which it is commenting upon and which it can never express.[41]

If the primal discourse needs restoration at all, quite obviously it means, as Foucault seems to suggest, that this discourse is already lost in the written text, and the language of commentary sets itself the unattainable goal of reclaiming that lost discourse through its trace in writing. Thus understood, writing signifies not only what it records but the loss of what was originally contained in thought as internal speech—the loss or absence of that primal discourse which the written text fails to preserve and commentary fails to retrieve. But inasmuch as both text and commentary exist as writing, the distinction between them becomes blurred and insignificant vis-à-vis the internal speech which alone holds the ideal harmony of the sign and the thing. In this sense, all writing is nothing but commentary called upon to reclaim speech, but it only generates more writing and more commentaries. Foucault has aptly described this unavoidable process of self-reduplication. Since writing in Western culture "refers not to a thing but to speech," he remarks, "a work of language only advances more deeply into the intangible density of the mirror, calls forth the double of this already doubled writing, discovers in this way a possible and impossible infinity, ceaselessly strives after speech, maintains it beyond the death which condemns it, and frees a murmuring stream." Foucault goes on to add that such a "presence of repeated speech" exists in Western writing alone, which has "an ontological status unknown in those cultures where the act of writing designates the thing itself, in its proper and visible body, stubbornly inaccessible to time."[42] Obviously, Foucault is referring to nonphonetic writings like Egyptian hieroglyphs or Chinese characters, which are allegedly direct representation of things, unchanged and inflexible, totally oblivious of the revolution of time. In the course of this study, I hope it will become clear that such sweeping generalizations about East-West cultural differences are very much the result of misconceptions or of a wilful projection of the desire to differentiate the Western Self from a non-Western Other. In Chinese commentaries on the Confucian *Analects* and on other works, there is also the desire to rescue the original speech from the death which condemns it, also the possible or impossible infinity, the endless reduplication of writing. As the external form of language, writing in Chinese as well as in Western culture constantly invites comment and interpretation, constituting the center of all hermeneutic investigation. "Thus written texts [or fixed texts, *fixierte Texte*]," as Gadamer says, "present the real hermeneutical task. Writing is self-alienation. Overcoming it, reading the text, is thus the highest task of understanding."[43]

Conversation and Transcription

Philosophers, at least ancient philosophers, apparently prefer to commit their thoughts to living discourse rather than to writing. When we think of an ancient philosopher, be it Socrates or Confucius, the image that readily comes to the mind is a master talking to his disciples as they walk along, trying out ideas that occur to them at the moment, revising and polishing those ideas till truth unfolds and shines out in the succession of questions and answers. Words are spoken to the right audience, understood in the immediacy of a dialogue, and the plenitude of meaning is warranted by further questions and answers, explanations and modifications. Once a thought is put in writing, however, it loses connection with the living voice and the dialogic context, and is exposed to the violence of misunderstanding. In the last part of the Platonic dialogue *Phaedrus*, Socrates dwells on the vulnerability of writing and its inferiority to oral speech. "You know, Phaedrus, that's the strange thing about writing," he says; "once a thing is put in writing, the composition, whatever it may be, drifts all over the place, getting into the hands not only of those who understand it, but equally of those who have no business with it; it doesn't know how to address the right people, and not address the wrong." When confronted with violence, "ill-treated and unfairly abused," writing is "unable to defend or help itself."[44]

For Plato, to address the right audience is important in order to have meaningful communication, and the same is true for Confucius. "Failure to converse with the one to whom you can talk is to lose the person," says Confucius; "conversing with the one to whom you cannot talk is to lose the word. A wise man will lose neither the person nor the word."[45] But how does one know whether one can or cannot talk to a person without first trying him out in conversation? And that is precisely the point: only through conversation will one know and decide what to do with the person. Like Socrates, Confucius is concerned not with the written but the spoken word. If to talk to the wrong person is to waste one's words, imagine how much worse it would be when the word is written down and addresses everybody promiscuously! Confucius, to be sure, did talk to his disciples, though at one point he desired to keep silent, but the source of our knowledge about him and his thoughts, the *Analects*, does not come from his hand. The curious fact that the thoughts and sayings of many ancient philosophers often come to us not in their own writing but as recorded by their disciples, when put in the context of Plato's or Confucius' concern for the right audience, seems to reveal more of their doubt about the usefulness of writing, their skeptical attitude toward language, than of their lack of concern about authorship in a time when authorship was not yet an issue.

If the form of writing is designed to record speech by putting it down permanently, can we then say that writing helps us remember what we hear only momentarily by changing it into something we can always come back to and see again? Not so, according to Plato. For him, memory has a peculiar significance, and instead of being an aid to memory, the invention of writing threatens to impair it: "If men learn this, it will implant forgetfulness in their souls; they will cease to exercise memory because they rely on that which is written, calling things to remembrance no longer from within themselves, but by means of external marks."[46] For Socrates, memory is not just the recollection of diurnal experiences but recovery of the true knowledge of eternal forms the soul once possessed in preexistence: we know by remembering what we once knew in a purer state. Therefore, by implanting forgetfulness, writing obstructs our way to true knowledge and blots out with its indelible stains the inward vision obtained through a mnemonic recuperation. The concept of knowledge as recollection of the soul lies at the center of Platonic mysticism; it forms the basis of rejecting writing as external marks, since memory works "from within" and "may be said as it were to write words in our souls."[47] In other words, truth resides only in the internal speech as intuition and memory of the soul, but never in writing as an unreliable form of transcription.

That may explain why Socrates never wrote down his ideas himself and why Plato denies that he is writing when writing is precisely what he does. For Plato, recording philosophical conversations poses an embarrassing question about the reliability of his writing, and the solution he comes up with is to minimize his role as writer, insisting that "there is not and will not be any written work of Plato's own. What are now called his are the work of a Socrates embellished and modernized."[48] In other words, Plato wants to present himself as a mere scribe who transmits the speech of his master in a form as transparently faithful as possible, trying to keep the living word intact in his transcription. For Plato, the only form of writing that allows such life-preserving transcription is that of the dialogue. As Schleiermacher observes, "the dialogistic form, necessary as an imitation of that original and reciprocal communication, would be as indispensable and natural to his writings as to his oral instruction."[49] Gadamer also notes that the hermeneutic significance of the Platonic dialogue lies in its emphasis on the art of questioning, which is also the art of dialectics. In contrast to the rigid form of assertive statement in writing, the dialogue embodies the art of dialectics by seeking truth in an exchange of questions and answers, by its open-ended orientation and the formation of concepts as the working out of specific problems. We can see, says Gadamer, "how Plato tries to overcome the weakness of the logoi, especially the written logoi, through his own dialogues. The literary form of the dialogue places language and concept back within the original movement of the conversation. This protects words from all dogmatic abuse."[50] As a form of writing, the Platonic dialogue thus overcomes the weakness of the logoi by self-effacement, presenting itself not as writing but as an accurate live transcription of what is actually spoken.

In Plato, as later on in the whole tradition of Western philosophy, there is evidently what Jacques Derrida calls a metaphysical hierarchy, which privileges the silent grasp of thinking in transparent speech at the cost of writing. The spoken word is regarded as adequate insofar as it immediately realizes inner speech, but writing is discredited as the external form of expression, a kind of secondary signifier. In the Hegelian system, for example, we can find one of the most impressive formulations of this metaphysical hierarchy. Hegel maintains that thinking as the inner is necessarily alienated when it is externalized into language, which, as an "outer expression," conceals as much as it reveals and never quite expresses the inner to the precise point. "For that reason," says the philosopher, "we might just as truly say that these outer expressions express the inner too much as that they do so too little."[51] And yet, Hegel does not so much devalue language per se as its outer form, which is writing. In living speech, the inner self as "pure ego" is immediately present and the force of mind acquires the form of reality, "the form in which *qua* language it exists to be its content, and possesses authority, *qua* spoken word." Any other form would be inadequate, for only the form of oral speech "contains this ego in its purity; it alone expresses I, I itself."[52] In contradistinction to the spoken word, the written form of language seems only to provide a concrete, finite, and dispensable shape in which the self is not immediately present and the personal voice is not heard. But philosophy, as Richard Rorty contends, is also a kind of writing; in its debasement of writing, therefore, philosophy seems only trying to put an end to itself. Rorty sees it as "characteristic of the Kantian tradition that, no matter how much writing it does, it does not think that philosophy *should* be 'written,' any more than science should be. Writing is an unfortunate necessity; what is really wanted is to show, to demonstrate, to point out, to exhibit, to make one's interlocutor stand at gaze before the world."[53]

Nevertheless, it is important to note that for Hegel the problem of writing does not lie in writing as such but only in the kind of writing that fails to represent logos or truth as self-presence in the inner speech. In his Eurocentric and ethnocentric view, German is the perfect language for philosophy, and it is only the language of the East, especially the nonphonetic Chinese written script, that exemplifies the problems of writing. Hegel formed his notoriously denigrating view of the Chinese language in the light of a metaphysical hierarchy. In his philosophical system, world history itself takes on a hierarchical shape in space as well as in time: "The History of the World travels from East to West, for Europe is absolutely the end of History, Asia the beginning."[54] He goes on to argue that history does not travel in a circle around the globe but moves dialectically from the lower phase to a higher one. This hierarchical movement applies to the development of language as well, for while German and Western alphabetic writing at large exists, as it were, merely for the purpose of registering sound, the voice, the inner speech and so is by far the better form of writing, the ideographic Chinese writing—which lacks the appropriate "means of orthoepic development" and "does not express, as ours does, individual sounds—does not present the spoken words to the eye, but represents the ideas themselves by signs"—becomes Hegel's classic example of an underdeveloped language.[55] In his preface to the second edition of *Science of Logic*, Hegel exalts German for having "an abundance of logical expressions" and "many advantages over other modern languages; some of its words even possess the further peculiarity of having not only different but opposite meanings," but he claims that the Chinese language "is supposed not to have developed to this stage or only to an inadequate extent."[56] Thus, ultimately, it is writing that separates itself from logos, or from truth grasped in inner speech, that is to be discarded. For Hegel, the nonphonetic Chinese script is exemplary of such inadequate writing—the external form of language which obscures the voice, the inner speech, the "pure ego," by its opaque externality.

For any attempt at an East-West comparative study, Hegel's challenge has to be reckoned with before any comparison can be considered meaningful, because such intercultural comparisons would make no sense at all if the difference between Western and Chinese writings is absolute, and if problems of language and interpretation discussed in the Western philosophical tradition are thought to be uniquely Western and inconceivable on the same level when related to the language and philosophy of the East. That is why Qian Zhongshu, by far the most learned scholar in modern China, takes issue with Hegel and his denigration of the Chinese language at the very beginning of *Guan zhui bian* or *Pipe-Awl Chapters*, which comments on important ancient Chinese texts from a truly global perspective. For Hegel, the philosophical superiority of the German language is epitomized by the protean word *Aufhebung*, which, as a perfect embodiment of Hegelian dialectics, means both "preserving" and "putting an end to," or "coming-to-be" and "ceasing-to-be," the wonderful "one and the same word for two opposite meanings."[57] Nevertheless, words with opposite meanings are not exclusively under German monopoly. Stephen Ullmann, for instance, mentions "a special case of bisemy" where we find "*antonymous senses* attached to the same name," and the examples he gives include the Latin *sacer* and the French *sacré*, meaning both "sacred" and "accursed."[58] In reviewing Karl Abel's *Über den Gegensinn der Urworte*, Freud notices that it is precisely in the Egyptian language that "we find a fair number of words with two meanings, one of which says the exact opposite of the other," and he compares such hieroglyphs with the language of dreams in which any two things can coexist without being contradictory to one another.[59]

In confronting Hegel, Qian Zhongshu demonstrates with formidable erudition and a wealth of examples how some of the Chinese characters may simultaneously possess three, four, or even five different and contradictory meanings. The Chinese character *yi* [易], for instance, could mean "conciseness" or "change" or "constancy"; therefore the famous *Yi jing*, or *I Ching*, may just as properly be translated as the "Concise Book of Constancy" as its better-known title, the *Book of Changes*, since it is essentially a book about changeless presence in a world of always changing configuration. We need not blame Hegel for his ignorance of the Chinese language, nor should we feel surprised that he would so unjustifiably philosophize on Chinese writing based on his very meager knowledge, "but it would cause a scholar to feel sorry for him," says Qian Zhongshu, "that he has made things that are common to both the East and the West to appear as though they were totally incommensurate."[60] For many scholars, whether they accept or reject the Hegelian view, incommensurability or fundamental difference between cultural systems is still very much the accepted working assumption. Of course, difference is what makes things identifiable, interesting, even aesthetically appealing, and hermeneutic difference is where understanding begins, but total difference without any common ground would make hermeneutics utterly impossible. We may recall Dilthey's remarks on the realm of hermeneutics as a locale between the two extremes of total difference and total identity. The object of all hermeneutic activities, a speech or a text that calls for interpretation, is always some kind of expression of life (*Lebensäusserung*). "Interpretation would be impossible," says Dilthey, "if the expressions of life were totally foreign. It would be unnecessary if there were nothing foreign in them. Interpretation therefore resides between the two opposed extremes. It is needed wherever there is something foreign, which the art of understanding should make one's own."[61]

The Tao and The Logos

The need to answer Hegel's challenge and to deal with the alleged incommensurability between the East and the West becomes even greater when we realize that not only does the traditional Hegelian debasement of writing consider the nonphonetic Chinese as different in kind from any Western language, but contemporary critique of the Hegelian prejudice also adopts such a misguided view as its premise. This can be seen clearly in Derrida's deconstructive critique of Western philosophical tradition and its ethnocentric-phonocentric view of language, which he regards as an inveterate prejudice in Western culture and terms "*logocentrism*: the metaphysics of phonetic writing."[62] According to Derrida, Western alphabetic writing as total transcription of the living voice inscribes a logocentric prejudice which privileges speech over writing, regarding the truth of logos as "the articulated unity of sound and sense within the phonie. With regard to this unity, writing would always be derivative, accidental, particular, exterior, doubling the signifier: phonetic. 'Sign of a sign,' said Aristotle, Rousseau, and Hegel."[63] By invoking the names of three important philosophers from different moments in the Western tradition, Derrida wants to emphasize the powerful and thorough permeation of the logocentric prejudice through the entire history of Western philosophy. The word *Western* here is significant, for it is Derrida's belief that logocentrism in metaphysics is manifested in Western writing as phonocentrism; it is therefore a purely Western phenomenon related to Western thinking and to Western thinking alone. "Almost by a reverse ethnocentrism," as Gayatri Chakravorty Spivak notes in the translator's preface to *Of Grammatology*, "Derrida insists that logocentrism is a property of the West. . . . Although something of the Chinese prejudice of the West is discussed in Part I, the *East* is never seriously studied or deconstructed in the Derridean text."[64] As a matter of fact, not only is the East never seriously studied or deconstructed but Derrida sees in the nonphonetic Chinese writing "the testimony of a powerful movement of civilization developing outside of all logocentrism."[65] When he looks within the Western tradition for a breakthrough, he finds it in nothing other than the poetics of Ezra Pound and his mentor, Ernest Fenollosa, who built a graphic poetics on what is certainly a peculiar reading of Chinese ideograms: "This is the meaning of the work of Fenellosa [*sic*] whose influence upon Ezra Pound and his poetics is well-known: this irreducibly graphic poetics was, with that of Mallarmé, the first break in the most entrenched Western tradition. The fascination that the Chinese ideogram exercised on Pound's writing may thus be given all its historical significance."[66]

Since Chinese is a living language with a system of nonphonetic scripts that function differently from that of any Western language, it naturally holds a fascination for those in the West who, weary of the Western tradition, try to find an alternative model on the other side of the world, in the Orient. This is how the so-called Chinese prejudice came into being at the end of the seventeenth and eighteenth centuries, when some philosophers in the West, notably Gottfried Wilhelm Leibniz, saw "in the recently discovered Chinese script a model of the philosophical language thus removed from history" and believed that "what liberates Chinese script from the voice is also that which, arbitrarily and by the artifice of invention, wrenches it from history and gives it to philosophy."[67] That is to say, what Leibniz and others saw in the Chinese language was what they desired and projected there, "a sort of European hallucination," as Derrida rightly calls it. "And the hallucination translated less an ignorance than a misunderstanding. It was not disturbed by the knowledge of Chinese script, limited but real, which was then available."[68]

Now the question that may be put to the contemporary effort to deconstruct the metaphysics of phonetic writing is whether such an effort has safely guarded itself against the same prejudice or hallucination that annulled the Leibnizian project and finally trapped it in the old snare of logocentrism. A more fundamental question that necessarily follows is whether or not logocentrism is symptomatic only of Western metaphysics, whether the metaphysics of Western thinking is really different from that of Eastern thinking and is not simply the way thinking is constituted and works. If, as Spivak suggests, "this phonocentrism-logocentrism relates to centrism itself—the human desire to posit a 'central' presence at beginning and end," then how can such a desire ever be successfully suppressed or totally choked off, however much the deconstructionists try?[69] In other words, if logocentrism is found present in the East as well as in the West, in nonphonetic as well as in phonetic writing, how is it possible for us to break away from, or through, its enclosure?

Since Derrida has given credit to Fenollosa and Pound for accomplishing "the first break in the most entrenched Western tradition," looking into this break ought to help us find an answer to the above questions. Fenollosa's influence on Pound and his poetics is well known indeed, but among people who know Chinese and therefore can judge the matter, it is well known to be a misleading influence insofar as it concerns sinology. Under that influence, Pound's understanding of the Chinese script is notoriously shaky and whimsical. A note in the Derridean text leads us to the statement that "Fenollosa recalled that Chinese poetry was essentially a script."[70] The idea here is that Chinese poetry, written in ideograms which Fenollosa believed to be "shorthand pictures of the operations of nature," explores the pictorial values of the characters to the utmost.[71] Each line of a Chinese poem becomes a string of thought-pictures or images that bring the independent visual aspect of the sign into prominence. Following this concept, Pound dissected the Chinese script into its pictographic components and was fascinated by the images he discovered there. For example, the Chinese character *xi* [習] is composed of two elements, a "feather" on top of "white." It does not mean "white feather," however, but "to practice." This character appears in the first sentence of the Confucian *Analects*, which could be translated as: "The Master says: to learn and to practice from time to time—is this not a joy?" In his fervent anatomy of Chinese script, however, Pound seized upon the feather image and rendered the line as: "Study with the seasons winging past, is not this pleasant?"[72] In Chinese the word *xi* or "practice" is often preceded by the word *xue* or "learn," and as the sinologist George Kennedy wittily comments, "The repeated idea is that learning is fruitless unless one puts it into practice. Pound sacrifices this rather important precept for the sake of a pastoral where the seasons go winging by. Undoubtedly this is fine poetry. Undoubtedly it is bad translation. Pound has the practice, but not the learning. He is to be saluted as a poet, but not as a translator."[73]

In a totally different context and with different intention, T. S. Eliot also denied Pound the title of translator. He predicted that Pound's *Cathay* "will be called (and justly) a 'magnificent specimen of XXth Century poetry' rather than a 'translation.'"[74] With his notion of tradition as the corpus of all the canonical works simultaneously shaping and being shaped by the new work of art, Eliot tried to place Pound in the tradition of European literature, identifying Robert Browning, William Butler Yeats, and many others as predecessors who had exerted strong influence on Pound's works. As for Chinese, Eliot insisted that what appeared in Pound's work was not so much Chinese per se as a version or vision of Chinese from the Poundian perspective. Eliot's well-known and pretty little aphorism that "Pound is the inventor of Chinese poetry for our time" contains more insight than perhaps Eliot himself was aware of.[75] The point is that neither Pound nor Fenollosa should be regarded as free from the sort of Chinese prejudice Derrida has detected in Leibniz, because for them, as for Leibniz more than two centuries earlier, "what liberates Chinese script from the voice is also that which, arbitrarily and by the artifice of invention, wrenches it from history and gives it to [poetry]."

Curiously enough, just as Hegel alleged that "the reading of hieroglyphs is for itself a deaf reading and a mute writing," so Fenollosa believed that "in reading Chinese we do not seem to be juggling mental counters, but to be watching *things* work out their own fate."[76] The pros and cons here are equally misconceived because reading Chinese, like reading any other language, is a linguistic act of comprehending the meaning of a succession of signs, either with silent understanding or with utterance of the sounds; it is not an archaeological act of digging up some obscure etymological roots from underneath a thick layer of distancing abstraction. Derrida reminds us with Ernest Renan that "in the most ancient languages, the words used to designate foreign peoples are drawn from two sources: either words that signify 'to stammer,' 'to mumble,' or words that signify 'mute.'"[77] But this practice seems by no means solely ancient, for did not Hegel in the nineteenth century and Fenollosa in the twentieth take Chinese for a mute language? The irony in Hegel's case is that he probably did not know that his favorite German *Muttersprache* is called in Russian *nemetskij jazyk*, which literally means "language of the dumb." As for Fenollosa, it is almost unnecessary to point out that Chinese poetry is essentially *not* a script to be deciphered but a song to be chanted, depending for its effect on a highly complicated tonal pattern. In discussing Fenollosa and Pound with special reference to Derrida's statement in *Of Grammatology*, Joseph Riddel reproves Fenollosa for his "incoherence or blindness that permits him . . . to forget that his own reading of the ideogram is a purely western idealization."[78] This seems to call Derrida's statement into question and put "the first break" in the Western tradition back into that tradition. One may begin to wonder, Is it possible that logocentrism or the metaphysical hierarchy with regard to thinking, speaking, and writing also exists in the Eastern tradition? Do the nonphonetic Chinese scripts really mark the outer boundaries of all logocentrism? And finally, Is there a Chinese word that denotes, as the word *logos* does, something equivalent or similar to the Western metaphysical hierarchy?

By a most curious coincidence, there is indeed a word in Chinese that exactly captures the duality of thinking and speaking. Schopenhauer remarks, by citing Cicero (*De Officiis*, 1.16), that the Greek word *logos* means both *ratio* and *oratio*, both reason and speech.[79] Stephen Ullmann also observes that *logos* as a notoriously ambiguous word has a serious effect on philosophical thought because it "has two chief meanings, one corresponding to Latin *oratio*, 'the word or that by which the inward thought is expressed,' the other to Latin *ratio*, 'the inward thought' itself."[80] In other words, *logos* means both thinking (*Denken*) and speaking (*Sprechen*).[81] Gadamer also reminds us that *logos*, though often translated as "reason" or "thinking," originally and chiefly means "language," and that human being as *animal rationale* [*das vernünftige Lebewesen*] is actually "animal that has language [*das Lebewesen, das Sprache hat*]."[82] In this wonderful word, then, thinking and speech literally fuse into one.

Significantly, the Chinese word *tao*, which also represents the foremost
Chinese philosophical concept, contains in one word the same duality of
thinking and speaking. In English, *tao* (or *dao*) is usually translated as
"way."[83] Though not exactly a mistranslation, "way" is only one of the
meanings of this polysemous Chinese character but not the crucial meaning which bears directly on the complexity of the interrelationship between
thinking and language. It is important and especially relevant to our discussion here to note that *tao* as used in the philosophical book *Laozi* has
two other meanings: "thinking" and "speaking." In an extremely insightful
explication of the opening lines of the *Laozi*, Qian Zhongshu has already
pointed out that *tao* and *logos* are remarkably comparable.[84]

The word *tao* is repeated three times in the first line of the *Laozi*, and
the repetition certainly makes a serious point by playing on the two meanings of *tao*—*tao* as thinking and *tao* as the verb "to speak":

> The *tao* that can be *tao*-ed ["spoken of"]
> Is not the constant *tao*;
> The name that can be named
> Is not the constant name.[85]

Puns like this are really untranslatable, and the point gets completely lost
in English translation which usually reads, "the way that can be spoken
of is not the constant way." The problem is that "way" and "to speak" in
English have nothing in common, but in the Chinese original they are one
and the same word. So, in the above translation, I try to make *tao* look
like a verb in order to capture the point of the pun in the original text.
According to Laozi the philosopher, *tao* is both immanent and transcendent; it is the begetter of all things; therefore, it is not and cannot be
named after any of these things. In other words, *tao* is the ineffable, the
"mystery of mysteries" beyond the power of language. Even the name *tao*
is not a name in itself: "I do not know its name; so I just call it *tao*." "The
tao is for ever nameless." Laozi makes it clear that the totality of the *tao* is
kept intact only in knowing silence; hence this famous paradox that "the
one who knows does not speak; the one who speaks does not know."[86]

One might protest that the *Laozi*, despite its extreme conciseness, is
after all a "book of five thousand characters," and thus Laozi has not only
spoken but has written a whole book about what he believes to be ineffable. This paradox, however, as though anticipated, may be partly recon-
ciled by the legendary genesis of the book as recorded in the biography of
Laozi by the great historian Sima Qian (145?–90? B.C.):

Laozi cultivated the *tao* and virtue; and his teachings sought to achieve seclusion and self-effacement. He lived in Zhou for a long time, but he left the place when he saw that it was in deterioration. As he reached the Pass, the Keeper there joyfully said to him, "Now you are going to live in seclusion, will you please write a book for me?" Thus Laozi wrote a book of some five thousand characters, explaining the *tao* and virtue in two parts, and then departed. No one knows where he went to in the end.[87]

We learn from the story that the *Laozi* was written at the request and for the benefit of the Pass Keeper, who was apparently not a philosopher capable of intuitive knowledge of the mysterious *tao*. In order to enlighten him and the world, Laozi was confronted with the difficult task of speaking of the unspeakable and describing the indescribable. As the commentator Wei Yuan (1794–1856) explains,

> The *tao* cannot be manifested through language, nor be found by following its trace in name. At the coercive request of the Pass Keeper, he was obliged to write the book, so he earnestly emphasized, at the very moment he began to speak, the extreme difficulty of speaking of the *tao*. For if it could be defined and given a name, it would then have a specific meaning, but not the omnipresent true constancy.[88]

This commentary succinctly brings out the point of the pun in the first line of the *Laozi*, showing that there is in Chinese a word that tries to disclose the same paradoxical relationship between thinking and speaking as we find in the logos and the whole Western problematic of inner *ratio* versus outer *oratio*, and that this paradoxical relationship is laid out clearly in one of the most important ancient texts of the Chinese philosophical tradition. Thus Laozi emphasizes, at the very beginning of his writing, the inadequacy and even futility of writing, and he does so by playing on the two meanings of *tao*: the *tao* as thinking denies the *tao* as speaking, and yet the two are interlocked in the same word. According to Laozi, then, the moment an internally grasped conception gets outside as a verbal expression, it loses its plenitude or, in Laozi's term, constancy (*chang*). The *tao*, like the Platonic idea, is constant and invariable; so in the second sentence, Laozi claims that no concrete and changeable name can do justice to constancy. We may recall that for Laozi *tao* is not a name and is forever nameless. Similarly, in the seventh philosophical epistle, Plato maintains that "no intelligent man will ever be so bold as to put into language those things which his reason has contemplated, especially not into a form that is unalterable. . . . Names, I maintain, are in no case stable."[89] "This passage," says Qian Zhongshu after quoting it, "may almost be translated to annotate the *Laozi*."[90] Indeed, there is no reason why Plato should not be considered as in harmonious company with Laozi in the contemplation of logos or the *tao*, given that for both philosophers and the traditions they represent, the relationship between thinking and language is so antithetical that it may be indicated in terms of conceptual opposites like inner / outer, intuition / expression, and signified / signifier. Moreover, for both philosophers and the traditions they represent, writing is even more suspicious and inadequate than the spoken word for conveying thinking as inner speech.

According to Derrida, metaphysical conceptualization always proceeds by hierarchies: "In a classical philosophical opposition we are not dealing with the peaceful coexistence of a *vis-à-vis*, but rather with a violent hierarchy. One of the two terms governs the other (axiologically, logically, etc.), or has the upper hand."[91] In the case of language, then, the metaphysical hierarchy is established when meaning dominates speech and speech dominates writing. Derrida finds such a hierarchy in the Western tradition since the very beginning in Plato and Aristotle, especially in the notion of phonetic writing as the first and primary signifier: "If, for Aristotle, for example, 'spoken words (ta en te phone) are the symbols of mental experience (pathemata tes psyches) and written words are the symbols of spoken words' (*De interpretatione*, 1, 16a 3) it is because the voice, producer of the *first symbols*, has a relationship of essential and immediate proximity with the mind."[92] This Aristotelian hierarchy seems to apply, however, not only to phonetic writing but to nonphonetic as well. When we look at the oldest Chinese dictionary, the *Shuowen jiezi* (second century A.D.), we find a similar hierarchy in the very definition of "word" (*ci*), which is described as "meaning inside and speech outside." In the appendixes to one of the ancient Chinese classics, the *Book of Changes*, we find a much earlier and even more clear formulation of this hierarchy: "Writing cannot fully convey the speech, and speech cannot fully convey the meaning."[93] Here the debasement of writing is based on the same consideration as in the West: written words are secondary signifiers; they are further removed than speech from what is conceived in the interiority of the mind, and they constitute a dead and empty shell from which the living voice is absent. "The epoch of the logos thus debases writing considered as mediation of mediation and as a fall into the exteriority of meaning."[94] Exactly! And that is why the wheelwright in the *Zhuangzi* told Duke Huan that "what you are reading, my lord, is nothing but the dregs of the ancients."[95] For Zhuangzi as for Aristotle, words are external and dispensable signs; they should be cast aside once their meaning, content, or signified has been extracted. Thus we have this beautiful passage from Zhuangzi that finds many an echo in classical Chinese poetry and philosophy:

> It is for the fish that the trap exists; once you've got the fish, you forget the trap. It is for the hare that the snare exists; once you've got the hare, you forget the snare. It is for the meaning that the word exists; once you've got the meaning, you forget the word. Where can I find the man who will forget words so that I can have a word with him?[96]

The man Zhuangzi calls for should indeed be the ideal addressee of a philosophical message, the perfect receptacle of the *tao* or logos that keeps the inner meaning but not the outer form, a man who forgets the word as expression but remembers what is grasped within. We may compare this with Heraclitus' fragment 36, "Listening not to me but to the logos," and with Ludwig Wittgenstein's metaphor at the end of his *Tractatus Logico-Philosophicus*—that the reader who has comprehended his propositions should throw them away as he should, so to speak, "throw away the ladder, after he has climbed up on it."[97] It is obvious not only that the dichotomy of meaning and word, content and form, intention and expression, is deeply rooted in both the Chinese and Western traditions, but that the two terms always stand in a hierarchical relation. Therefore, the metaphysical hierarchy of thinking, speech, and writing exists not only in the West but in the East as well, and logocentrism does not just inhabit the Western way of thinking but constitutes the very way of thinking itself.

If that is the case, is there then any other way that thinking may operate beyond or outside the enclosure of logocentrism? Derrida himself seems to doubt the possibility when he says that, operating necessarily from the inside and unable to isolate the elements and atoms of the old structure, "deconstruction always in a way falls prey to its own work."[98] The elements and atoms are so much constituent of the whole structure of thinking, every bit of it, that it becomes impossible for the deconstructionist to single out one element or atom of thinking and purge the rest of logocentrism. Derrida takes great pains to coin new words which might, one hopes, take on meanings yet uncontaminated by the old structure of metaphysical thinking—words like *trace, archiécriture* and, most notably, *différance*. He then hastens to insist that *différance*, like the other Derridean terms, "is literally neither a word nor a concept"; meanwhile his vocabulary keeps moving on to some newer coinage.[99] Nevertheless, such painstaking effort seems to be of little avail, and the terminology of deconstruction simply becomes another set of terminology in due time— that is, both words and concepts. The only way out of such a circle seems to lie in giving up the feat of naming altogether and leaving all those nonconceptual terms unnamed. Yet even that would hardly be the solution, since it would be going to the other end of logocentrism, indeed the oldest form of it—namely, the unnamed and unnameable *tao* or logos itself.

On the other hand, the terms of deconstruction become interesting and useful when they begin to function as words and concepts. *Différance*, for example, plays a very vital part in the strategy of deconstructing the metaphysical hierarchy in language. By pushing further Ferdinand de Saussure's proposition that "in language there are only differences *without positive terms*,"[100] Derrida proves that the meaning or the signified is never a transcendental, self-contained presence, never an entity that becomes visible in the form of a signifier, but, like the signifier, is always already a trace, a mark of the absence of a presence and therefore a trace always "under erasure." Language as a sign system is but a system of different and mutually defining terms, and this is true in speaking as well as in writing. Therefore, there is no ground on which the superiority of speech to writing, of the phonetic to the nonphonetic, could be established. The Hegelian prejudice is exposed as philosophically untenable, based on a false conception of the nature of writing, since logos as inner speech is already implicated and traversed by *différance*, which makes conceptualization possible in the first place. Similarly, Plato's fear of writing can also be exposed as untenable. Though Gadamer acknowledges the hermeneutic significance of the form of the Platonic dialogue, his discussion eventually leads up to an attempt to correct Plato's misguided view that sees writing only as an external moment of dubious equivocation, eventually to be discarded by true dialectics. The form of the dialogue is intended to emulate the silent grasp of pure thought, as "a dialogue of the soul with itself." The inner dialogue is immediately articulated in the spoken word: "The logos is the stream that flows from this thought and sounds out through the mouth." But, Gadamer goes on to argue, "audible perceptibility involves no claim that what is said is true. Plato undoubtedly did not consider the fact that the process of thought, if conceived as a dialogue of soul, itself involves a connection with language." In *Cratylus* and the seventh epistle, therefore, Plato did not actually grapple with "the real relationship between words and things," and his debasement of writing "conceals the true nature of language."[101]

Evidently, not only in the Western logos but also in the Chinese character *tao* we can find a word that endeavors to name the unnameable and to inscribe the problematic relationship between thinking and language: a single word that signifies, with its remarkable double sense, a hierarchical relation between inner reality and outer expression. The striking similarity of *tao* and logos certainly invites and encourages further exploration. The presence in both China and the West of largely the same kind of metaphysical hierarchy, the same concern about the loss of inner reality in outer expression, already provides a fertile ground for comparison that may help us expand our horizon and finally understand the nature of language beyond the arbitrary phonocentric distinctions. The Chinese script as a form of nonphonetic writing, however, does differ from the Western alphabetical writing in a significant way that may overturn the metaphysical hierarchy more easily and efficiently than Western phonetic writing does, and there is something in the Chinese script that does appeal to the Derridean grammatology. In the legendary account of its origin, Chinese writing is never conceived as a mere recording of oral speech but as originating independently of speech; writing imitates the pattern of traces left by birds and animals on the ground or by natural phenomena in general. A widespread tradition has it that when the creator of the Chinese script, Cangjie, invented writing by observing such patterns: "Millet grains rained down from heaven and the ghosts wailed at night." A commentator explains that the invention of writing marked the loss of innocence and the beginning of guile and that "heaven foreknew that people were to starve, so it let millet grains rain down; and the ghosts were afraid to be condemned by written verdict, so they wailed at night."[102] On the one hand, the commentator here conceives of writing as the loss of innocence that incurs great disasters, but, on the other hand, he recognizes that man has gained power in writing to such an extent that even the ghosts are afraid of him. It is interesting to note that the same passage has been reinterpreted in the light of modern archaeology and anthropology by K. C. Chang, who understands the raining of millet grains and the wailing of the ghosts as one of the "very few happy incidents" described in ancient Chinese mythology and considers Chinese writing "the path to authority."[103]

The power of Chinese writing is certainly substantiated by the large amount of inscriptions on pottery and bronze utensils, on tortoise shells and oracle bones, on bamboo slips and stone tablets. There is further evidence in the importance and high prestige which the Chinese accord calligraphy as a traditional form of art and in the predominant influence of ancient writing as canonical classics. Anyone who has visited a Chinese palace, temple, or garden can hardly fail to notice the manifold inscribed characters on the gates, pillars, and walls. Anyone who has seen a Chinese painting knows that writing and the seal-stamp form an integral part of the finished picture. Indeed, as it is created by observing the pattern of traces, Chinese writing tends to project the nature or quality of trace in writing better than any phonetic writing does and thus reveals language as a system of differential terms. The convention in ancient China of naming a book after its author and the settled practice of ancient writers quoting earlier writings do not so much emphasize the origin of writing in its author, but rather make authors identifiable first in their writing and transform the writings of philosophers like Laozi and Zhuangzi into great sourcebooks, origins of authority, and the ultimate texts of reference in the intertextuality of Chinese writing. It is quite true that almost every ancient Chinese text is an intertext, but an intertext significantly different from that understood in deconstructive criticism. While a deconstructive *intertexte* is a trace without origin, a Chinese intertext is always a trace leading back to the origin, to the fountainhead of tradition, the great thinkers of Taoism and Confucianism. In this sense, the power of Chinese writing transforms the author into authoritative text, and when quoting from ancient writings, there is no difference between quoting, for example, Laozi the author or *Laozi* the book. In the Chinese tradition, therefore, the power of writing as such avenged itself the very moment it was debased; the metaphysical hierarchy was thus already undermined when it was established. Perhaps this is precisely where the *tao* differs from the logos: it hardly needed to wait till the twentieth century for the dismantling of phonetic writing, for the Derridean sleight of hand, the strategy of deconstruction.

2

Philosopher,

Mystic,

Poet

I sometimes hold it half a sin
To put in words the grief I feel;
For words, like Nature, half reveal
And half conceal the Soul within.
—Alfred Tennyson, *In Memoriam*, 5

elle balance
Sur le plumage instrumental,
Musicienne du silence.
—Stéphane Mallarmé, *Sainte*

The Ironic Pattern

We start this chapter with some of Ludwig Wittgenstein's propositions because in them the central issues that concern us here — that is, thinking, speaking, silence, and the like — are so well formulated that it would be difficult to find any other formulation that may claim to have the same depth of insight put in such a highly condensed form. In the preface to *Tractatus Logico-Philosophicus*, Wittgenstein sums up the whole point of his book in this famous statement: "What can be said at all can be said clearly; and whereof one cannot speak thereof one must be silent."[1] Underlying this statement, we probably sense the same suspicion of the inadequacy of language that we find in the writings of Plato, Laozi, and others, since Wittgenstein says explicitly that the limit drawn here is "not to thinking, but to the expression of thoughts."[2] In his introduction to this book, Bertrand Russell explains that Wittgenstein is here concerned with an ideal, logically perfect language which has eliminated the source of ambiguity and confusion in daily speech, that is, the gaps between thinking and expression. The business of philosophy, says Wittgenstein, is to "make clear and delimit sharply the thoughts which otherwise are, as it were, opaque and blurred." Nevertheless, very little of what we usually say lives up to the standard of the ideal language. Much of our talk, including what we say about the good and the beautiful, or ethics and aesthetics, is opaque, blurred, and, from the vantage point of the ideal language, senseless.[3] The only thing that can be said with precision, the "totality of true propositions," says Wittgenstein, is "the totality of the natural sciences" — that is, something that does not depend on language for its effectiveness but shows its presence extralinguistically.[4] Yet philosophy is not a natural science; so eventually even philosophy and the whole of logic must fall under the inexpressible. Following Fritz Mauthner, Wittgenstein declares that all philosophy is

"critique of language," although "not at all in Mauthner's sense." Unless
the logic of language is understood through such a *Sprachkritik*, most
philosophical propositions and questions can only be "senseless."[5] What,
one may ask, are the things that can be said at all? Or, to put it differently,
what are the things that can be thought and that, through thinking, find
their clear expression? Wittgenstein insists that they can only be "the
propositions of natural science, i. e. something that has nothing to do
with philosophy."[6] This makes Russell feel quite puzzled, for Wittgenstein's
view would lead to the inevitable conclusion that "nothing correct can be
said in philosophy. Every philosophical proposition is bad grammar, and
the best that we can hope to achieve by philosophical discussion is to lead
people to see that philosophical discussion is a mistake." Nevertheless,
Russell goes on to say, "after all, Mr Wittgenstein manages to say a good
deal about what cannot be said, thus suggesting to the sceptical reader
that possibly there may be some loophole through a hierarchy of languages, or by some other exit."[7]

It seems an inevitable irony that the philosopher always has to say a
good deal about what he believes to be ineffable and to write a good deal
to elucidate what is supposedly absent in writing. Instead of being silent,
Wittgenstein writes about the inexpressible in epigrammatic propositions
which he acknowledges to be ultimately senseless (*unsinnig*) and which
he urges the reader to throw away once he has understood them. Similarly, Laozi composes a book of five thousand characters to speak of the
tao that cannot be *tao*-ed (spoken of), and Zhuangzi tries to demonstrate
the ineffable in a dazzling display of metaphors, parables, and images,
while searching for the man who will forget his words once he has got the
meaning. The loophole or exit Russell mentions turns out to be nothing
but speaking and writing, something these philosophers did not mean to
use but all ended up using profusely. They all have to *say* that they mean
to be silent, and they all have to *write* to declare that they do not trust
writing. Yet nothing abides but writing; even the debasement of writing
has to survive in writing. Philosophers' anxiety over writing begins with
their misgivings concerning the discrepancy between thoughts and words,
especially words used figuratively, but in the end they all use words, and
use them in all kinds of rhetorical ways. The dream of a univocal language without any figure or metaphor, as Derrida says, remains a "dream
at the heart of philosophy."[8] Derrida attempts to expose the emptiness of
this dream, the philosopher's futile search for a language of unmediated
presence, by quoting Anatole France that "the very metaphysicians who

think to escape the world of appearances are constrained to live perpetually in allegory. A sorry lot of poets, they dim the colours of the ancient
fables, and are themselves but gatherers of fables. They produce white
mythology."[9]

Indeed, in using images and analogies, philosophical discourse at times
verges on the intense metaphoricity of poetry. Kant points out the inescapable figurative nature of all philosophical expressions when he observes
that language is replete with indirect exhibitions which "express concepts
not by means of a direct intuition but only according to an analogy with
one, i.e., a transfer of our reflection on an object of intuition to an entirely
different concept, to which perhaps no intuition can ever directly correspond."[10] He sees clearly that the inescapable metaphoricity of language
constitutes the very substance of philosophical discourse, and puts the
distinction between philosophical and poetic expressions in question. An
examination of the language philosophers use can bear this out. The epigrammatic form of Wittgenstein's writing has a touch of wit and raciness
reminiscent of many of Schiller's aphorisms or Novalis's fragments. In turning out numerous metaphors in quick succession, Zhuangzi, as he himself
describes, uses words like wine goblets to be filled or emptied as the occa-
sion requires, achieving a highly literary kind of writing that is richly
packed with "airy and fantastic sayings, absurd and bombastic phrases,
and words without ends or boundaries."[11] Even Plato, who accuses poets
of lying and banishes them from his ideal state, expounds the Socratic
philosophy in the form of dialogues which Aristotle classifies as a literary
genre "between poetry and prose."[12] In many ways Aristotle's *Poetics* is a
defense of poetry against Plato's rationalistic attack, and ever since the
Renaissance many apologists of poetry have claimed that Plato himself is
a poet, for "whosoever well considereth shall find," as Sir Philip Sidney
contends, "that in the body of his work, though the inside and strength
were philosophy, the skin as it were and beauty depended most of poetry."[13]
In much the same vein, Shelley also claims that "Plato was essentially a
poet," for "the truth and splendour of his imagery, and the melody of his
language, is the most intense that it is possible to conceive."[14]

If Sidney still locates the metaphoricity of Plato's writing in the frame
of an inner/outer dichotomy, considering it as the mere outside, long before
him Dante already realizes that metaphor is more than just embedded in
the texture of philosophical discourse but may be said to constitute the
very philosophical discourse itself. In his well-known "Letter to Can
Grande," Dante argues that it is metaphor that enables the philosopher to

express thoughts that must otherwise remain silent and inexpressible: "For we see many things with the intellect for which there are no verbal signs. This fact Plato makes plain enough by the use he makes of metaphors in his books: for he saw many things by the light of the intellect which he was unable to express in the appropriate words."[15] Therefore, it is through images, metaphors, analogies, and other figures of speech that philosophical conceptions take graspable shape and become intelligible. We can almost say that metaphor, in philosophy as well as in poetry, "gives to aery nothing / A local habitation and a name."[16] The unnamed is inconceivable, and philosophy as such exists only in words and names. Despite Zhuangzi's advice to forget the word, it is ironically his words that have made him best remembered, for many people read Zhuangzi as one of the greatest prose writers in classical Chinese literature: they admire the grandeur of his imagination and the beauty of his language, even though they do not care about his Taoist ideology. That is to say, people tend to remember his words while forgetting his meaning, and Zhuangzi's advice functions against itself as a poetic trope, an irony. And his philosophy of self-effacement, like that of Laozi, is thus overturned by his own writing.

Zhuangzi's highly figurative text shows clearly how the play of metaphor blurs the usual distinction between philosophy and literature. In this particular case, however, the mythology emerging from the text is by no means white, but of a very robust and sanguine color. Neither is Zhuangzi unaware of the irreducible metaphoricity of his writing, but he would take it as an unfortunate necessity. Hui Shi, a rival philosopher, challenges Zhuangzi that he does, after all, use many words despite his protest that words are quite useless. In response to that challenge, Zhuangzi answers wittily in a typical irony: "But you must know they are useless, and then you can talk about their use." He seems to argue that once you know that the use of words is provisional, you are freed, as it were, from the infatuation with words and are thus capable of using words as expedient "non-words." "Speaking those non-words," Zhuangzi argues, "you may talk all your life without having said anything. Otherwise, even if you never speak in all your life, you may still have said too much."[17] So the issue at stake is not so much speaking itself as the right kind of medium one uses in speaking. By using words as "non-words," Zhuangzi carries out a double-edged argument, for on the one hand, language becomes for him a mere instrument to convey meaning, like the trap for catching fish or the snare to get the hare: a disposable instrument once its purpose is served; while on the other hand, the philosopher has the excuse to use language any way he pleases to convey the meaning, including using all sorts of rhetorical devices and maneuvers. But what exactly are Zhuangzi's "non-words"? What else, if not the irreducible metaphors necessary for bringing the unnamed and the unnameable into existence, metaphors the philosopher has to smuggle back into his writing after he has denied their usefulness? When Zhuangzi called for the man who would forget his words while preserving his meaning, he seemed to know that he was never to find such a man. We may also recall that Confucius, despite his wish to be silent, nevertheless acknowledges the necessity of speaking to transmit what the sages have already said in the past. Much as they would desire a transparent and wordless transmission of truth and knowledge, philosophers, no less than the poets, thus find themselves deeply immersed in language and its inescapable metaphoricity. Apparently, the desire for silence will find catharsis in an ironic pattern, for the more one craves silence, the more desperately one must speak and write. To some extent, Richard Rorty argues that it is recognition of this ironic pattern that differentiates deconstruction from traditional philosophy. "Philosophical writing, for Heidegger as for the Kantians," he puts it summarily, "is really aimed at putting an end to writing. For Derrida, writing always leads to more writing, and more, and still more."[18] Perhaps we may say that Zhuangzi, by using words as "non-words," also recognized this ironic pattern, offering philosophers an excuse to recuperate writing, a license to proliferate writing even to infinity, because Zhuangzi's use of "non-words" can be understood as essentially a move to reclaim language and to acknowledge the inevitable metaphoricity of all philosophical discourse.

"Metaphor," Derrida writes in summing up the traditional view, "is determined by philosophy as a provisional loss of meaning, an economy of the proper without irreparable damage, a certainly inevitable detour, but also a history with its sights set on, and within the horizon of, the circular reappropriation of literal, proper meaning."[19] He rejects such a view as a distortion of the nature of both metaphor and of philosophy, maintaining that not only is our language—which philosophers also use—a storehouse of dead metaphors, but the very concepts of philosophy, in their origin and history, are also metaphorical. We know from etymological studies that words denoting spiritual or abstract notions usually derive from words originally signifying sensuous objects. Giambattista Vico, for example, thus formulates "the universal principle of etymology in all languages: words are carried over from bodies and from the properties of bodies to signify the institutions of the mind and spirit."[20]

Interestingly, there is a very similar formulation of the same principle in the appendix to the *Book of Changes*, where it is said that the ancient king Pao Xi invented the hexagrams by observing the configuration of heaven and earth, and imitating the pattern of traces left by birds and animals on the ground. "By taking hint near at hand from his body and farther away from external things, he then created the hexagrams to make the virtue of gods comprehensible and the nature of all things known in signs."[21] Thus, in both Vico and the Chinese classic, signs and words are recognized as originally signifying something sensuous, especially the human body, out of which the spiritual or abstract meanings develop as transferred, figurative, and hence metaphorical. The physiology of the body contains the origin of all abstract words and meanings. As long as philosophy is written in words, it can never rid itself of all metaphors; it can never escape from this irreducible physicality to acquire absolute clarity. "How could a piece of knowledge or a language be properly clear or obscure?" Derrida asks. "Now, all the concepts which have operated in the definition of metaphor always have an origin and an efficacity that are themselves 'metaphorical.'"[22]

Derrida, however, does not keep the issue simply within the range of etymology. He tries, rather, to reveal the metaphoricity of essential philosophical concepts in the texts of major philosophers in the Western tradition: Plato, Aristotle, Descartes, and Hegel. He calls our attention especially to the perennial heliotrope, which appears so often in philosophical writings. Descartes' hyperbolic doubt, for instance, put in question not only those ideas that have a sensory origin but also abstract ideas, refusing to take any of the ideas as the proper foundation for philosophical reasoning. Descartes, however, found himself unable to doubt the "natural light" that enabled him to "see" the fact that he was doubting. And yet, Derrida argues, what is "natural light" if not another use of the sun metaphor? To conceive of the mind as some kind of an intellectual light is of course making a metaphor. Thus, Descartes' radical skepticism is disclosed as coming out of the heliotrope; the Cartesian *cogito* and the whole edifice of rationalist philosophy are found to have been built squarely on metaphorical grounds. This may also help us expose the metaphorical foundation of Hegel's Eurocentric-ethnocentric view of world history, because he symbolizes the course of history and contrasts the East and the West in terms of the outer and the inner "Sun," the former being the lesser light of inactive contemplation and the latter the greater light of free spirit. In the East or Asia "rises the outward physical Sun, and in the West it sinks down: here consentaneously rises the Sun of self-consciousness, which diffuses a nobler brilliance."[23] As Derrida comments, here the "sensory sun, which rises in the East, becomes interiorized, in the evening of its journey, in the eye and the heart of the Westerner. . . . Philosophical discourse—as such—describes a metaphor which is displaced and reabsorbed between two suns."[24] The disclosure of the heliotrope at the heart of philosophical discourse has profound implications for our understanding of the nature of philosophy itself: "Metaphor," Derrida maintains, "is less in the philosophical text (and in the rhetorical text coordinated with it) than the philosophical text is within metaphor." As metaphor so closely intertwines with, and within, the texture of philosophy, it becomes impossible to separate it from philosophy, and no ontology will ever be able to reduce its play to the purity of proper meaning. For philosophy, therefore, any attempt to efface metaphor would be suicidal, because the death of metaphor, Derrida declares, will also be "the death *of* philosophy."[25]

From *Sprachkritik* To Mysticism

From Wittgenstein's imperative to keep silent to Zhuangzi's use of "nonwords" as a license to speak without saying, we see, in both the East and the West, philosophy wrestling with its own metaphoricity, trying in vain to get rid of it, to escape from its implications. Against this background, the effort to rehabilitate metaphoricity and to rescue it from the oblivion that philosophy tries to put it in certainly sets deconstruction off strikingly from the tradition of the metaphysics that it severely criticizes. Without discounting the original contributions of this deconstructive valorization of metaphor, however, we may note that in his project to carry out a consistent critique of language, Fritz Mauthner, an interesting cultural figure in Vienna at the turn of the century, already adumbrated the view that philosophy is nothing but language and, as such, is by nature metaphorical. It is important to realize, Mauthner maintains, "that understanding or human thinking or language is metaphorical through and through."[26] Just like Vico or the legendary account in the *Book of Changes*, Mauthner holds that signs, words, and their meanings all originate in sensory experiences of the outside world, including observations of the human body; they are therefore incapable of adequately representing the inner experiences of the mind: "Nothing in the human mind or in language has not previously been in the senses; and the senses, as I said, do not look inward. There is not one word in language that did not originate in observations of the physical world [*Beobachtungen der Körperwelt*], including our own body and bodily experiences."[27]

Our language is thus implicated by the external, the material, the bodily, and owing to its origin and history, it is thoroughly metaphorical. We have no adequate means to describe our inner experiences, Mauthner argues, so psychology as a discipline is impossible. Moreover, to the extent that it claims to be the "self-knowledge of human intellect," philosophy is also impossible.[28] Since philosophical propositions use a metaphorical language to talk about the metaphysical, they are simply senseless. Only through a rigorous critique of language, Mauthner declares, can philosophy make significant progress, and in fact philosophy ought to be nothing but such a critique. "In the beginning was the Word"—Mauthner starts his *Kritik der Sprache* by quoting the first verse of St. John. There is the need to transcend the beginning, but human beings would forever remain in the beginning, and their knowledge of the world forever arrested from growing, if they were still bound to the word. Miraculously, the word has an uncanny power over us, says Mauthner; whoever wants to step out of its spell and make progress in thinking "must free himself from the word and word-superstition, must try to deliver his world from the tyranny of language."[29] The goal of his critique is precisely liberation from such a tyranny of language; it will eventually lead to the negation of all words and all linguistic expressions. Mauthner characterizes his own philosophy as "out of the death-wish of thinking, a suicide of language," for to be consistent in such a critique, one must give up language altogether.[30] Whoever still sets out to write a book out of his "hunger for words, love of words, and vanity of words" cannot yet accomplish the task of this liberation. Whoever carries out an uncompromising critique of language must destroy the very language with which he carries out the critique, like smashing the ladder after one has climbed up on it—a memorable image Mauthner borrows from Sextus Empiricus, and Wittgenstein in turn borrows from him at the end of his *Tractatus Logico-Philosophicus*. Mauthner writes: "If I want to climb upwards in the critique of language, which is the most important business of thinking mankind, I must then destroy the language behind me, before me, and in me step by step, I must then smash each rung of the ladder on which I just stepped. Whoever wishes to follow will fix the rungs again only to smash them yet once more."[31]

As Allan Janik and Stephen Toulmin show convincingly, Mauthner's critique of language forms part of the Viennese milieu of the 1890s and

1900s, within which Wittgenstein's *Tractatus*, a key work in modern philosophy but also one of the most enigmatic ones, becomes comprehensible. They read the *Tractatus*, among other things, as a response to Mauthner, an effort "to defend the adequacy of language as a scientific instrument from Mauthner's skepticism."[32] But in his later works, they argue, when he no longer believed in the self-evident correlation between language and reality as he had posited in the *Tractatus*, Wittgenstein "revived many positions and arguments already put forward by Mauthner in 1901."[33] In a study of Mauthner's *Sprachkritik*, Gershon Weiler also notes that both Mauthner and Wittgenstein "see the critique of language as an inquiry into the limits of what can be and what cannot be said." The two philosophers differ in their opinions so far as natural science is concerned, but they both share the view that ultimately philosophy belongs to the unsayable, and they both "conclude their works by a commitment to mysticism."[34]

Insofar as both philosophy and mysticism claim to have something that cannot be put in words, they are never far from each other. The quintessential mystic moment, as Martin Buber notes, is that of a union with God, a truly ineffable moment of ecstasy, when "one is removed from the commotion, removed into the most silent, speechless heavenly kingdom —removed even from language."[35] Admittedly, Mauthner's critique of language operates totally outside the concerns of religious mysticism; it is, as Mauthner himself admits, a "godless" mysticism, but it is mystic in the sense that it leads to a moment of complete speechlessness, as it steers "through a mistrust of language to silence."[36] We have Mauthner's own testimony: "Critique of language was my first word and is still my last. Looking backward, critique of language is all-crushing skepticism [*alles zermalmende Skepsis*]. Looking forward and playing with illusions, it is a longing for unity, it is mysticism."[37]

Nevertheless, Mauthner calls his own mysticism "godless" in order to differentiate it from other kinds of mysticism, for the concept of God, like all other concepts, when put in the perspective of his critical theory, is only a word without substance. Critique of language must therefore lead to the negation of theology as well as philosophy, to the destruction of all concepts and words. The final result can only be a moment of complete silence wherein nothing is conceptualized, nothing is said. This is the moment when one realizes, as Laozi puts it, that "the one who knows does not speak; the one who speaks does not know"; or, as Zhuangzi remarks, that "to explain is not as effective as to keep silent"; and that "the *tao* cannot be heard, what is heard is not *tao*. It cannot be seen, what is seen is not *tao*. It cannot be spoken, what is spoken is not *tao*."[38] In fact, it is Mauthner himself who cited these words from Laozi and Zhuangzi and referred to *tao* as "the puzzling word [*Rätselwort*], coined or used two thousand and five hundred years ago by the Chinese sage Laozi to capture in a human sound the most profound self-communion of the East, the feeling of unity with a world without God."[39] Not surprisingly, Mauthner's reflections on the meaning of *tao* are historically limited and ill-informed, but we must admit that he has a remarkable insight in seeing an affinity between the *tao* and logos, and claiming to "discover in Tao a primeval critique of language [*in Tao eine uralte Sprachkritik zu entdecken*]; for Laozi says: 'The name that can be named is not the constant name.'"[40]

Mystics, whether religious or godless, in the East or the West, all claim that the feeling of unity they experience or the spiritual reality they have come to know is so unique that it cannot be put in words. Meister Eckhart, for example, distinguishes between word as outside expression and the divine Word as inward silence when he claims, "St. Paul said to Timothy: 'Beloved, preach the word!' Did he mean the audible word that beats the air? Certainly not! He referred to the inborn, secret word that lies hidden in the soul."[41] In the Buddhist tradition, inward silence is also held as the state of mind to be achieved at the final moment of enlightenment, for the nature of things or dharmas is beyond language, as the great second-century Buddhist thinker Nagarjuna pointed out. In order to attain to perfect wisdom, one must be free from the habitual clinging to words because such wisdom does not transmit in language, but will "put an end to the entire network of words (*prapañca*)."[42] So Buddha, as Nagarjuna notes, "delighted at heart in keeping silent" when approached by the uninitiated with questions, for "he knew that it is difficult for ordinary minds to comprehend the profound *dharma*."[43] With so much emphasis on intuitive apprehension, transmission of wisdom in Buddhism becomes very difficult and teaching virtually impossible. A Chan (or Zen) master would thus prefer "a special transmission outside the scripture," with "no dependence upon words and letters." That, as D. T. Suzuki notes, "sums up all that is claimed by Zen as religion."[44] And yet teaching without using language is certainly characteristic not just of Zen but also of Taoist teaching, which is set forth by Laozi as "teaching without words."[45] In fact, it is an attitude shared by all mystics, a critique of language shaped by the very sense of the mysterious:

It is especially the cult of mysticism, in all ages and among all peoples, that grapples again and again with this intellectual double problem—the task of comprehending the Divine in its totality, in its highest inward reality, and yet avoiding any particularity of name or image. Thus all mysticism is directed toward a world beyond language, a world of silence. As Meister Eckhardt has written, God is the "simple ground, the still desert, the simple silence."[46]

The critique of language, however, whether in Mauthner's or Wittgenstein's sense, must be carried out in and with language; thus their works exemplify, of necessity, the irony of all mysticism, that is, the irony of silence. The words we use may be inadequate for whatever purposes they are meant to serve, but they are the only means of conveying what we have to say, and the mystic who negates words has to use words to say what he holds as beyond language. Mauthner is of course aware of this contradiction when he declares: "I shall try once more to say the unsayable, to express with poor words whatever I have to give pious unbelievers in nominalistic mysticism, in skeptical mysticism."[47] He uses a great deal of words as if they were Zhuangzi's "non-words," continuously turning mystic silence into thick volumes of philosophical writing. It seems that mystic silence, whether the religious or the linguistic kind, really generates a strong repressed desire to speak, and that its fulfillment must follow the ironic pattern as we have delineated it, for the mystic is always torn between the plenitude of silence and the human need for communication. As Martin Buber remarks, "Even the innermost experience is not kept safe from the drive to expression." The ecstatic "must speak, because the Word burns in him," because "he wants to create a memorial for ecstasy which leaves no traces, to tow the timeless into the harbor of time; he wants to make the unity without multiplicity into the unity of all multiplicity."[48]

For philosophers and mystics, the necessity of reconciling unity and multiplicity and of catching silence in speech poses an insoluble problem. The nature of things or the ecstatic experience may remain forever ineffable, but philosophers and mystics will still try to approximate to it by all means, allowing their effort at saying the unsayable to move incessantly from the depth of reticence to the peak of loquacity. Zhuangzi's "non-words" provide one way out of this metaphysical-metaphorical dilemma; so do the Buddhist *prajñapti* or "provisional names." Nagarjuna maintains that one can speak neither of the positive nor of the negative, nor even of the negation of the negative, but one can speak of all these when speaking with provisional names. His philosophy is known as the Middle Way (*madhyama pratipat*) because it transcends the absolute by way of the provisional, subsuming all binary categories under an ambivalent non-category. Thus beyond silence and speech, the Nagarjunian provisional names build up a sort of mental ladder upon which we may climb beyond our finite, historically limited understanding toward ultimate infinity. The Middle Way in his philosophy, as Venkata Ramanan puts it, is the way "to recognize the possibility of determining things differently from different standpoints and to recognize that these determinations cannot be seized as absolute. This is the way that realizes the relativity of specific views and of determinate entities."[49] The Middle Way, in other words, advocates a kind of hermeneutic pluralism that will free the wayfarer from extremes and absolutes by acknowledging the local values of different views and positions without imposing commitment to any one of them. Absolute silence for Nagarjuna would be as untenable as blind adherence to words; thus with provisional names, one is able to attain to *upaya* or skillful nonclinging, the ability to reclaim language as something useful though limited and expedient.

No matter how they are called, "non-words" or "provisional names," these are all strategies that mystics in the East employ to justify their use of language, even the excessive verbosity so often found in their writings. In Western mysticism, as Karl Vossler observes, there is also a similar move. The mystics insist, on the one hand, that "no name fits God, because he stands above all things that have names," while on the other, that "since he is the creator of all things, all names of all things could be applied to him." As a result, "mystics have never tired of glorifying God as the highest and the lowest, the greatest and the smallest, the day and the night, all and nothing; they have surrounded him with a wild dance of words where each negates the one before it."[50] These words cannot but remind us of what Zhuangzi says about the *tao*, that if *tao* is nowhere, then it is everywhere; if nothing contains it in totality, then everything bears it in part. When pressed to name the site of *tao*, Zhuangzi declares, in a deliberate decrescendo, that it exists in ants, in weeds, in earthenware, even in urine and excrement.[51] Commenting on such moves, Qian Zhongshu sees the circular cancellation of words as a unique method mystics use in speaking of the ineffable. Citing copious examples from Buddhist sutras, Taoist books, and Western mystic writings, he shows clearly that anonymy and polynomy are complementary to one another in all mystic pronouncements. Perhaps the most revealing of these examples is an interesting passage quoted from a Taoist book, *Guan yinzi* (c. third century B.C.), where the circular negation of words is compared to the precarious balance kept among three creatures: the cricket, the snake, and the frog. According to an old superstition, these three were believed to be deadly one to the other:

> The cricket preys on the snake, the snake preys on the frog, and the frog preys on the cricket: one preying on the next. So do the words of the sages: they speak of the imperfection of being and nonbeing, then they speak of the imperfection of the negation of being and nonbeing, and then they speak of the imperfection of the negation of that negation. They are, so to speak, sawing up words; only the good ones will leave no word behind.[52]

From this, Qian Zhongshu maintains, we should see the crucial difference in the use of words and images between the mystic or the philosopher on the one hand and the poet on the other. In the *Book of Changes*, a set of archetypal images are used to help bring out the meaning of the hexagrams, of which *Qian*

for example, is symbolized by horse, head, sky, father, etc.; and *Kun*

by cow, belly, earth, mother, etc.; and *Zhen*

by dragon, foot, thunder, the eldest son, etc. The meaning of *Qian* cannot be put in language, but it is something common to horse, head, sky, father, etc.; and the meaning of *Kun* is suggested likewise by cow, belly, earth, mother, etc. What *Qian* is to *Kun* is analogous to what horse is to cow, head to belly, sky to earth, father to mother, and the like. Each of these images in isolation does not seem to make much sense, but when they are juxtaposed in such pairs, some kind of a pattern manifests itself that renders those signs intelligible; something emerges as a shared quality or property: something strong and masculine about *Qian*, or meek and feminine about *Kun*, becomes conceivable. Yet the meaning of *Qian* is not exhausted by masculinity, nor is *Kun* mere femininity. None of these images is really able to claim to have a natural relation with the concept it helps to articulate. *Qian* is neither horse nor any of the other images for suggesting its meaning, nor is *Kun* a cow or mother. All the images illustrate or symbolize the concept, but they all differ from its totality and from one another; thereby they negate and cancel one another out, quite like the cricket, the snake, and the frog, in their different symbolism. Insofar as they are all figures and metaphors, images can do no better than words in getting to the ultimate and unmediated signified. To grasp a concept, one has to go beyond the image—to throw it away, as it were, and to forget it. The advice of Zhuangzi to forget words thus applies to images as well, for images are just as provisional and dispensable as words: if words cancel one another out, so do images. For the hexagram *Qian*, horse may be replaced by head, sky, or father; and for *Kun*, cow may be replaced by belly, earth, or mother. Such replacement and mutual cancellation indeed characterize words and images used in philosophical discourse, and this is where the philosopher and the mystic differ from the poet in the use of language. The words and images in lines from the *Book of Poetry*, such as "Neigh, neigh cries the horse," or "Dewy damp are ears of the cow," as Qian Zhongshu points out emphatically, cannot possibly allow such replacement. Thus, horse differs from horse, and cow from cow: "The image the philosopher wants us to forget once we've got the word, and the word he wants us to forget once we've got the meaning, are precisely what the poet cherishes and relishes."[53] Wittgenstein also points out the crucial difference between philosophical and literary discourse according to whether the form of expression itself is replaceable:

> We speak of understanding a sentence in the sense in which it can be replaced by another which says the same; but also in the sense in which it cannot be replaced by any other. (Any more than one musical theme can be replaced by another.)
>
> In the one case the thought in the sentence is something common to different sentences; in the other, something that is expressed only by these words in these positions. (Understanding a poem.)[54]

We may very well agree with Derrida that "metaphor seems to involve the usage of philosophical language in its entirety."[55] Given the above distinction, however, it should also be clear that we must take into consideration the different functions of metaphor and the different degrees of its irreducibility in literary and philosophical texts, as well as the different ways those texts demand to be read. Words and images in mystic or philosophical writings are like blurred traces or a kind of palimpsest through which one tries hopelessly to see the ultimate signified, which is what matters. It is only in poetry or literary texts in general that words and images become truly irreducible, because we may paraphrase a philosophical proposition to get its tenor, but if we change the wording or the specific sequence of words in a poem ever so slightly, what makes it uniquely poetic will immediately be affected, altered, even completely destroyed. Poetry, as Robert Frost's often-quoted definition has it, is what gets lost in translation. This is, however, not meant to be a disparagement of the literary value of translation but rather an affirmation of what we have indicated all along—that is, the uniqueness of words in a poem or the impossibility of their replacement. Therefore, Frost's definition should read, as Stanley Burnshaw notes, "*The poetry of the original* is the poetry that gets lost from verse or prose in translation."[56]

The Tongue-tied Muse

When Homer begins his epics by invoking the muse to help him tell the story of gods and heroes, he is making a sort of theoretical statement about the art of poetry. In a way, he is acknowledging his inability to speak or to portray actions of a gigantic proportion—the will of gods, the adventures of heroes, the course of capricious fate, and all those splendid things that make up the sublime text of an epic. He is saying that he cannot accomplish the composing of poetry without the help he now hopes to enlist from the goddess of song, and that whatever comes out of his mouth owes its origin not to the poet but to the muse, for his poems are words not his own but uttered by divine inspiration. The invocation to the muse later becomes a poetic convention, but with the passing of time, a poet with a strong sense of the belatedness of his own time, a "sentimental" poet like Friedrich Schiller, may feel very sharply that the invocation has now lost its real sense and become a meaningless gesture. Gone is the Homeric past, the "naive," mythological past, when creative collaboration with gods did not seem so unthinkable,

> Da der Dichtung zauberische Hülle
> Sich noch lieblich um die Wahrheit wand.

> When the magic fold of poetry
> Still charmingly wound around truth.[57]

The naive, simple, and more homogeneous past may very well be Schiller's idealizing fantasy, but he is painfully conscious of the fact that without the aid of divine power, it is now much more difficult for a modern poet to establish the perfect connection between reality and his own writing, which seemed once attainable in remote antiquity. Not surprisingly, it is Schiller—the great German poet, playwright, and philosopher—who has voiced the difficulty of articulation, the poet's inability to speak:

> Warum kann der lebendige Geist dem Geist nicht erscheinen?
> *Spricht* die Seele, so spricht, ach! schon die *Seele* nicht mehr.

> Why cannot a living spirit to another spirit appear?
> When the soul *speaks*, alas! the *soul's* no longer speaking.[58]

The difficulty Schiller speaks about is not just a matter of technical perfection—the problem of seeking the right word, a happy turn of phrase, or *le mot juste*—though that is undeniably difficult, too. It is rather a far more fundamental problem, namely, the problem of articulation or the inadequacy of all linguistic expressions, with which philosophers and mystics have been grappling all along. Schiller is of course not the only one to complain about this inadequacy, for the difficulty of articulation is indeed as old as poetry itself. No matter how hard they try, even with the "poetic license" to do some violence to words and syntax, poets still find their actual saying less than perfect and their written text a falling off from what they originally conceived in the intensity of imagination. "For the mind in creation," Shelley puts it elegantly, "is as a fading coal, which some invisible influence, like an inconstant wind, awakens to transitory brightness." And that brightness is quickly dimmed the very moment the poet begins to translate what seems to have taken shape in his mind, for "when composition begins, inspiration is already on the decline, and the most glorious poetry that has ever been communicated to the world is probably a feeble shadow of the original conception of the Poet."[59]

Though truthfulness in the representation of reality or the expression of emotions is a perennial question in the history of art, it becomes a matter of special acuteness and urgency for the theory of literature whenever the question is raised specifically as a problem of representation in language. In China during the third and fourth centuries, in that intellectually stimulating and intriguing Wei-Jin period (220–420), there was a philosophical debate among the literati about whether words could fully convey meaning. After four hundred years of scholastic studies in the Confucian classics during the Han dynasty (206 B.C.–220 A.D.), freed from all those repressive moralistic and utilitarian ordinances, this was a truly refreshing moment of intellectual emancipation in Chinese history when the concept of literature finally came into being not as a didactic tool for moral edification, but as expression of profound and genuine feelings, valuable in its own right. It was a time when the books of Laozi and Zhuangzi were read with rather sophisticated understanding and elicited a great deal of metaphysical discussion, when the sense of the self began to manifest in Chinese poetry along with a very keen sense of the complexity of language and expression. The debate on language ultimately originates from Taoist thinking, especially from Zhuangzi's radical linguistic skepticism. We may recall his famous parable of Pian the wheelwright, who tells Duke Huan that all books are merely dregs of the ancients because, so the wheelwright argues, even the simple craft of wheel making cannot be put into words and taught to his own son; how can something so complicated as ancient wisdom be transmitted to posterity across the enormous gaps in time and space by means of the lifeless signs of a written language? "The world likes to talk about books," says Zhuangzi, "yet books are nothing but words. Though words have value, what is valuable in words is meaning. There is something to which meaning adheres, but what meaning adheres to cannot be transmitted in language." The art of wheel making provides an analogy, for even such a simple craft is something the wheelwright "has got at his fingertips, secured in his heart, but cannot speak out of his mouth."[60] In such a view, words can never fully convey meaning because "of all things, words can discuss the coarser ones, and the mind can grasp the finer ones. But what words cannot discuss and mind cannot grasp is neither coarse nor fine."[61]

Zhuangzi is of course talking about the ineffable *tao* that transcends dimension, language, and comprehension. His words, however, are resonant with overtones obviously crucial and relevant to poetry, because poets, more than philosophers, undertake not only to grasp but also to describe in words the coarse, the fine, as well as what transcends the coarseness and fineness of things—to put in beautiful language all that is profound, subtle, probable, or improbable within the wide range of human experience and imagination. If the language of philosophy fails to describe the ineffable *tao*, it is hardly surprising that the language of poetry would seem especially inadequate for the purpose the poet has set in mind.

Against the background of the debate on language around the third century, we may understand why one of the earliest critical essays in China,

"Wen fu" [Rhymeprose on Literature] by Lu Ji (261–303), would begin with some prefatory remarks on the problem of poetic articulation. In studying the works of gifted writers, says Lu Ji, he often feels that he has grasped something of the workings of their minds. Whenever he himself takes up writing, he can see even more clearly how those writers strove for articulation, for "constantly one feels the anxiety that meaning does not match with things, and writing does not convey meaning. And this results not so much from the difficulty of knowing as from the limitation of one's ability."[62] The hierarchic relationship Lu Ji describes among writing, meaning, and things may remind us of the hierarchy established in that passage in the appendix to the *Book of Changes*, where it is stated that writing cannot fully convey speech and speech cannot fully convey meaning. Lu Ji hopes that some day the art of poetry may be fully understood, but he knows very well that it is not at all easy to put one's knowledge into words or practice, for "the knack in accommodating writing to the changing circumstances is indeed difficult to describe in words."[63] In the text of the "Fu" [Rhymeprose] itself, he further develops the idea that not only do poets find it difficult to conceive things adequately and put their conception in adequate language, but also the critic finds it difficult to put into words the diverse ways in which one perceives generic or stylistic excellence, the mystery of poetic art:

> Whether exuberant or concise in style,
> Shape the text in this or that fashion—
> All depends on the needs of the while
> To capture the subtlety of emotion.
> Clumsy expressions may disclose an ingenious idea,
> While plain truths in frivolous words may hide.
> Out of old models a newer piece may be wrought,
> Amidst a muddy stream clearer water may glide.
> A work may be understood at a mere glance,
> Or be comprehended with sustained efforts;
> Like the dancer's sleeves moving with rhythmic beat,
> Or the singer's voice in tune with the chords,
> Art is unsayable, as Pian the wheelwright knows,
> Nor explicable in any eloquent words.[64]

The allusion to Pian the wheelwright is a significant indication of how influential Zhuangzi or Taoist philosophy in general is in the tradition of Chinese poetics, in spite of the fact that for most of China's history,

Confucian ethics and politics dominate Chinese thinking in its moral and social aspects. James J. Y. Liu is quite right to claim that the book of Zhuangzi "has influenced Chinese artistic sensibility more profoundly than any other single book."[65] In fact, there are so many references to Pian the wheelwright in traditional Chinese criticism that this particular figure may be said to have become an archetypal image of the tongue-tied poet or critic, who finds his intimate knowledge of poetry hardly communicable. For example, Liu Xie (c. 465–522) writes in the well-known and most comprehensive work in traditional Chinese criticism *Wenxin diaolong* [The Literary Mind or the Carving of Dragons] that poetry has its mystery "as exquisite as the taste in the cauldron Yi Zhi fails to describe or the knack of using the axe Pian the wheelwright cannot put into words."[66] When he first takes up the writing brush, the poet is full of ideas yet to be verbalized, but "when the writing is completed, half of what he had conceived in the beginning disappears. Why is it so? For ideas, soaring high, easily tend towards the wondrous, but words, bound to reality, can rarely attain to equal ingenuity."[67] Writing a thousand years after Liu Xie, another critic Xu Zhenqing (1479–1511) also relates the archetypal wheelwright with the hierarchy of linguistic expressions, maintaining that the various manifestations of poetic excellence are "inexplicable as what Pian the wheelwright has intuitively apprehended. It is said in the *Book of Changes*, 'Writing cannot fully convey the speech, and speech cannot fully convey the meaning.' Then, how can one get the meaning if one seeks it in words?"[68] This radical doubt of the adequacy of language appears to be one of the deep-seated cultural notions in the Chinese mind. That may explain why traditional Chinese criticism is largely written in the same kind of figurative language as poetry itself. Knowing that they can hardly speak of poetry in a metapoetic language, Chinese critics either quote exemplary lines to demonstrate what they believe to be an exquisite nature or indescribable quality, or try to suggest that nature or quality by means of images and metaphors, that is, by showing rather than speaking. Instead of analysis and argumentation, Chinese critics tend to write poetry about poetry, and many insightful comments on the art of poetry are found not in criticism as such but in poetry itself. Indeed, many poems can be read as commenting on the problem of poetic language. For example, Qian Zhongshu quotes two lines from a poem by Liu Yuxi (772–842) to underscore an idea that strongly reminds us of Schleiermacher's basic assumption for hermeneutics, namely, that misunderstanding occurs as a matter of course, which makes interpretation an absolute necessity:

However meticulously and scrupulously the creator of texts may pon-
der over the use of words and the shape of sentences, more often
than not the receiver of those texts may still fall short of a thorough
understanding, or even lapse into distortion and misunderstanding.
"How often I regret that words are too shallow / Ever to reach the
depth of human feelings!" Does that lamentation refer only to love?[69]

Indeed, of all our emotions it is love that often reaches such intensity of
feeling that it would leave the poet utterly frustrated in his attempt to
speak. In love poems, therefore, the difficulty of poetic articulation becomes
a particularly urgent issue. But again, the poet's expression of his frustration is essentially ironic, for not only must he speak about the fact that he
cannot speak, but in doing so, he is able to achieve a special eloquence in
poetry. This pattern of poetic irony is clearly discernible in many great
love poems. In some of his most beautiful sonnets, Shakespeare, for example, gives a powerful expression to the frustration in articulating the emotion of love, and he does this by ironically commenting on his own inadequacy as a poet. He complains that his language lacks inventiveness:

> Why is my verse so barren of new pride?
> So far from variation or quick change?
> Why with the time do I not glance aside
> To new-found methods and to compounds strange?
> [Sonnet 76]

As the poet is supposedly dependent on divine inspiration, he blames his
muse for the failure of poetry. And in this case, Shakespeare complains
that his muse is "tongue-tied," so his thoughts remain unexpressed,
"dumb":

> My tongue-tied Muse in manners holds her still,
> While comments of your praise, richly compil'd,
> Reserve their character with golden quill
> And precious phrase by all the Muses fil'd.
> I think good thoughts whilst other write good words,
> And like unlettered clerk still cry "Amen"
> To every hymn that able spirit affords
> In polish'd form of well-refined pen.
> Hearing you prais'd, I say, "'Tis so, 'tis true,"
> And to the most of praise add something more,
> But that is in my thought, whose love to you

(Though words come hindmost) holds his rank before.
Then others for the breath of words respect,
Me for my dumb thoughts, speaking in effect.
[Sonnet 85]

This sonnet has of course complicated levels of meaning, and the poet is not just saying that he is dumb and illiterate, "like unlettered clerk," a statement that the very existence of the sonnet implicitly impugns and denies. However, its literal, obvious level of meaning is precisely such a statement, and the effect of the sonnet depends on the subversion of this obvious meaning by the hierarchy of thoughts over words. Resting on the deep level of the poem, the metaphysical hierarchy is reified as a rivalry between our poet of "good thoughts" and other poets of "good words," between his "tongue-tied Muse" and all the other Muses of "precious phrase," all the while privileging the seemingly dumb and speechless. In the final couplet, this hierarchy is reinforced to give credit to the "dumb thoughts," while "the breath of words" implies not only the superficiality of articulated words but also their fleeting, ephemeral existence. If our poet finally claims to be a better lover than the others, however, he can do so only at the cost of his capacity as a poet—namely, at the cost of poetic language—because the triumph of love rises eloquently only from the failure of language: that he loves most deeply is indicated only by his inability to express that love in poetry.

The poet's inability or frustration becomes even more intense when the task he faces, properly speaking, is not so much saying as showing, when he wants to describe the beauty of his love rather than to profess his own thoughts and feelings. His muse appears even less competent, and he blames her again for the poverty of his expression and the narrow scope of his vision. There is almost a crisis of writing:

Alack, what poverty my Muse brings forth,
That having such a scope to show her pride,
The argument all bare is of more worth
Than when it hath my added praise beside.
O, blame me not if I no more can write!
Look in your glass, and there appears a face
That overgoes my blunt invention quite,
Dulling my lines, and doing me disgrace.
Were it not sinful then, striving to mend,
To mar the subject that before was well?

> For to no other pass my verses tend
> Than of your graces and your gifts to tell;
>> And more, much more than in my verse can sit,
>> Your own glass shows you, when you look in it.
> [Sonnet 103]

The tone of this sonnet, so far as it concerns the poet's skills, is of course totally ironic, but the hierarchy which gives the poem its structural tension is serious. It is the hierarchy of things over words, showing over speaking, and the mirror image that faithfully reflects the beautiful face over verbal expression that tries in vain to represent beauty in deficient ways. In the middle of a crisis when the poet cries out, "I no more can write," in the very source of his failure, he claims to have found his excuse, for the splendor of his love simply surpasses all description. The mirror image is privileged for a much closer representation of the original than any verbal description. The final couplet fully recognizes the superiority of images to words, or that of showing to speaking:

> And more, much more than in my verse can sit,
> Your own glass shows you, when you look in it.

The contest between image and verbal representation, as W. J. T. Mitchell notes, is entrenched in the very history of perception and understanding. It takes roots in many of our age-old notions of reality and representation, in the ways we think about the relations between symbols and the world, signs and their meaning. Very often we too quickly assume a natural connection between pictorial image and the thing it represents, imagining the gulf between words and images to be "as wide as the one between words and things, between (in the larger sense) culture and nature," thus degrading the value of words: "The word is its 'other,' the artificial, arbitrary production of human will that disrupts natural presence by introducing unnatural elements into the world—time, consciousness, history, and the alienating intervention of symbolic mediation."[70] But according to Mitchell, there is also a countertradition that privileges verbal rather than pictorial imagery. The history of culture, Mitchell maintains, is a competition, a protracted struggle for dominance between pictorial and linguistic signs, and what is most interesting and complex about this struggle is a "relationship of subversion, in which language or imagery looks into its own heart and finds lurking there its opposite number."[71]

In Shakespeare's sonnets, the hierarchy of mirror image over verbal representation is subverted in many subtle ways, in which we certainly find what Mitchell calls the countertradition being invoked to justify the higher value of poetic language. A wonderful example is Sonnet 76, which we must now look at more closely in its entirety:

> Why is my verse so barren of new pride?
> So far from variation or quick change?
> Why with the time do I not glance aside
> To new-found methods and to compounds strange?
> Why write I still all one, ever the same,
> And keep invention in a noted weed,
> That every word doth almost tell my name,
> Showing their birth, and where they did proceed?
> O, know, sweet love, I always write of you,
> And you and love are still my argument;
> So all my best is dressing old words new,
> Spending again what is already spent:
> > For as the sun is daily new and old,
> > So is my love still telling what is told.

What immediately strikes one as the potential power for subversion is the sun image in the final couplet. While the poet ostentatiously admits that his verse lacks inventiveness and variation, the final couplet undermines that literal level of meaning by drawing on the positive associations of the sun metaphor to declare that his verse has the rejuvenating power we usually attribute to the rising sun. After all those questions and complaints, language reaffirms its power as the source of light and illumination.

The fact that the language at the poet's disposal antedates poetry, that it exists *a priori* as a historical given with ready-made grammatical rules and a well-defined vocabulary, seems to impede the poet's effort to achieve originality, as it only allows him to dress old words new and spend what is already spent. In a recent study of the Shakespearean sonnet cycle, Joel Fineman argues that Shakespeare invents poetic subjectivity by *re*-writing the conventional poetry of praise; so in Sonnet 76 and similar poems that speak precisely about the lack of inventiveness, he can only find "elegiac pathos" and a "tired 'love'" compared to "the ancient sun."[72] It is true that the opportunity language offers seems too limited to satisfy the need for ever new expressions, but it seems to me a very simplistic reading of the final couplet if we understand it, as Fineman apparently does, as the poet taking "the ever-renewed sameness of the sun, its perennially revivified vivacity, as a dead metaphor for the animating *energeia* and *enargia* of an ideal metaphoricity," or as the poet identifying himself with "the afterlight and aftermath of this dead metaphoric sun," "an aged eternality."[73] The final rhymed couplet in the English sonnet, as Barbara Herrnstein Smith points out, is a powerful device to close the poem with "striking resolution, finality, punch, pointedness, and so forth," and it does this not so much by its formal effectiveness per se as by "its effectiveness in relation to the formal structure that precedes it."[74] With regard to Shakespeare's sonnets in particular, she argues that in most cases "the conclusion of the poem coincides with the resolution of the dialectic process"; in other words, "the dialectical complexity of thought" is represented only insofar as it is represented "as ultimately resolved."[75]

Unless we want to argue that Sonnet 76 fails to work out the resolution of its dialectical process and thus also fails to close the poem effectively, we must reread the final couplet more carefully in relation to the formal structure of the preceding lines. The sonnet begins with a significant "Why" ("Why is my verse so barren of new pride?"), and indeed the octave consists of four successive questions that seriously challenge the poet's ability to write anything original. The tone of the poem, however, shifts a bit in the quatrain that immediately follows when the poet tries to come up with an answer:

> Now, sweet love, I always write of you,
> And you and love are still my argument;
> So all my best is dressing old words new,
> Spending again what is already spent.

The answer may not acquit the poet of all charges of poetic sterility, but the quatrain evidently builds up an antithesis to the compelling interrogation in the octave, setting up the virtue of constancy in love to contrast with the pressure for rhetorical and stylistic "variation or quick change." The questions and the answer nicely illustrate the contour of the dialectic process of the sonnet, and the resolution of that process is summed up in the final couplet in which, as Hallett Smith remarks, "the assertion of constancy in love is related to the consistency of the poet's style."[76]

> For as the sun is daily new and old,
> So is my love still telling what is told.

The last line refers of course both to the poet's love as a constant devotion and to his love poems as repeated praise. The dialectic complexity as shown in the question-and-answer structure in the first twelve lines, or the tension between the demand for rhetorical innovations and the constancy of love, is ultimately resolved in favor of constancy both in love and in writing about love. Thanks to the positive associations of the sun metaphor, the complaint voiced against language in the preceding lines suddenly breaks down in the final couplet, overturned by the sun/verse analogy, which bestows on the poet's writing the virtue of endurance, thus closing the sonnet on a positive note by revealing the value of its seemingly barren language.

In Shakespeare's sonnets, then, the final couplet often forms a contrast to the structure of the preceding lines, and when the poet complains about the inadequacy of his language, that complaint is likely to be undercut or overturned by the concluding lines. The same may be said of Sonnet 105, in which the poet admits that his verse is "to constancy confin'd." In Sonnet 123, he cries out, "No! Time, thou shalt not boast that I do change," and significantly the triumph of constancy over mutability is simultaneously the triumph of poetry as verbal representation over material, visual images that decay in time. Though in Sonnet 76 the poet acknowledges that his best is only "dressing old words new," in Sonnet 123 he discovers that, after all, everything that exists in time, everything that enters into Time's "registers" and "records," represented by the "pyramids built up with newer might," is nothing but "dressings of a former sight." It is interesting to note that the rejection of time and change is expressed in this sonnet as the negation of visual imagery; the "former sight" or something we see is something whose impressive appearance is only deceptive:

> For thy records and what we see doth lie,
> Made more or less by thy continual haste.

This is a crucial point because it helps set a higher value on verbal signs than visual imagery, thus invoking what Mitchell calls the countertradition to exalt the language of poetry in its repetitive constancy. In this poetics of repetition, visual images, rhetorical innovations, and stylistic changes are equated with mutability and even mortality. The obsession with the *memento mori* in Elizabethan literature puts physical beauty and its mirror image in the precarious condition of a feeble existence, forever exposed to the threat of devouring Time, from which only the language of poetry can offer the hope of redemption. Both *memento mori* and *carpe diem* are familiar themes that speak of essentially the same thing: the fear as well as the joy of being confined in the cycle of life. This naturally leads us to the appreciation of another familiar theme in the Shakespearean sonnet cycle: the immortalizing power of poetic language. The well-known lines in Sonnet 18 can serve as an example, in which the poet assures his love that however the world may change,

> thy eternal summer shall not fade,
> Nor lose possession of that fair thou ow'st,
> Nor shall Death brag thou wand'rest in his shade,
> When in eternal lines to time thou grow'st.
> So long as men can breathe or eyes can see,
> So long lives this, and this gives life to thee.

In the paradoxical statement—"in eternal lines to time thou grow'st" —timeless eternity and temporal growth are yoked together, and the nature of language is revealed as at once immutable and capable of accommodating to the evolution of time. For in each reading—no matter by whom, where, and when—poetry, if it is read as poetry, is experienced not as something from the past but in the present, establishing an immediate relationship with the reader. Contemporaneity (*Gleichzeitigkeit*), as Gadamer says, "belongs to the being of the work of art. It constitutes the essence of 'being present.'"[77] Poetry, and for that matter all works of art, represent "an overcoming of time," and "endow the ephemeral and the transient with a new form of permanence."[78] This applies, of course, to both verbal and pictorial art, and here, as Mitchell puts it, poetry and visual art form an interesting "relationship of subversion, in which language or imagery looks into its own heart and finds lurking there its opposite number."[79] Thus, poetry and painting, like all other kinds of art, endow a form of permanence to the fleeting moment of human experience, taking it out of the cycle of birth, decay, and death to a form that is enduring and becomes alive every time the work is being experienced. Poetry thus awaits its reader to live the moment again, for which both the art of writing poetry and the art of reading are needed. The poet's "tongue-tied Muse" has not been able to speak eloquently, but eventually the written text of the sonnets, the wonderful "book" of poetry, proves to be more eloquent than the tongue. It may be said that in Shakespeare the metaphysical hierarchy is finally subverted, for it is not the tongue but the pen, not speech but writing, that turns out to be the better vehicle of communication:

> O, let my books be then the eloquence
> And dumb presagers of my speaking breast,

Who plead for love, and look for recompense,
More than that tongue that more hath more express'd.
    O, learn to read what silent love hath writ:
    To hear with eyes belongs to love's fine wit.
[Sonnet 23]

Raid on the Inarticulate

In a poetics that recognizes the creative role of constitutive repetition, language in Shakespeare's sonnets proves to be eloquent without being particularly flamboyant, and its value is quietly affirmed in the combination of structural and thematic development in the sonnet form, in which the final couplet is especially important in subverting the overt complaint about the inadequacy of language. Of course, the rehabilitation of language is ironically accomplished, because it is the effect of a subverted critique of language, as if the poet finally realizes that his "tongue-tied Muse" has actually achieved the persuasive power of poetic innovation he so desperately sought in following the norms and conventions of the time. Thus we realize that the complaint about inadequacy is yet another brilliant performance of the poet, and Shakespeare proves himself beyond any doubt to be the lord of language.

In modern poetry, however, it seems much more difficult to assume such a positive attitude toward language. If in Shakespeare we find a "tongue-tied Muse," in Mallarmé we have an impotent one, the anxiety-ridden "Muse moderne de l'Impuissance."[80] If it is largely a conventional gesture for Shakespeare to complain about the weakness of his language, that complaint seems to sound more real and to indicate a more urgent problem with modern poets. For Mallarmé, the task of the poet is "Donner un sens plus pur aux mots de la tribu,"[81] which T. S. Eliot paraphrases as "purify the dialect of the tribe." In fact, as Eliot says repeatedly in *Four Quartets*, a major concern of the modern poet is precisely the status of poetic language in our times:

> our concern was speech, and speech impelled us
> To purify the dialect of the tribe
> And urge the mind to aftersight and foresight.
> ["Little Gidding," 2.73−75][82]

As Shakespeare in the sonnets, the poet in *Four Quartets* is very much conscious of the problem of time and desperately seeks poetic innovations, a new language that would give voice to new vision and new experiences, a language of the present that speaks of the here and now:

> For last year's words belong to last year's language
> And next year's words await another voice.
> ["Little Gidding," 2.65−66]

Throughout *Four Quartets*, however, the search for a new, precise, and adequate language finally turns out to be a lost battle. In the last section of "Burnt Norton," the poet seems to suggest at first that there is still some hope of achieving permanence in the silent form of art:

> Words move, music moves
> Only in time; but that which is only living
> Can only die. Words, after speech, reach
> Into the silence. Only by the form, the pattern,
> Can words or music reach
> The stillness, as a Chinese jar still
> Moves perpetually in its stillness.
> ["Burnt Norton," 5.1−7]

What Eliot talks about here is again the overcoming of time in art, which endows the ephemeral and the transient with a new form of permanence. The fleeting sound of words or music, like all that is only living, dies away and is forever lost as soon as it is heard, but it can transcend time and step out of the cycle of life and death once it has acquired a pattern or artistic form, when it can grow to time and move, as it were, "perpetually in its stillness." As a symbol of artistic permanence, the "Chinese jar" in Eliot's poem reminds us of the figures of the "two Chinamen" carved in stone in W. B. Yeats' "Lapis Lazuli," the two figures in "the little half-way house," who, while contemplating "all the tragic scene" amid the world's "mournful melodies," remain nevertheless calm and cheerful, happily out of the world's worries and miseries, in their transcendent state of artistic tranquility, almost a stasis of bliss:

> Their eyes mid many wrinkles, their eyes,
> Their ancient, glittering eyes, are gay.[83]

Or better still, Eliot's poem reminds us of "the artifice of eternity," the golden bird in Yeats' imaginary Byzantium, the bird that "once out of nature," sings paradoxically of "what is past, or passing, or to come."[84] If we trace the imagery of poetic immortality to its romantic forebears, we may perhaps find the most appropriate analogy in Keats' Grecian urn, that graceful "Attic shape," the "silent form" that does "tease us out of thought / As doth eternity."[85] The stillness of artistic form, Eliot continues, is "not the stillness of the violin, while the note lasts." In other words, the stillness of artistic form is not caught in the flux of time but is a permanent "co-existence," the unique contemporaneity of the work of art, or, as Eliot puts it astutely, a stillness in which "all is always now" ("Burnt Norton," 5.13).

As a modernist poet, however, Eliot differs from the romantic Keats, or even from Yeats, in his agonizing awareness of the inadequacy of language in modern times. For him, poetic language can no longer sustain the burden of promised permanence but falls apart under the strain of precision, the inevitable discrepancy between the poet's vision and diction:

> Words strain,
> Crack and sometimes break, under the burden,
> Under the tension, slip, slide, perish,
> Decay with imprecision, will not stay in place,
> Will not stay still.
> ["Burnt Norton," 5.13–17]

These choppy, ragged lines with monosyllabic verbs bumping along their lengths perfectly mimic the disintegration of language, and apparently there is little hope for the modern poet ever to accomplish his self-appointed mission "to purify the dialect of the tribe." This hopelessness is further intensified in "East Coker" where Eliot tries to describe his vision of the cosmic flux and reflux, in which the beginning and the end reciprocate, only to find his description at best a feeble shadow of his original conception, just "a way of putting it—not very satisfactory," a trace of his imaginative vision that leaves many desires yet unfulfilled:

> A periphrastic study in a worn-out poetical fashion,
> Leaving one still with the intolerable wrestle
> With words and meanings. The poetry does not matter.
> It was not (to start again) what one had expected.
> ["East Coker," 2.19–22]

Here Eliot, as David Spurr comments, "ultimately arrives at an artistically suicidal position that sees the poetic ideal as beyond thought and language, in fact, beyond poetry itself."[86] For Barbara Herrnstein Smith, the "suspicion of language" revealed in this passage is symptomatic of the modern age, when language becomes "the badge of our suspect reason and humanity."[87] The failure of the poet's language to match his imaginative vision is of course his failure as a poet; it is also a waste of some twenty years he has spent "trying to learn to use words," "the years of *l'entre deux guerres.*" The military associations of this phrase dominate Eliot's portrayal of his effort to use words, for "the psychological war between intellectual order and the visionary imagination," as Spurr puts it aptly, "translates into an artistic war between the creative will and linguistic disorder. . . . Thus the language and imagery of warfare provide an extended metaphor for the poet's struggle with language."[88] Indeed, the poet's "intolerable wrestle / With words and meanings" becomes even more intolerable, as he realizes that it is almost definitely a losing battle:

> And so each venture
> Is a new beginning, a raid on the inarticulate
> With shabby equipment always deteriorating
> In the general mess of imprecision of feeling.
> Undisciplined squads of emotion. And what there is to conquer
> By strength and submission, has already been discovered
> Once or twice, or several times, by men whom one cannot hope
> To emulate—but there is no competition—
> There is only the fight to recover what has been lost
> And found and lost again and again: and now, under conditions
> That seem unpropitious.
> ["East Coker," 5.7–17]

There is something specifically modern about the poet's frustration at the collapse of language, something that perhaps we may justly call modernity. There is first this anxiety of influence, for there is no frontier left for the modern poet to discover and conquer: all has already been discovered and conquered several times by powerful precursors whom, as Eliot reminds us, the modern poet cannot hope to emulate because he has to carry out "a raid on the inarticulate" not only with shabby and always deteriorating equipment but in an "unpropitious" time which is our own. Spurr argues that a dramatic conflict between an intellectual order and an imaginative one permeates Eliot's consciousness as well as the corpus of his poetry. In fact, by frequently referring to the "dissociated sensibility" in the English tradition since the Metaphysical poets, Eliot had already situated himself historically in a context that to some extent anticipates and justifies Spurr's argument. "In the seventeenth century," says Eliot, "a dissociation of sensibility set in, from which we have never recovered."[89] For Eliot, then, modernity is not without its own past, and the problem of language in modern poetry is rooted in the dissociation of sensibility which began in the seventeenth century, but the intensity with which the poet senses the language problem and the difficulty of articulation is certainly characteristic of modern times. In a discursive passage of "The Dry Salvages," Eliot speaks again of such a disunity of his poetic world, the discrepancy between experience and meaning, or between meaning and form:

> We had the experience but missed the meaning,
> And approach to the meaning restores the experience
> In a different form, beyond any meaning
> We can assign to happiness.
> ["The Dry Salvages," 2.45–48]

In the last section of "Little Gidding," which is also the end of *Four Quartets*, the poet tries to impose a unity on his disjointed poetic universe by reiterating the theme of the cosmic cycle, the merging of the beginning and the end, "where every word is at home," and poetry proclaims both death and birth:

> Every phrase and every sentence is an end and a beginning,
> Every poem an epitaph. And any action
> Is a step to the block, to the fire, down the sea's throat
> Or to an illegible stone: and that is where we start.
> ["Little Gidding," 5.11–14]

The language of poetry finally arrives at its origin or point of departure, which is only a hieroglyphic "illegible stone" and can speak only in the elegiac tone of the epitaph. But in the cyclical movement that runs throughout the text, the poem somehow comes to a mystic reconciliation, where the voice is "half-heard, in the stillness / Between two waves of the sea," and somehow everything seems all right:

> And all shall be well and
> All manner of thing shall be well
> When the tongues of flame are in-folded
> Into the crowned knot of fire
> And the fire and the rose are one.
> ["Little Gidding," 5.42–46]

In emphasizing Eliot's effort to reunite dissociated sensibility, traditional readings tend to ignore his express confessions of the impossibility
of appropriate language and communication, while celebrating, even
though without much textual confirmation in Eliot's work, an alleged
success of that reunion of intellect and emotion, language and experience.
Helen Gardner, for instance, offers a wonderful analysis of the musicality
of *Four Quartets* but dismisses Eliot's explicit comments on his own
language as "passages that are in themselves flat, prosaic and inexpressive."[90] She claims that Eliot is unique among English poets in having
achieved the balance between his vision and his art: "When we read *Four
Quartets* we are left finally not with the thought of 'the transitory Being
who beheld this vision,' nor with the thought of the vision itself, but with
the poem, beautiful, satisfying, self-contained, self-organized, complete."[91]
If we do not presuppose the textual coherence of *Four Quartets* as a
criterion of its value, however, we must challenge both the unification of
sensibility in Eliot's poem and the traditional criticism that celebrates
such a unification at the cost of sensitivity to the language problem the
poem itself persistently raises. We must ask, with Spurr, "whether the text
actually brings about this unification or whether, on the other hand, the
poet simply invokes this ideal as an impassioned response to the actual
experience of textual, psychological, and metaphysical disunity."[92] For
traditional critics, any textual fissure and any self-doubt of language are
disturbingly alien to the autonomy of poetry and the harmony of the
aesthetic form, and any "thought" that cannot be comfortably absorbed in
a holistic form only threatens to lower the intrinsic value of the poem. Gardner insists that *Four Quartets* is not a poem of philosophic argument, as
though the poem would be worth much less if it were adulterated with the
base metal of philosophizing. She compares Eliot favorably with Tennyson as a writer of long poems with philosophic ideas, but while "Tennyson can hardly save *In Memoriam* as a whole from the monotony of life
and give it the coherence of art," Eliot "transforms living into art, not
thought, gives us a sense of beginning and ending, of the theme having
been fully worked out, which is rare in the long poem."[93] And yet Eliot
himself speaks very highly of *In Memoriam*, finding in its 132 passages
"never monotony or repetition," though he deplores the dissociation of refined language and genuine feeling in Tennyson and Browning when compared with Donne or Herbert.[94] But insofar as both *In Memoriam* and *Four
Quartets* are thematically concerned with the anxiety of language, we
may agree with Harold Bloom that, in spite of Eliot's own assertion, the

actual forerunners of his poetry are not the Jacobean dramatists or Meta-physical lyricists, but "Whitman and Tennyson."[95]

At any rate, Eliot does not seem to shun the temptation of philosophizing in poetry, nor does he regard commenting on language in poetry as prosaic or inexpressive, for he might, as many contemporary critics certainly do, take a great interest in the language problem for its hermeneutic implications not only in discursive writing but in poetry itself. In this connection, the following remark Eliot made in 1933 still has relevancy today:

> The critical mind operating *in* poetry, the critical effort which goes to the writing of it, may always be in advance of the critical mind operating *upon* poetry, whether it be one's own or some one else's. . . . And when I speak of modern poetry as being extremely critical, I mean that the contemporary poet, who is not merely a composer of graceful verses, is forced to ask himself such questions as 'what is poetry for?'; not merely 'what am I to say?' but rather 'how and to whom am I to say it?' . . . *If* poetry is a form of 'communication', yet that which is to be communicated is the poem itself, and only incidentally the experience and the thought which have gone into it.[96]

Here, Eliot shows how highly self-conscious modern poetry is of its own linguistic nature, its mode of existence as a verbal artifact, and its paradox as both the means and the content of communication. The self-critique of poetic language in *Four Quartets*, therefore, does not just attach to the more lyrical and imagistic part as a sort of discursive accessory, but constitutes as integral a part of the poem and sets up the dialectic structure of language's movement which, indeed, thematically as well as semantically, is at the heart of the poem.

Spurr maintains that Eliot's great poem ends with "the final obituary on language," that it "proclaims the death of language, and stands as a commitment to his search for unity of the self in 'the constitution of silence.'"[97] The near despair in the line that "poetry does not matter" strikes him as "an artistically suicidal position."[98] However, the seemingly indifferent tone in this abandonment of the search for poetic expressiveness may ironically conceal in its depth the conviction that poetry is all that matters, even though its imperfect medium, the corrupted words and meanings, may at best suggest what is to be desired in poetry. As Barbara H. Smith argues, Eliot's poem not only expresses the problem of language but also embodies the paradox it entails: "Language is what fails us and fails between us; but language is also the material of poetry."[99] This is of course the paradox of language that not only poets but also philosophers and mystics have to reconcile in one way or another. By claiming that "poetry does not matter," Eliot probably meant to solve the problem by something like the mystic strategy of provisional names or Zhuangzi's "non-words"—something that tries to make words both present as meaningful signifiers and infinitely receding as empty traces of an absent signified, both that which literally matters as poetic icons and that which literally does not matter as mere signs. After all, language is the being of poetry, and the poet, however frustrated and disappointed with words he may be, has to use words for what they are worth. In the end, the poet realizes that language as such is all we have for expression and communication; so he declares, rather like Tennyson's Ulysses, that "We shall not cease from exploration" ("Little Gidding," 5.26). He has always to try, to make one effort after another, while hoping that someday, somehow, he may find a way to make his effort successful. As Eliot himself says,

> But perhaps neither gain nor loss.
> For us, there is only the trying. The rest is not our business.
> ["East Coker," 5.17–18]

3
The
Use of
Silence

Elected Silence, sing to me
And beat upon my whorlèd ear,
Pipe me to pastures still and be
The music that I care to hear.
—Gerard Manley Hopkins,
  "The Habit of Perfection"

Schweigen. Wer inniger schwieg,
rührt an die Wurzeln der Rede.
Be silent. Who keeps silent inside
touches the roots of speech.
—Rainer Maria Rilke,
  "Für Frau Fanette Clavel"

Rilke: Alienation from Angels

Commenting on T. S. Eliot's controversial enunciation in *Four Quartets* that "the poetry does not matter," Stephen Spender aptly points out that such a statement can only be ironic, for the poet's dismissal of poetry is "itself an artistic device."[1] When he compares *Four Quartets* with another important work in twentieth-century literature, Rainer Maria Rilke's *Duino Elegies*, however, Spender acknowledges that the two poetic works have indeed more to offer than the usual significance of the aesthetic form, that they share a tendency to go beyond textual symbolism toward a goal other than the pure display of rhetorical virtuosity, so much so that "the poetry itself is, one might say, not the only goal of the poems: or, perhaps one should say there is a goal beyond the one of pure poetry—religious vision."[2] Of course, Rilke's vision may differ from that of Eliot, but at the time of writing these works, Spender argues, both authors have come to believe in certain ideas which are more important to them than poetry itself and to which their poetry constantly refers. In such works, says Spender, "The symbol is no longer an end in itself, the poetry is no longer self-sufficient; it is a point of departure to the expression of supernatural values."[3] According to Spender, then, the difficulty of poetic articulation, so self-consciously commented on by the poets themselves in both *Four Quartets* and the *Duino Elegies*, has to do with the problem of representing a religious vision or supernatural values in language, the problem of expressing the divine Word which is ultimately inexpressible. One may of course disagree with Spender on the exact nature of the poets' vision, and may not even call it religious, but one thing is certain—namely, the poets' desire to give their vision an appropriate poetic form is frustrated by their awareness that the language at their disposal is inadequate for carrying out such a mission.

We have seen how the poet's awareness of the limitation of language persistently raises self-doubt in Eliot's *Four Quartets*. Similarly in Rilke's *Duino Elegies*, such self-doubt, which contributes to the elegiac tonality of the entire poetic cycle, sets in immediately when the poet begins the "First Elegy" with an outcry, an agonizing question about the efficacy of poetic articulation: "Wer, wenn ich schriee, hörte mich denn aus der Engel / Ordnungen? [Who, if I cried out, would hear me among the angels' / hierarchies?]."[4] Inevitably overhearing this question, readers of Rilke's poetry are given to understand that when the poet speaks, his voice should presumably be heard by the angels, but now, in Rilke's time, this intimate relationship between the poet and his celestial listeners is no longer attainable. The poet's alienation from angels reminds us of Schiller's lament over the deplorable loss of the "naive," mythological past, but the significance of Rilke's question can be fully appreciated not just in general terms as a post-Schillerian sensibility in modern poetry, but more specifically in the context of Rilke's personal vision, the peculiar cosmology of his imaginative world, in which angels form a higher order of beings against whom the abilities of men are to be tested and judged.

The angel of the *Elegies*, as Rilke explains in a letter to his Polish translator, is "that creature in whom the transformation of the visible into the invisible, which we are accomplishing, already appears in its completion . . . that being who guarantees the recognition of a higher level of reality in the invisible." The angel is *schrecklich* (terrifying) because we, "its lovers and transformers, still cling to the visible."[5] In a recent book on Rilke's *Duino Elegies*, Kathleen Komar suggests that the relationship between man and angel in Rilke's poetry can be fully understood in the light of Heinrich von Kleist's theory of the progression of consciousness, put forward in his famous essay, "Über das Marionettentheater." In that essay, a dancer expounds a theory of graceful movement and claims that self-conscious human beings, ever since the eating of the forbidden tree and the loss of innocence, have lost the ability to achieve the highest degree of gracefulness, which can now be attained only by unconscious or super-conscious means: "Grace appears purest in that human form which has either no consciousness or an infinite one, that is, in a puppet or in a god."[6] Both this theory and the images of puppet and god find manifestation in Rilke's works, though the image of god is there displaced by that of the angel with the capacity of recognizing "a higher level of reality in the invisible." Such a progression of consciousness, Komar argues, is "well established in Christian tradition," based on the biblical myth that "man moves from the prelapsarian innocence and unity through self-conscious

alienation (the knowledge of good and evil) toward a transcendent reuni-
fication with existence as a whole after death." Man's alienation from
angels in Rilke's poetry is thus put in a context with religious implications. "It is against the background of this movement of consciousness,"
says Komar, "that Rilke's *Elegies* are acted out."[7] Though Rilke himself
claims that the angel of the *Elegies* is inspired by the angels of Islam, the
iconography of Christian angels certainly provides the poet with basic
ideas and motifs.[8] Perhaps it is in this sense that Spender sees the *Elegies*
as striving to express a religious vision. And yet, as Ursula Franklin argues,
it is possible to see Rilke's angel not as a figure of the religious mystery of
transcendence, but as "a symbolic vehicle which, secularized and trans-
muted, conveys [the poet's] intellectual and artistic essence."[9] For Rilke as
a poet, the difficulty of speaking to the angel is first of all the difficulty of
speaking, specifically, that of poetic articulation. The rich content of poetic
themes and images in the *Elegies* has of course been variously interpreted,
but the emphasis on the difficulty of speaking, the significance of the
poet's comment on the impossibility of poetry itself, can be fully recognized only in the context of a study of hermeneutics that understands the
problem of transformation, which thematically sets the whole cycle of the
Elegies in motion, as above all a problem of language and communication, with regard to which human inadequacy is exposed vis-à-vis the
angel.

For Rilke, the task that makes man's life meaningful is that of the transformation of the visible into the invisible, an important task nature itself
urges the poet to fulfill:

> Erde, ist es nicht dies, was du willst: *unsichtbar*
> in uns erstehn?—Ist es dein Traum nicht,
> einmal unsichtbar zu sein?—Erde! unsichtbar!
> Was, wenn Verwandlung nicht, ist dein drängender Auftrag?

> Earth, isn't this what you want: to arise within us,
> *invisible*? Isn't it your dream
> to be wholly invisible someday?—O Earth: invisible!
> What, if not transformation, is your urgent command?
> [9, 67–70]

In addition to interpretations that emphasize the religious implication of
transcendence, there are readings that understand Rilke's idea of the transformation largely in terms of philosophical conceptualization. Richard

Jayne maintains that to transform the earth into the invisible, to let it "arise within us," can be understood as essentially a Hegelian *Aufhebung* of the phenomenal world into the inward vision of poetic subjectivity, as the process of internalization in the romantic period when the world spirit moves away from the unification of the idea and its sensuous appearance, the perfect form of beauty accomplished in classical art, toward a purely internalized world, the *Weltinnenraum*. Though Rilke is heir to the symbolist tradition, Jayne argues, his vision of transformation has its historical antecedent in German romanticism, notably the works of Novalis, in which we already find "a latent awareness of the precariousness of the union of inner and outer reality in the inwardness of poetry."[10] In such a Hegelian reading, the poet's alienation from angels is said to be dialectically inevitable when the spirit moves beyond its realization in sensuous appearance, beyond materiality toward the inside—a movement which, according to Hegel, characterizes all art and literature ever since the end of classical antiquity. Like religious readings, however, such a philosophical interpretation is liable to overlook the visible/invisible opposition in Rilke's work as specifically put in terms of a poetic transformation; it tends to neglect the insistent claim Rilke's poetry makes for the importance of things, and it fails to account for the ubiquitous presence in that poetry of a typically Rilkean trope: the overturning of figural oppositions of the visible/invisible, inside/outside, subject/object and so forth in what Paul de Man calls "the chiasmic reversal."[11] In short, a strictly Hegelian interpretation tends to loose sight of the fact that it is precisely things and the sayable, the phenomenal world and language, that are finally vindicated in the *Duino Elegies* as well as in Rilke's other works.

The difficulty of transformation is indeed put in terms of a problem of language in the *Elegies* from the very start. The poet laments that we can no longer reach the angels because we depend so much on the performance of a dubiously equivocal language, that "wir nicht sehr verlässlich zu Haus sind / in der gedeuteten Welt [we are not really at home in / our interpreted world]" (1, 12–13). In the light of Kleist's essay, the "interpreted world" would be the fallen world distanced from its pure, prelapsarian origin, the dim place betwixt puppet and god, where the truth of the world, revealed either through its undifferentiated thingness or by the kind of angelic inner speech, is inevitably obscured by human consciousness and language. Therefore, the task of transforming the visible into the invisible as Rilke describes at the beginning of the *Elegies*, insofar as it is conceived in terms of an inside/outside opposition, predicates itself on a truly *logocentric* view of language and expression. Indeed, in the "Seventh Elegy," Rilke speaks of transformation as a translation of the visible into a transparent inner speech, for "doch das sichtbarste Glück uns / erst zu erkennen sich giebt, wenn wir es innen verwandeln [even the most visible happiness / can't reveal itself to us until we transform it, within]" (7, 48–49). But if the visible can be revealed to us only in its transformation, wherein the outside world shrinks and even completely vanishes, how can the poet still avail himself of images and symbols to convey his inward vision? The effacing of the visible and the external to attain to an inner world, the *Weltinnenraum*, makes the writing of poetry a self-defeating and almost impossible task, since the language the poet uses—all the words, images, and metaphors that constitute his language —are deeply rooted in the visible world of concrete things. The difficulty of transformation, as Rilke puts it clearly, is due to the inevitable human limitation that we "still cling to the visible," that our language still depends on the material as the ultimate source of its symbolic, signifying power. In this sense, then, the poet, like the philosopher and the mystic, finds himself facing the difficulty of using an inadequate language to express what is beyond language, to say what is unsayable.

Although most of the *Duino Elegies* do not address the problem of human deficiencies and limitations explicitly in terms of linguistic inadequacy, the lament resounding throughout the poems is ultimately due to the poet's regret that language has lost its power to unify the inner and outer worlds by means of images and metaphors, by the symbolism of poetry; and eventually the solution to the initial problem of human limitations is to be found in a reaffirmed sense of the power of language to create things in evocation. As Kathleen Komar also notes, "the *Duino Elegies* are a metapoetic text. These poems take up the question of the function of the poet and poetry and conclude that the poet's task is to transform the physical world into the more durable and invisible realm of aesthetic space."[12] The inadequacy of language certainly constitutes part of man's limitations, and the split of the spirit and the phenomenal world is always related to our inability to grasp and express the inward vision. In Rilke's mythological world, only angels, those superhuman beings and "Verwöhnten der Schöpfung [Creation's pampered favorites]" (2, 10), can dispense with language in their silent grasp of unmediated inwardness, while human beings, caught in the brevity of a transient life, are bereft not only of angelic eternity but also of the ability to find adequate means to convey their inward experience. The poet seems to resign himself to this situation: "Und so verhalt ich mich denn und verschlucke den Lockruf / dunkelen Schluchzens [And so I hold myself back and swallow the call-note / of my dark sobbing]" (1, 8–9). He is made particularly aware of his verbal inadequacy when he looks at some ancient Attic gravestones and contemplates the perfect figures carved on them. The difference between the classical and the modern is strongly felt:

> Denn das eigene Herz übersteigt uns
> noch immer wie jene. Und wir können ihm nicht mehr
> nachschaun in Bilder, die es besänftigen, noch in
> göttliche Körper, in denen es grösser sich mässigt.
>
> For our own heart always exceeds us
> as theirs did. And we can no longer follow it, gazing
> into images that soothe it or into the godlike bodies
> where, measured more greatly, it achieves a greater repose.
> [2, 76–79]

Those "godlike bodies" of Greek sculpture with their cathartic effect of soothing the aching heart can no longer be created and emulated in modern poetry. The poet can no longer objectify the world of inwardness by taking images from the outside world. The "Second Elegy," says E. L. Stahl, thus gives two reasons for lament: first, the "transient and evanescent" nature of man, and second, "the absence of valid external symbols for the inward actions of his soul," for the poet is now "unable to create new objects of an intimately human value."[13] The loss of symbolic correspondence, the poet's inability to express inward actions by means of external symbols, is of course not just a motif in the "Second Elegy" but a theme developed throughout the entire poetic cycle.

The "Fourth Elegy" laments the distractedness of the mind and its transiency and oscillation: "Uns aber, wo wir Eines meinen, ganz, / ist schon des andern Aufwand fühlbar [But we, while we are intent upon one object, / already feel the pull of another]" (4, 9–10). These lines, like Shelley's in the famous "To a Skylark"—"We look before and after / And pine for what is not"—vividly present a picture of anxiety and desire that render the human mind forever unsatisfied and unhappy. Rilke, however, does not as quickly aestheticize sorrow as Shelley does in acknowledging that "our sweetest songs are those that tell of saddest thought." Instead, Rilke further explores the implications of the distraction of the mind in a metaphysical manner, on the model of the argument and imagery of Kleist's essay "On the Marionette Theater." Because of the perpetual hesitation of a split mind, says the poet, we are unable to know the inner self without first depending on some external signs: "Wir kennen den Kontur / des Fühlens nicht: nur, was ihn formt von aussen [We never know / the actual, vital contour of our own / emotions—just what forms them from outside]" (4, 17–18). Unlike the inanimate puppet, we are not at one with the world: "Wir sind nicht einig [We are not in harmony]" (4, 2). For this particular reason, man turns out to be inferior to the puppet whose lack of consciousness draws it closer to the angel, and the poet feels that he needs to overcome self-consciousness, and indeed life itself, in order to accomplish the task of transformation:

> Engel und Puppe: dann ist endlich Schauspiel.
> Dann kommt zusammen, was wir immerfort
> entzwein, indem wir da sind. Dann entsteht
> aus unsern Jahreszeiten erst der Umkreis
> des ganzen Wandelns.

> Angel and puppet: a real play, finally.
> Then what we separate by our very presence
> can come together. And only then, the whole
> cycle of transformation will arise,
> out of our own life-seasons.
> [4, 57–61]

The poet finds it hard to understand "Den Tod, / den ganzen Tod, noch vor dem Leben so / sanft zu enthalten und nicht bös zu sein [that one can contain / death, the whole of death, even before / life has begun, can hold it to one's heart gently, and not refuse to go on living]" (4, 82–84).

In the negation not only of an inadequate language but of life itself, the poet seems to come close to a suicidal position, and his self-doubt reaches its nadir in the "Fifth Elegy," which is inspired by Picasso's painting *Les Saltimbanques*.[14] A group of wandering acrobats in Picasso's painting represents for the poet the whole of humanity, whose meaning, or the lack of it, is evasive and enigmatic. It is again to the angel that the poet suddenly turns during a frustrated effort to depict the jaded acrobats and their unenthusiastic onlookers, calling on the celestial power to seize the smile on the face of a little boy, to immortalize that momentary, fleeting smile in a vase or urn:

Engel! o nimms, pflücks, das kleinblütige Heilkraut.
Schaff eine Vase, verwahrs! Stells unter jene, uns *noch* nicht
offenen Freuden; in lieblicher Urne
rühms mit blumiger schwungiger Aufschrift: "Subrisio Saltat."

Oh gather it, Angel, that small-flowered herb of healing.
Create a vase and preserve it. Set it among those joys
not *yet* open to us; on that lovely urn
praise it with the ornately flowing inscription: "Subrisio Saltat."
[5, 58–61]

Since the poem is based on an artist's work that has already permanently
gathered and preserved the boy's smile in color and form, the apostrophe
to the angel seems especially puzzling. The poet's desire to preserve the
young boy's smile in "a vase" is reminiscent of Keats' "Grecian urn" or
Eliot's "Chinese jar," which both symbolize the power of art to transform
the ephemeral and the transient into the permanence of aesthetic form,
the contemporaneity of the work of art. For Rilke, however, not only is
the poet unable to gather that "small-flowered herb of healing," but the
smile itself may have lost its meaning and sincerity among jaded adults;
even the desire to preserve the boy's smile in an urn bearing the Latin
inscription is not without some tragic pathos, a shadow of morbid imagination. The acrobats are tired and bored, doing their routine gymnastic
feats like automatons with no real interest, no smile. So are their audiences:
"die Rose des Zuschauns: / blüht und entblättert [the rose of Onlooking /
blooms and unblossoms]" (5, 19–20); they come and go, "glänzend mit
dünnster / Oberfläche leicht scheinlächelnden Unlust [their thin / sur-
faces glossy with boredom's specious half-smile]" (5, 24–25). It is in this
rather gloomy ambience that the little boy's innocent smile, despite "das
Brennen der Fusssohln [stinging in his soles]" (5, 53), shows its special
cathartic value, its "healing" effect. Rilke later describes the lovers in their
passionate lovemaking as a "wahrhaft lächelnde Paar [genuinely smiling
pair]" (5, 106). Thus the smile, the simple sign of joy and human affec-
tion mentioned several times in this poem, takes on a special meaning and
points to a moment of true emotion without conscious calculation, a
moment that breaks the daily routine of studied activities. That may
explain why the poet wants to preserve the boy's smile and inscribe it as
"Subrisio Saltatorum [the Acrobats' Smile]," and why he wants to know
the place where young acrobats are still novices whose tricks are not yet
totally automatic:

wo die Gewichte noch schwer sind;
wo noch von ihren vergeblich
wirbelnden Stäben die Teller
torkeln . . . . .

where the weights are still heavy; where
from their vainly twirling sticks
the plates still wobble
and drop . . . . .
[5, 77–80]

The poet, however, can neither know the place nor immortalize the smile. The place where the novices become jaded performers is "die unsägliche Stelle [the unsayable spot]" (5, 82); only angels know on what "unsäglichem Teppich [unsayable carpet]" (5, 96) lovers embrace and lean on each other. Here the recurrent word "unsägliche [unsayable]" is crucial, for it clearly defines the difficulty the poet experiences as the loss of language's symbolic power. As Eliot says in *Four Quartets*:

> Words strain,
> Crack and sometimes break, under the burden,
> Under the tension, slip, slide, perish,
> Decay with imprecision, will not stay in place,
> Will not stay still.
> ["Burnt Norton," 5.13–17]

For Rilke, the crisis of language ultimately comes from the opposition or dichotomy of the visible and the invisible, the subject and the object, from which there is no escape. This opposition as the root of human limitations figures repeatedly in Rilke's poems. In the "Eighth Elegy," "das Offene [the Open]" (8, 2) or the freedom of all creatures—plants, animals, and young children—is brought into comparison with man's tragically narrow and schismatic perspective, because for the grown-up man "dieses heisst Schicksal: gegenüber sein / und nichts als das und immer gegenüber [that is what fate means: to be opposite, / to be opposite and nothing else, forever]" (8, 33–34). The mind's doomed dichotomy of subject and object can hardly be put more strongly than in these words. The difference here, Rilke explains, is that "the animal is *in* the world; we stand *in front of* the world because of the peculiar turn and heightening which our consciousness has taken."[15] We are, in other words, not one with the world because of the intervention of consciousness, and the dichotomy is not merely a separation of man from the world, but a split within the human mind itself, a split that has become our unavoidable fate. In the *Duino Elegies*, this fated opposition is represented on a cosmic level as man's alienation from angels and microcosmically as the mind's internalized dichotomy; opposition on both levels is brought into focus as a crisis in poetic articulation, the difficulty of saying what is unsayable. Insofar as this opposition is put in terms of a metaphysical hierarchy of inner vision and its always inadequate outer expression, there is no hope that the poet can bring the task of transformation to a satisfactory solution. That appears to be much of what Rilke says in the *Elegies*, but that is not what the work as a whole promises. Eventually, the poet will find a specifically *poetic* solution to the problem he tries to tackle here, and the real drama unfolding in the poetic cycle will show the reader how the poet is to overcome the dichotomy, to transcend angels, and to find ways to say what is unsayable.

Poetry as Praise

In reading Rilke for his rhetorical ingenuity, Paul de Man notes that most critics have accepted Rilke's words without questioning the possible discrepancy between the meaning and the linguistic devices used to convey the meaning, and he wonders "whether the poetry indeed shares in the conception of language that is attributed to it," and "whether Rilke's text turns back upon itself in a manner that puts the authority of its own affirmations in doubt, especially when these affirmations refer to the modes of writing that it advocates."[16] On the most obvious level, the effectiveness with which Rilke's language speaks of its own inadequacy already puts the confession of inadequacy in question. This is so not because the poet speaks in bad faith, but because poetry works best with irony and litotes not merely as rhetorical devices but as structural principles, as powerful means to convey what would otherwise remain inexpressible. Indeed, the negative way of speaking is typical of Rilke's poetry. In a brilliant reading of several of Rilke's poems, de Man shows how a specifically Rilkean "chiasmic reversal" works to undo the various oppositions that make up the rhetorical structure of the poems. The way Rilke reaffirms the power of language by such reversal again demonstrates the forming of an ironic pattern which necessarily occurs in all writings that question the adequacy of language and writing. While the ironic pattern in the discourse of philosophy or mysticism may reveal an unwanted necessity, in poetry it is more likely a conscious strategy, a rhetorical device with a liberating effect that enables the poet to achieve by evocation and suggestion what cannot be attained in direct expression.

In his earlier poems, Rilke had already tried to transcend the fated dichotomy by reversing the position of subject and object, by assuming a kind of inner sight of the blind, the vision or sensibility of a panther, a gazelle, a swan, or a cat. The reversal reappears in different forms in many of the *New Poems* (1907, 1908), of which perhaps the most famous example is "Archaïscher Torso Apollos [The Archaic Torso of Apollo]," a poem in which the viewer and the viewed change places, and transformation of our ordinary life becomes art's compelling imperative:

> Wir kannten nicht sein unerhörtes Haupt
> darin die Augenäpfel reiften. Aber
> sein Torso glüht noch wie ein Kandelaber,
> in dem sein Schauen, nur zurückgeschraubt,
> sich hält und glänzt. Sonst könnte nicht der Bug
> der Brust dich blenden, und im leisen Drehen
> der Lenden könnte nicht ein Lächeln gehen
> zu jener Mitte, die die Zeugung trug.
> Sonst stünde dieser Stein entstellt und kurz
> unter der Schultern durchsichtigem Sturz
> und flimmerte nicht so wie Raubtierfelle;
> und bräche nicht aus allen seinen Rändern
> aus wie ein Stern: denn da ist keine Stelle,
> die dich nicht sieht. Du musst dein Leben ändern.

> We cannot know his legendary head
> with eyes like ripening fruit. And yet his torso
> is still suffused with brilliance from inside,
> like a lamp, in which his gaze, now turned to low,
> gleams in all its power. Otherwise
> the curved breast could not dazzle you so, nor could
> a smile run through the placid hips and thighs
> to that dark center where procreation flared.
> Otherwise this stone would seem defaced
> beneath the translucent cascade of the shoulders
> and would not glisten like a wild beast's fur:
> would not, from all the borders of itself,

burst like a star: for here there is no place
that does not see you. You must change your life.

The poem begins with a typically Rilkean negative statement that presents before our eyes what is absent: we are told that the fragmented statue
of Apollo is without head and eyes, and yet it is radiant with an inward
light. In fact, the negative mode predominates throughout the text, even
the reversal of the viewer and the viewed at the end of the poem is put in a
slightly eccentric litotes, a negative way of expression: "here there is no
place / that does not see you." Looking at the statue, the viewer's eye
follows the guiding voice speaking in the poem and sees "the curved breast,"
the "placid hips and thighs," and then, literally at the center of the poem,
the "dark center where procreation flared." The light flooding down the
torso is affirmed all the while as radiance coming from inside, though in a
negative manner; suddenly the viewer becomes the viewed, and it is the
eyeless torso of Apollo that sees and reveals the necessity of transformation. The very absence of the head and eye become the source of an inner
presence of light, around which the voice speaking to the reader (who is
also the viewer of the statue) can build up the reversal at the end of the
poem. "The reversal is possible," as de Man comments, "only because the
sculpture is broken and fragmentary; if the statue had actually represented the eye of Apollo, the chiasmus could not have come about. The
absent eye allows for an imaginary vision to come into being, and it makes
the eyeless sculpture into an Argus eye capable of engendering, by itself,
all the dimensions of space."[17] But the absent eye is of course present in
the text, only in a negative mode, because "die Augenäpfel [eyes like
apples]" literally exist from the very start; and the conjuncture of eye
and apple into one word effectively aestheticizes the absent eye, making
it tangibly present and turning its absence into a positive, almost sensuous experience. By naming an absent object, the poet in fact makes
it present in language; the chiasmic reversal thus becomes a powerful
means of creating things out of nothing and thereby fulfilling the task of
transformation.

Rilke calls such verbal creation of things by the act of naming an act of
praise. In "The Fifth Elegy," when the poet calls on the angel to immortalize the little boy's smile, "rühms [praise]" (5, 61) is the key word. If by an
act of praise the angel is able to preserve the smile, so will the poet. For
Rilke, poetry as praise is capable of all sorts of miracles: it is the poet's
vocation, his answer to the question of how to create things in language:

Oh sage, Dichter, was du tust?—Ich rühme.
Aber das Tödliche und Ungetüme,
wie hältst du's aus, wie nimmst du's hin?—Ich rühme.
Aber das Namenlose, Anonyme,
wie rufst du's, Dichter, dennoch an?—Ich rühme.
Woher dein Recht, in jeglichem Kostüme,
in jeder Maske wahr zu sein?—Ich rühme.
Und dass das Stille und das Ungestüme
wie Stern und Sturm dich kennen?:—weil ich rühme.

Oh, speak, poet, what do you do?—I praise.
But the deadly and the monstrous,
how do you bear them, how do you take them?—I praise.
But the nameless, the anonymous,
how do you, poet, still invoke them?—I praise.
Whence your right, in each costume,
in every mask, to be true?—I praise.
How do the quiet and the vehement
like star and storm all know you?:—for I praise.[18]

Poetry as praise becomes for Rilke a kind of verbal magic that helps invoke the nameless and the unnameable, the magic of incantation in which the ordinary word takes on the great evocative power to summon the invisible: "wirklich wie der Ruf des Taubers, / der nach der unsicht-baren Taube ruft [real as the cock pigeon's cry, / that calls for the invisible dove]."[19] The magic of words definitely opens the possibility of reversing what the poet has complained about, the impossibility of addressing angels and transforming the visible into the invisible, the difficulty of poetic articulation. The concept of poetry as praise thus brings the reversal to completion not just in a single poem but in the total structure of the *Elegies* in its evolution from complaint to joy.

In the "Seventh Elegy," the transition from lament to praise is clearly signaled when the poet no longer looks up to the angel but affirms what belongs to man, boldly declaring that "Hiersein ist herrlich [*Truly* being here is glorious!]" (7, 39). He is able to point out things in this human world to the angel and say: "O staune, Engel, denn wir sinds [Be aston-ished, Angel, for we / *are* this]" (7, 75). The contrast between angel and man, which is reinforced throughout the *Elegies*, reaches a turning point where the human voice becomes more courageous, confident, even defiant:

> Glaub *nicht*, dass ich werbe.
> Engel, und würb ich dich auch! Du kommst nicht. Denn mein
> Anruf ist immer voll Hinweg; wider so starke
> Strömung kannst du nicht schreiten.
>
> Don't think that I'm wooing.
> Angel, and even if I were, you would not come. For my call
> is always filled with departure; against such a powerful
> current you cannot move.
> [7, 85–88]

The general tone of the last two elegies evidently differs from that of the earlier ones, for we clearly hear a joyful voice of praise, the triumphant jubilee of the here and now that celebrates the human condition despite all its deficiencies and limitations. The poet no longer woos the angel but sees man's brief life span as almost standing against the angelic eternity. Though we exist but once and never again, says Rilke, to have lived once fully is in itself worthwhile: "Wenn auch nur ein Mal: / irdisch gewesen zu sein, scheint nicht widerrufbar [even if only once: / to have been at one with the earth, seems beyond undoing]" (9, 15–16). In the "Ninth Elegy," man's limitations and the way to overcome them are all put in terms of what is said and not said, the sayable and the unsayable. The hardships in life and the joy of love are unsayable, but language is the only means to register all our feelings, our actions and experiences. The traveler coming back from the mountain slope does not bring a handful of unsayable earth but some pure words like wildflowers. The combination of words and flowers, or language and things, is especially significant because it shows a renewed confidence in language to unify the outer and the inner worlds, the realization that to say what can be said is the poet's mission:

> Sind wir vielleicht *hier*, um zu sagen: Haus,
> Brücke, Brunnen, Tor, Krug, Obstbaum, Fenster,—
> höchstens: Säule, Turm. . . . aber zu *sagen*, verstehs,
> oh zu sagen *so*, wie selber die Dinge niemals
> innig meinten zu sein.
>
> Perhaps we are *here* in order to say: house,
> bridge, fountain, gate, pitcher, fruit-tree, window—
> at most: column, tower. . . . But to *say* them, you must understand,

oh to say them *more* intensely than the Things themselves
ever dreamed of existing.
[9, 31–35]

Here we have one of the most powerful pleas in modern poetry for the power of language. Saying is conceived as more intensely ontological than things themselves could have ever dreamed of being: it is language, the naming of simple things—house, bridge, fountain, gate, pitcher—that brings things into existence and defines what is uniquely human. Rilke proclaims:

> *Hier* ist des *Säglichen* Zeit, *hier* seine Heimat.
> Sprich und bekenn.

> *Here* is the time for the *sayable*, *here* is its homeland.
> Speak and bear witness.
> [9, 42–43)

The word "das Sägliche," as H. E. Holthusen comments, "becomes the mythical key-word to describe man's position vis-à-vis the Angel, while 'das Unsägliche' comes to stand as the Angel's attribute, a kind of pseudonym of transcendence."[20] Against the angel's mystic silence, the poet is here to speak and praise, and his saying affirms the value of simple, concrete words and things. Compared with the elegiac tonality in earlier poems, the "Ninth Elegy" boldly reaffirms the creative power of poetry as praise. "Preise dem Engel die Welt, nicht die unsägliche [Praise this world to the angel, not the unsayable one]," the poet declares. "Sag ihm die Dinge. Er wird staunender stehn [Tell him of Things. He will stand astonished]" (9, 52 and 57). Now the position of the poet vis-à-vis the angel is reversed, for it is the poet that shows the angel

> wie glücklich ein Ding sein kann, wie schuldlos und unser,
> wie selbst das klagende Leid rein zur Gestalt sich entschliesst,
> dient als ein Ding, oder stirbt in ein Ding—, und jenseits
> selig der Geige entgeht.

> how happy a Thing can be, how innocent and ours,
> how even lamenting grief purely decides to take form,
> serves as a Thing, or dies into a Thing—, and blissfully
> escapes far beyond the violin.
> [9, 59–62]

To earth's command of transformation, the poet can now give a confidently positive answer; for man now assumes the role of the deliverer of things from *their* transience: "Und diese von Hingang / lebenden Dinge verstehn, dass du sie rühmst; vergänglich, / traun sie ein Rettendes uns, den Vergänglichsten, zu [And these Things, / which live by perishing, know you are praising them; transient, / they look to us for deliverance: us, the most transient of all]" (9, 63–65). As Walter Strauss remarks, here Rilke is making "a deeply felt plea to awaken the silent voice of things in their relatedness to man, to break out of the prison-house of interpretation into the openness of mutuality with objects."[21] In the celebration of things and the sayable, the poet is no longer confined in the concept of a metaphysical transcendence that paralyzes his ability to transform the visible into the invisible and weakens his voice before angels. If saying and praise is what the poet can and must do, then earth's command of transformation, its desire to "arise within us" and be "invisible," cannot be a negation of language. On the contrary, it can only be earth's arising in language by the incantation of verse. The dismissal of language proves to be self-ironic, and the poet who seems to have negated language must reclaim it, following the same ironic pattern as we have described earlier with regard to philosophers and mystics.

At the same time, the language in which earth arises invisibly is language internalized, a language that does not merely refer to the outward appearance as the ultimate signified or ultimate justification, but a language that awakens the silent voice of things, a suggestive language that points beyond the visible object to the invisible and the unsayable. The German "Sag ihm die Dinge" contains a direct relationship between saying and things that is more emphatic than can be conveyed in the English version "*Tell* him *of* Things" (9, 57). It is a transitive relation that emphasizes the power of language to create, to bring things into existence. Only with a language that can create *ex nihilo*, that brings things into being simply by naming them, can the poet wish to address the angels' hierarchies:

> Dass ich dereinst, an dem Ausgang der grimmigen Einsicht,
> Jubel und Ruhm aufsinge zustimmenden Engeln.

> Someday, emerging at last from the violent insight,
> let me sing out jubilation and praise to assenting angels!
> [9, 1–2]

Such is the wish expressed in the last of the elegies; such is also the project of Rilke's *Sonnets to Orpheus,* of which the cheerful tone of praise and celebration contrasts strikingly with the lament of the *Duino Elegies.* The myth of Orpheus the divine singer—his power to tame wild animals with music, his descent into Hades, and his being torn to pieces by the wild Maenads—provides Rilke with an excellent *fabula* for putting together the various aspects of his vision of the poet as the singer of praise. Orpheus is the archetypal poet, the image of the poet as one who praises: "Rühmen, das ists! Ein zum Rühmen Bestellter, / ging er hervor wie das Erz aus des Steins / Schweigen [Praising is what matters! He was summoned for that, / and came to us like the ore from a stone's / silence]" (1, 7).[22] It is important to note that it is out of "a stone's silence" that the poet in the Orphic mask is summoned to praise and make music. We may recall that the poet proposes in the "Ninth Elegy" that man as the singer of praise should show the angel "das Einfache, das, von Geschlecht zu Geschlechtern gestaltet, / als ein Unsriges lebt, neben der Hand und im Blick [something simple which, formed over generations, / lives as our own, near our hand and within our gaze]" (9, 55–56). The Orphic language that makes divine music "like the ore from a stone's silence" is therefore not an elaborate language that attempts exhaustively to name all and describe all, but a language of reticence that says little but suggests the plenitude of things in its appeal to the animated imagination. Eventually, it is by naming the finite and the nameable that the poet can speak of the infinite and the unnameable, yet every name is invested with such power of symbolic representation, every word endowed with such magic of invocation, that poetry coming out of the silence is far richer than what its simple language literally contains. Rilke says in the first Orphic sonnet:

> Da stieg ein Baum. O reine Übersteigung!
> O Orpheus singt! O hoher Baum im Ohr!
> Und alles schwieg. Doch selbst in der Verschweigung
> ging neuer Anfang, Wink und Wandlung vor.

> A tree ascended there. Oh, pure transcendence!
> Oh Orpheus sings! Oh tall tree in the ear!
> And all things hushed. Yet even in that silence
> a new beginning, beckoning, changes appeared.
> [1, 1]

The tall, ascending tree that rises up in the ear as Orpheus sings gives Rilke's poetic theory a graphic expression in a striking image. As a symbol of life and growth, the tree represents the concrete world of things, a world that now exists no longer as the outer realm opposed to man's inner vision but that is brought into being by the power of language, by the evocation of poetic articulation. The silence of things promises new beginnings and changes, beckoning the poet to speak, to bring the unsayable into the circle of communication. In the form of an Orphic song, words and music attain to artistic permanence, or as Eliot puts it, "as a Chinese jar still / Moves perpetually in its stillness" ("Burnt Norton," 5.6–7). The poet may still have doubt and hesitation, but his definition of poetry as an Orphic praise, as presence out of absence or nothingness, is all the more convincing, as it is not a facile solution to the difficulties so deeply felt and expressed in his earlier poems:

> Ein Gott vermags. Wie aber, sag mir, soll
> ein Mann ihm folgen durch die schmale Leier?
> Sein Sinn ist Zwiespalt. An der Kreuzung zweier
> Herzwege steht kein Tempel für Apoll.
>
> Gesang, wie du ihn lehrst, ist nicht Begehr,
> nicht Werbung um ein endlich noch Erreichtes;
> Gesang ist Dasein. Für den Gott ein Leichtes.
> Wann aber *sind* wir? Und wann wendet er
>
> an unser Sein die Erde und die Sterne?
> Dies *ists* nicht, Jüngling, dass du liebst, wenn auch
> die Stimme dann den Mund dir aufstösst,—lerne
>
> vergessen, dass du aufsangst. Das verrinnt.
> In Wahrheit singen, ist ein andrer Hauch.
> Ein Hauch um nichts. Ein Wehn im Gott. Ein Wind.

> A god can do it. But will you tell me how
> a man can enter through the lyre's strings?
> Our mind is split. And at the shadowed crossing
> of heart-roads, there is no temple for Apollo.
>
> Song, as you have taught it, is not desire,
> not wooing any grace that can be achieved;
> song is reality. Simple, for a god.
> But when can *we* be real? When does he pour

the earth, the stars, into us? Young man,
it is not your loving, even if your mouth
was forced wide open by your own voice—learn

to forget that passionate music. It will end.
True singing is a different breath, about
nothing. A gust inside the god. A wind.
[1, 3]

This sonnet admirably recapitulates what we have discussed so far: the difficulty of speaking, the split of the human mind, and poetry as originating from inner silence and nothingness. In his autobiographic novel, *The Notebooks of Malte Laurids Brigge*, Rilke has formulated a poetics of impersonality, asserting that "poems are not, as people think, simply emotions (one has emotions early enough)—they are experiences."[23] The theory is reiterated here that one must forsake "desire" and "wooing," forget the personal "passionate music" that naturally bursts out of the mouth, and learn to sing in "a different breath, about / nothing. A gust inside the god. A wind." While the sonnet begins at a moment where, like the earlier *Elegies*, the poet still finds it difficult to "enter through the lyre's strings," it quickly learns from Orpheus to sing the song of silence, the song about nothing, until the poet can do what a god can and realizes the creative power of poetry in the famous line "Gesang ist Dasein [Song is being]." What is decisive in all the arts, as Rilke says himself, "is not their outward appearance, not what is called the 'beautiful'; but rather their deepest, most inner origin, the buried reality that calls forth this appearance."[24] The idea expressed here is very different from a romantic internalization of art and rather advocates a poetics of silence. Only when the poet has reached the inner origin, the silence and nothingness that call forth the beautiful appearance, can he invoke the inexpressible and brings it into being. The evolution of Rilke as a poet is of course much more complex than our brief discussion can fully describe, but from the *Duino Elegies* to the *Sonnets to Orpheus*, just as in many single poems, there is structurally as well as thematically a reversal of what the poet explicitly says about poetry and language, and there is finally a reaffirmed confidence in the magic power of poetic language.

In the light of the Orphic sonnets, we may understand what exactly Rilke means by praise. If the act of praise helps the poet call on the nameless and the anonymous, we may wonder whether its magic is not essentially a result of the same kind of strategy to reclaim language as we have seen in both the West and the East, something not unlike Zhuangzi's "non-words," the Nagarjunian "provisional names," or Meister Eckhart's command to preach the "silent word." As Joachim Storck argues, silence is of paramount significance in the works of Rilke after he has completed *The Notebooks of Malte* (1910) and gone through a crisis of creativity. "In this crisis of creativity, which grows into a crisis of existence for Rilke," Storck observes, "'silence' gains an ever greater importance." And this silence can be defined, he continues, as "the poetic possibility of a negatively put expression."[25] In "The Archaic Torso of Apollo," we have seen how the negative mode dominates the entire text and makes it possible for the poet to achieve the chiasmic reversal. That poem can indeed serve as a model of Rilke's works as a whole, in which the possibility of poetry, the potential of a reversal, is provided by an absence or silence which is always a "negatively put expression." Rilke formulates this poetics of silence in these famous lines:

> Schweigen. Wer inniger schwieg,
> rührt an die Wurzeln der Rede.
> Einmal wird ihm dann jede
> erwachsene Silbe zum Sieg.

> Be silent. Who keeps silent inside
> touches the roots of speech.
> Then each growing syllable
> becomes for him a victory.[26]

Silence, the apparent total negation of language, paradoxically contains the roots of speech, and Rilke's redemptive myth is significantly that of Orpheus, the divine singer born with a magic voice, making music out of stony silence. In order to sing, one must learn to be silent, for true singing is "about / nothing. A gust inside the god. A wind." In the famous line "Gesang ist Dasein," the name and the thing named are united and become identical in the poetic articulation, and poetry as inspired breath validates human existence from within, as internalized experiences. To praise a thing is therefore to name it, and by naming to bestow on it an ontological value. By defining poetry as praise in this special sense, Rilke reclaims the power of language to convey the truth of inwardness, making it a poetic equivalent of the philosophic and mystic logos, the unification of being and saying. The important difference between Rilke's *Gesang* and the mystic "non-words" is not to be overlooked, however, for the poet's song is not a provisional name of being to be replaced and cast away once its meaning is understood, but it is Being itself, albeit an ontologically limited being-there, an existential *Dasein*.

Sound and Sense

In *Truth and Method*, one of the main points Gadamer makes in his critique of romantic aesthetics is the validity of reintegrating art in historical experience as a kind of knowledge, and indeed truth. Starting from the theories of Kant and Kierkegaard, who both attempted to overcome the radical subjectivism of the aesthetic, Gadamer argues that aesthetic experience, far from being an experience of something outside our historicity, is "a mode of self-understanding." When we encounter a work of art, we are not magically transported into a totally different, strange world but a world continuous with our own; "We learn to understand ourselves in and through it, and this means that we sublate [*aufheben*] the discontinuity and atomism of isolated experiences in the continuity of our own existence."[27] The hermeneutic task of how to understand radically oppositional and discontinuous modern and contemporary art in the continuity of our historical existence becomes the major concern in some of Gadamer's essays written after *Truth and Method*, and repeatedly he points to the possibility of meaning—namely, something meaningful and to be understood in a work of art—as the binding element that provides for the continuity of the aesthetic world and the world of our daily existence. In a way reminiscent of Rilke, Gadamer acknowledges that "the poetry of our time has reached the limits of intelligible meaning and perhaps the greatest achievements of the greatest writers are themselves marked by tragic speechlessness in the face of the unsayable."[28] However, modern art and poetry can never completely rid themselves of meaning, no matter how nonrepresentational they are meant to be. Even absolute music as a form of nonobjective art retains "some obscure relationship with language," which ultimately accounts for our sense of its quality, the possibility for us to speak of its shallowness or depth. "In fact," Gadamer maintains, "all artistic creation challenges each of us to listen to the language in which the work of art speaks and to make it our own."[29]

The emphasis on language and meaning has special importance here because it highlights the hermeneutic significance of all works of art and makes the encounter with art analogous to the encounter with language. In this connection, the significance of poetry as the art of language becomes evident, for poetry can be seen as the model for the understanding of other forms of art. For Gadamer, the emphasis on language is also that on meaning, since the elements of language, he observes, can become the elements of poetic form only "by virtue of their meaning." Given the radically nonobjective and nonrepresentational claims of much of contemporary art, it is particularly important to recognize the presence of meaning in all forms of art, and to see them as speaking of something meaningful in their own languages. Gadamer is fully aware that "emancipation from an objectively interpreted experience of the world appears to be a basic principle of contemporary art," but he claims that poetry by its very nature cannot endorse this tendency. "The poet cannot participate in this process. Language as the medium and material of expression can never fully emancipate itself from meaning. A genuinely nonobjective poetry would simply be gibberish."[30] It is in the context of meaningful linguistic communication that Gadamer proposes to define the work of art: "For something can only be called art when it requires that we construe the world by learning to understand the language of form and content so that communication really occurs."[31]

With its emphasis on meaning and understanding, the hermeneutic concept of the work of art forms an interesting contrast to a very different kind of theoretical analysis of language: the deconstructive concept of text and writing. Having dismissed both formalism and the "moral imperative" to reach beyond formalism to the external, referential reality as two sides of the same coin—the opposing intrinsic and extrinsic approaches caught in "an inside/outside metaphor that is never being questioned"— Paul de Man declares that deconstructive semiology can now transcend meaning, interpretation, and paraphrase: "By an awareness of the arbitrariness of the sign (Saussure) and of literature as an autotelic statement 'focused on the way it is expressed' (Jakobson) the entire question of meaning can be bracketed, thus freeing the critical discourse from the debilitating burden of paraphrase."[32] The result of deconstructive reading is therefore not the possibility of meaning but a "negative assurance," a "suspended ignorance," "a rhetorical question which does not even know whether it is really questioning."[33] With such an agnostic presumption considered appropriate for critical discourse, de Man tries to delineate a "phonocentric poetics" in Rilke which "subordinates the semantic function of language to the phonic one" and which constructs, in one poem after another, elaborate structures of acoustic effect at the expense of semantic depth. According to de Man, language in Rilke's poetry becomes "a medium which deprives itself of all resources except those of sound. Possibilities of representation and of expression are eliminated in an askesis which tolerates no other reference than the formal attributes of the vehicle. Since sound is the only property of language that is truly immanent to it and that bears no relation to anything that would be situated outside language itself, it will remain as the only available resource."[34] In short, all good poems are poems of sound rather than sense, and for de Man's aesthetic sensibility, a poem becomes less interesting when it does promise to have a theme or meaning. For example, Rilke's "Quai du Rosaire" describes the reflection of the city of Brugge in the clear evening water as "die eingehängte Welt von Spiegelbildern [the suspended world of mirrored images]," which "so wirklich wird wie diese Dinge nie [becomes so real as things could never be]." The unreal world of mirrored images thus assumes a fantastic reality more real than the city aboveground, and this may strike the reader as the meaning the poem implies, that the poem is about Brugge, " 'Bruges la morte' as it is called by the poet Georges Rodenbach, a city that used to be prestigious but has become, by the loss of its natural harbor and medieval glory, an emblem for the transience of human achievement, a figure of mutability."[35] For de Man, however, this possibility of meaning or thematic interpretation is "banal" and "of minor interest," whereas "the true interest of the poem" stems from "the intricacy and the wealth of movements triggered by the original chiasmus."[36] The chiasmic reversal in Rilke's poetry is therefore not thematic but acoustic, not a matter of sense but purely of sound. De Man does not seem to differentiate the rhetorical in general from the acoustic in particular, and in his discussion of "phonocentric poetics," the autonomous world a poem creates within its linguistic boundary becomes identical with a world of pure sound with no sense. The nonrepresentation of "pure poetry" is for him the emancipation from meaning, and the play of signifier is considered absolute, pointing to nothing outside itself. The aesthetic world of poetry is thus completely cut off from the world of our daily existence, and the kind of continuity that Gadamer conceives between the experience of art and the experience of life becomes utterly inconceivable. In de Man's reading, a poem is successful only to the extent that it succeeds in emancipating itself from meaning, and "this 'liberating theory of the Signifier'," he maintains, "also implies a complete drying up of thematic possibilities. In order to be a pure poetry of what Rilke calls 'figures,' it should start on the far side of the renunciation which opens up its access to this new freedom."[37] Instead of seeing poetry as knowledge and truth, de Man declares that "the poetry gains a maximum of convincing power at the very moment that it abdicates any claim to truth."[38]

Rilke's "Gesang ist Dasein [Song is reality]" seems to put the idea of the self-referentiality of "pure poetry" in a succinct and memorable form. Song, we are told, is *Dasein*, reality, or rather, being-there or existence. For Gadamer, however, this line does not indicate the evaporation of meaning but precisely "combines meaning and being in one," because for him *Gesang* is necessarily meaningful. "'Song is existence.' But what kind of existence is this?" Gadamer raises the question in order to lead from a reading of this line as expressing the idea of a self-enclosed aesthetic world to the hermeneutic concept of poetry as grounded in our historical existence, as "meaning-gestures." "All intentional speech points away from itself," he continues. "Words are not simply complexes of sound, but meaning-gestures that point away from themselves as gestures do. We all know that the sound-quality of poetry only acquires definition through the understanding of meaning."[39] In Gadamer's reading, then, the *Dasein* in Rilke's line is not the aesthetic world of poetic language as completely different from the ordinary language, certainly not a conglomeration of sounds or sound effects, but existence that has an intimate relationship and continuity with the life of each of us—that is, existence as *reality*. Even sound quality, as he notes, can be differentiated and become phonetic units of language only through the understanding of meaning. In linguistics we learn that not all sounds are phonetically significant, but only those that are recognized within a certain linguistic system as making a difference, namely, capable of generating meaning. For example, pronouncing the same sound of a word in different tones does not change the semantic value of the sound in English, but the change of tone may be phonetically significant in Chinese as it may indicate different words with totally different meanings. From a linguistic point of view, therefore, de Man's idea of a "phonocentric poetics" as free from meaning is put on a rather dubious basis, and despite his brilliant discussion of the chiasmic reversal in many of the poems, his deconstructive reading fails to do justice to Rilke's poetry as a whole. The weakness of his critical approach becomes evident when he claims that "Rilke's most advanced poetic achievement" can be found only in poems that are "by necessity brief and enigmatic, often consisting of one single sentence," while ignoring or devaluating Rilke's major works, asserting that "the imperative tone of the *Elegies* is totally incompatible with the very notion of pure figure," or that the *Elegies* and the *Sonnets to Orpheus* fall short of Rilke's greatest achievement because of their "relapse from a rhetoric of figuration into a rheto-ric of signification."[40]

But is "pure poetry" really devoid of meaning? Or to put it differently, does the reading of "pure poetry" also pose the hermeneutic problems of understanding and interpretation? In a number of essays, Gadamer dis-cusses pure poetry several times and tries precisely to answer that ques-tion. He borrows a phrase from Martin Luther to characterize the poetic word as one "that stands written [*Es stehet geschrieben*]" in the sense that it is autonomous and self-fulfilling. And this self-fulfillment, Gadamer remarks, "appears at its most mysterious in lyric poetry, where we cannot even determine the unified sense of poetic speech, as is especially the case with 'pure poetry' since the time of Mallarmé."[41] Pure poetry as "pro-grammatically developed by Mallarmé" is thus an extreme case of "the inseparability of the linguistic work of art and its original manifestation as a language," which makes poetry virtually untranslatable. But "even in this extreme case, where the musicality of the poetic word is intensified to the very highest degree," Gadamer argues, "it is still a question of the musicality of *language*. The form of the poem is constructed by the con-stantly shifting balance between sound and sense," and it is in poetry that word and language become "word and language in a preeminent sense."[42] No matter how special the unity of poetic creation may be, it is still a unity that "at the same time possesses the unity of everyday speech," which means that "logico-grammatical forms of intelligible speech are also at work in the poem," and that "syntactic indeterminacy" is ultimately responsible "for the free play of both the connotations to which the word owes its rich content and, even more, for the semantic weight that inhab-its every word and suggests a variety of possible meanings."[43] Instead of being free from meaning, pure poetry in Gadamer's understanding con-tains a particularly rich possibility of different meanings, and in such poetry, "sound and sense are in perfect equilibrium as centers of gravity, so that the unity of speech is achieved without any other syntactic means whatsoever." This, says Gadamer, "was Mallarmé's ideal," but "that does not mean that the unified sense of speech has been endangered or eliminated."[44]

Every time Gadamer mentions "pure poetry," he invariably relates it to Mallarmé, and this, as Robert Bernasconi suggests, presents "the possi-bility of a challenging comparison with Derrida who offers a reading of Mallarmé's *Mimique* in 'The double session,' in *Dissemination*."[45] As we have seen in the contrast between Gadamer's and de Man's reading of

Rilke, the comparison with Derrida will also be a contrast between hermeneutics and deconstruction, revealing a theoretical difference and very
different approaches to the question of whether "pure poetry" has the
possibility of meaning and interpretation. The question of meaning, as
we shall see, is not simply a question involved in solving textual difficulties
in the reading process but is related to the whole problem of mimesis or
representation as understood in the Western philosophical tradition.

Mallarmé: The Importance of Blank

By juxtaposing an excerpt from Plato's *Philebus* and Mallarmé's essay,
"Mimique," thereby forcing them into an intertextual close combat,
Derrida questions the validity of a philosophical reading of Mallarmé as
well as the traditional notions of truth and representation. In Plato's text,
the question of mimesis or truth is raised when Socrates privileges "the
conjunction of memory with sensations" as a kind of internal writing,
which "may be said as it were to write words in our souls" and give us
"true opinion and true assertions," while he dismisses external writing as
untruth, which the "internal scribe" produces when he deviates from the
ideal forms already inscribed in his soul and "writes what is false."[46] Such
classical concepts of mimesis and truth predicate themselves on the assumption of an exact correspondence between copy and original, imitation and
imitated, signifier and signified: a correspondence that endeavors to emulate the ideal unification of meaning and speech in the logos. But here, by
the side of Plato's text, is Mallarmé's "Mimique," a text responding to
another text by another author and recounting the performance of a mime
whose unscripted gestures mimic at once Pierrot the murderer and his
murdered wife, carrying on, says Mallarmé, "a mute soliloquy that the
phantom, white as a yet unwritten page, holds in both face and gesture at
full length to his soul."[47] Mallarmé speaks of the pantomime in terms of a
gestural writing, and his own writing about this gestural writing is in turn
based on another writing, for he has not seen the mime's performance but
has read about it in a book.

Such stratification of writing in double and triple layers offers an excellent opportunity for Derrida to deconstruct traditional notions of origin,
mimesis, and truth. To read Mallarmé's "Mimique," Derrida argues, is to
enter "a textual labyrinth panelled with mirrors," where we find nothing
but "a self-duplication of repetition itself; *ad infinitum*, since this movement feeds its own proliferation."[48] In other words, both the mime's ges-

tural writing and Mallarmé's actual writing have no origin; they imitate nothing but their own textuality; they are not copies reproducing an original situated outside themselves. That the mime's gestures do not refer to any preexistent model or reality puts in question the very concept of mimesis as Plato and the whole philosophical tradition have defined it in terms of the correspondence of copy and the original. "The Mime imitates nothing," says Derrida. "There is nothing prior to the writing of his gestures. Nothing is prescribed for him. No present has preceded or supervised the tracing of his writing. His movements form a figure that no speech anticipates or accompanies. They are not linked with *logos* in any order of consequence."[49] The series of negative statements purports to emphasize the deconstructive concept of writing as nonrepresentational, as the free play of signifiers. According to Derrida, Mallarmé's "Mimique" exemplifies the nonreferentiality of writing as fully as any "pure poetry" does, and it undermines the concept of truth as defined in traditional philosophical terms. To be sure, Mallarmé often talks about truth, the Idea, the spiritual universe, and so forth, but Derrida insists that Mallarmé's talk only has the appearance of philosophical discourse; it only "preserves the differential structure of mimicry or *mimesis*, but without its Platonic or metaphysical interpretation, which implies that somewhere the being of something that *is*, is being imitated." What appears to be Mallarmé's literary version of philosophical idealism is a mere "simulacrum of Platonism or Hegelianism," and so it is "not simply false to say that Mallarmé is a Platonist or a Hegelian. But it is above all not true."[50] According to Derrida, the only truth about pure poetry is that it does not contain any truth as the representation of reality. From such a deconstructive reading, then, Mallarmé emerges as an antimimetic and antilogocentric poet, a deconstructionist *avant la lettre*. Indeed, together with Pound, Mallarmé is considered by Derrida himself as a precursor of deconstruction, for he has credited Mallarmé and Pound with inventing a graphic poetics and making "the first break in the most entrenched Western tradition."[51]

A direct consequence of Derrida's deconstructive reading of Mallarmé, like that of de Man's reading of Rilke, is a profound suspicion about the search for meaning in criticism. That explains why it is important for Derrida to include in his essay on "Mimique" a critique of Jean-Pierre Richard's thematic interpretation of Mallarmé. Derrida holds that "Mimique" and Mallarmé's other texts do not refer to anything outside themselves and that therefore it is impossible to see them as imitating, representing, or expressing anything. But to see them as representation and expression, Derrida argues, is precisely what thematic criticism does, since it "makes the text into a form of expression, reduces it to its signified theme, and retains all the traits of mimetologism. What it retains in particular is that *dialecticity* that has remained profoundly inseparable from metaphysics, from Plato to Hegel."[52] That is to say, thematic criticism, the search for meaning, and Richard's notion of theme as the sum of multiple meanings or the putting in perspective of that multiplicity are all related to traditional metaphysics, against which Derrida positions Mallarmé's works as antilogocentric, exemplifying the impossibility of meaning. For example, Derrida claims that the *blanc* ("blank" or "white") which often appears in Mallarmé's texts cannot be semantically determined in any perspective. This is so not because its semantic valences are inexhaustible but because there is always an extra or *plus* of blank beyond the sum of multiple meanings, "a blank *between* the valences," which makes the differentiation of meaning possible in the first place.[53] A blank is thus not a theme of the text but opens up the space and forms the very condition of textuality. Therefore Derrida maintains that any attempt to interpret Mallarmé's writing semantically or thematically might "arrest its play or its indecision," to subsume it "within a philosophical or critical (Platonico-Hegelian) interpretation of *mimesis*," and render it "incapable of accounting for that excess of syntax over meaning."[54] Eventually, Derrida's reading leads to the total erasure of meaning, to the free play of "signifiers unhooked, dislodged, disengaged from their historic polarization." What follows, then, is an inevitable theoretical move that will, Derrida claims, replace the "hermeneutic concept of *polysemy*" with the deconstructive "*dissemination*."[55]

One may agree that reducing the play of signifiers to a single meaning or theme from a limited and limiting perspective fails to do justice to the complexity of Mallarmé's text and impoverishes its rich syntactic potential. But one begins to wonder whether it is only confusing literary indeterminacy with mystic obscurantism if we insist that what we read in Mallarmé does not make any sense at all and that the blank, as Derrida argues, only "re-marks itself forever as disappearance, erasure, nonsense."[56] It is true that Mallarmé himself sets a high value on mystery in poetry, but the question remains whether and how we should differentiate poetic mystery from religious mysticism. In an essay written at the age of twenty, Mallarmé already realized that "everything sacred that wants to remain sacred envelops itself in mystery."[57] For him, art is sacred as religion, and its mysteries must be kept from the vulgar eye, revealed only to the elect few. The young poet cries: "O golden clasps on old missals! O inviolate hieroglyphs on papyrus scrolls!" This youthful manifesto of Mallarmé's artistic elitism and mysticism, according to Guy Michaud, "contains something approximating a key to his entire work."[58] As Mallarmé puts it in advocating the kind of writing that suggests a hidden and obscure mystery on the white page: "There must be something of the occult at the bottom of all things."[59] The mystery in poetry, however, as Mallarmé himself expounds it, is not the total absence of meaning but has a fairly definite meaning in his poetic theory—namely, the use of a suggestive language to create a certain mystique or atmosphere of something beautiful and indescribable. Suggestiveness, the indirect expression in an elliptical language, is for Mallarmé a creative principle, as he explains to his friend Jules Huret:

> To *name* an object is to suppress three-quarters of the enjoyment of the poem which is made to be divined little by little: to *suggest* it, that's the dream [*le* suggérer, *voilà le rêve*]. It is the perfect use of this mystery that constitutes the symbol: to evoke an object little by little in order to show a state of mind, or, inversely, to choose an object and bring forth from it a state of mind through a series of deciphering.[60]

From this famous passage it is clear that poetry is not something one can grasp at a glance, something directly named or explicitly stated, but something vaguely implied, enshrouded in the mist of evocative language that works to build up a state of mind or a mood, a certain atmosphere; and the pleasure of reading is a perception of something indefinite but beautiful, the experience of a mystery that can be deciphered only gradually, after much pondering and rumination. Mystery here has nothing in it that concerns the otherworldliness or the ineffable holy Word; it is rather a way of expression that suggests but never directly names the object that resides at the center of the poem as an absence or *blanc*. Like the silence in Rilke, mystery or the blank at the center of the text for Mallarmé simply means the evocation of something out of nothing, the poetic possibility of a negatively put expression and therefore a possibility deeply imbedded in language. In fact, Mallarmé's poetry and poetics had a significant influence on Rilke, and like Rilke's works, the pure poetry of Mallarmé does not abdicate the claim to truth or the rich possibilities of meaning. In a way that again reminds us of Rilke, Mallarmé explains to Verlaine that the task of the poet, "the only duty of the poet and the literary game par excellence," is "the Orphic explication of the earth

[*L'explication orphique de la terre*]."[61] The idea of poetry as "explication" already implies the unfolding of meaning, the recreation of the earth in an ideal, beautiful form, even if the Orphic ode does not refer to any definite object or reality outside itself. This is more clearly expressed in Mallarmé's definition of poetry, formulated at Léo d'Orfer's request:

> Poetry is the expression, through human language reduced to its essential rhythm, of the mysterious meaning of the aspects of existence: it thus bestows authenticity on our sojourn and constitutes the only spiritual task.[62]

Here, language stands out above all as the medium to express the mysterious meaning of life, thereby fulfilling the only spiritual task, and there is an unmistakable connection between poetry and our historical existence. By evoking the absent in language in its essential rhythm, the poet is able to create out of nothing, or as Mallarmé puts it, out of the poet himself as his own center, "like a sacred spider onto the principal threads already woven out of my spirit."[63] But what does it mean to say that poetry is the expression of the mysterious meaning of our existence? What constitutes the meaning poetry expresses, and how is it expressed? If the question of meaning and expression is related with that of representation or imitation, we must first of all make clear the meaning of the very term *representation* or *imitation*. Gadamer's discussion of mimesis aims precisely to revise the understanding of this key term in the Platonico-Hegelian idealist aesthetics and to suggest an answer from the perspective of hermeneutics to the questions raised above.

As we already mentioned, Gadamer maintains that the poetic word "stands written," that "it bears witness to itself and does not admit anything that might verify it." And it is in this ontological constitution of the poetic word that we must find the ground for the truth of poetry. "To speak of truth in poetry," says Gadamer, "is to ask how the poetic word finds fulfillment precisely by refusing external verification of any kind."[64] That the word in poetry "stands written" thus means that it stands true in and of itself. In the sense that it is ontologically significant and does not just bear a message as its vehicle, the poetic word is also what Gadamer calls a *symbol*, which stands for itself while at the same time pointing to something beyond itself and is thereby differentiated from *allegory*, which exists only for the message it refers to. It is to Heidegger, Gadamer maintains, that we owe this insight into the ontological nature of art, which helps correct idealist aesthetics and its simplification of mimesis as reproduction or the copy of an original. Meaning in symbolic representation is not a content that can be extracted from the work of art as its outer form. "The symbolic does not simply point toward a meaning, but rather allows that meaning to present itself. The symbolic represents meaning," says Gadamer. "Here 'representation' does not imply that something merely stands for something else as if it were a replacement or substitute that enjoyed a less authentic, more indirect kind of existence. On the contrary, what is represented is itself present in the only way available to it."[65] The symbolic representation, the specific nature of *repraesentatio*, is thus not to be understood as the substitute of being but as an overflow or extension of being, "that increase in being that something acquires by being represented."[66] Such an understanding gives a whole new meaning to the concept of mimesis or *imitatio* which, Gadamer declares, "has nothing to do with the mere imitation of something that is already familiar to us. Rather, it implies that something is represented in such a way that it is actually present in sensuous abundance."[67] The importance of the sensuous existence of things in symbolic representation implies that the understanding of art involves more than a simple recuperation of meaning, especially a recuperation in terms of abstract concepts. Gadamer's rejection of the Hegelian definition of the beautiful as "the sensuous showing of the Idea" can be understood in this connection, because that definition eventually privileges the abstract conceptualization of philosophy over the sensuous language of art. In asking what is communicated in the experience of art, Gadamer argues, the decisive and indispensable insight is that "one cannot talk about a simple transference or mediation of meaning there. For this would already be to assimilate the experience of art to the universal anticipation of meaning that is characteristic of theoretical reason." And that, Gadamer goes on to say, is precisely where Hegel errs:

> Hegel and the idealists defined the beautiful in art as the sensuous appearance of the Idea, a bold revival of Plato's insight into the unity of the good and the beautiful. However, to go along with this is to presuppose that truth as it appears in art can be transcended by a philosophy that conceives the Idea as the highest and most appropriate form for grasping truth. The weakness of idealist aesthetics lay in its failure to appreciate that we typically encounter art as a unique manifestation of truth whose particularity cannot be surpassed. The significance of the symbol and the symbolic lay in this paradoxical kind of reference that embodies and even vouchsafes its meaning. Art

is only encountered in a form that resists pure conceptualization. . . .
Thus the essence of the symbolic lies precisely in the fact that it is not
related to an ultimate meaning that could be recuperated in intellectual terms. The symbol preserves its meaning within itself.[68]

The concept of art as ontologically significant does not take a work of art
for the bearer of truth or meaning, but sees it as itself true and meaningful, and therefore never devoid of meaning. The self-fulfilling poetic word
stands true in itself and preserves meaning in its own being, and in this
sense we can read Rilke's line "Gesang ist Dasein" as speaking of its own
ontological status. It is in this context that Gadamer points out the inevitable relationship art maintains with language and claims that all artistic
creation challenges us to listen to the language in which it speaks. Even in
the extreme case of absolute music, the relationship still exists because
"we also hear the concentrated expression of music with the same ear with
which we otherwise try to understand language. There remains an inelim-
inable connection between what we like to call the wordless language of
music and the verbal language of normal linguistic communication."[69]
Poetry, more than any other form of art, is language-bound, that is, filled
with the potential of meaning. As Gadamer observes, "The language of
art means the excess of meaning that is present in the work itself. The
inexhaustibility that distinguishes the language of art from all translation
into concepts rests on this excess of meaning."[70]

   Gadamer's critique of idealist aesthetics and its recuperation of meaning in terms of abstract concepts exposes the weakness of the idea of
representation or mimesis as it has been traditionally understood from
Plato to Hegel. In this respect, hermeneutics and deconstruction seem to
share a good deal of discontent with the tradition of Western metaphysics, as Gadamer himself has argued.[71] A crucial difference exists between
hermeneutics and deconstruction, however. While Derrida rejects meaning along with the traditional philosophical concept of representation
and conceives of language as a free play of signifiers, Gadamer reclaims
the Greek term *mimesis* or *imitatio* from its idealist misuse and preserves
the possibility of meaning in art and literature. The hermeneutic emphasis on meaning, communication, the contemporaneity of art, and the fundamental continuity between the aesthetic experience of art and our everyday existence—all this has the virtue of making the experience of art part
of human experience as a whole and of still affirming the relevance of the
beautiful in this age of separation and self-enclosure. As Fred Dallmayr

observes, Gadamer's hermeneutic notion of experience as *Bildung* or an educational process and the formation of public character "is by no means synonymous with the imposition of an abstract-universal scheme or an external pedagogical system; rather, like Gadamerian dialogue, it involves mutual exposure and risk-taking—and above all, participation in the labor or travail of individual and communal transformation." And as such, it is "a far cry from the non-engagement and neutral indifference prevalent in liberal societies (a stance present implicitly or as a tendency in Derrida's occasional aestheticism)."[72] The hermeneutic emphasis on meaning, in other words, recognizes the important relationship of the individual and the communal and conceives of human experience as participation, as transformation of the Self in the encounter with the Other. Meaning exists not in and for itself but for the sake of a mutual engagement, in the fruitful exchange of ideas in communication.

In this connection, we may appreciate the importance of reading as the construction of meaning out of the hermeneutic circle of parts and whole. As Gadamer argues, "Reading is not just scrutinizing or taking one word after another, but means above all performing a constant hermeneutic movement guided by the anticipation of the whole, and finally fulfilled by the individual in the realization of the total sense."[73] The challenge of reading a difficult text like a Mallarmé poem, as well as the pleasure, lies precisely in deciphering its mystery and pattern of meaning—that is, in putting the enigmatic text in perspective when the floating mass of disparate signs and fragments finally falls in place. Meaning always arises in a certain perspective, even though momentarily, and however uncontrollable the play of signifiers, however diverse the channels and directions of their dissemination, semantic and syntactic elements will always form an intelligible pattern out of the free play of signifiers. A text may be made of multiple writings in a network of complex relationships, but as Roland Barthes suggests, "There is one place where this multiplicity is focused and that place is the reader. . . . The reader is the space on which all the quotations that make up a writing are inscribed without any of them being lost."[74] Even deconstructive critics seem to find it impossible to banish meaning completely. In the translator's introduction to *Dissemination*, Barbara Johnson tries specifically to dispel the suspicion that deconstruction is "a form of textual vandalism designed to prove that meaning is impossible." Deconstruction, in her felicitous phrase, is "the careful teasing out of warring forces of signification *within the text itself*." It is a critical approach that simply "implies that a text signifies in more

than one way, and to varying degrees of explicitness."[75] In his book on
Derrida, Christopher Norris also denies that deconstruction propagates
"the notion that texts cannot possibly 'refer' to any world outside their
own rhetorical domain."[76] Even Derrida himself seems to allow for the
inevitable rise of meaning when he concedes that although "strictly speaking," signifiers like "writing," "fold," "tissue," and "text" are *no longer*
signifiers, "a conceptual strategy of some sort can temporarily privilege
them as *determinate* signifiers."[77] In this connection, then, perhaps
deconstruction can be positively understood as operating in a negative
manner, as a mode of reading which, though not a total annihilation of
meaning, does question any particular meaning or theme a critic presents
without being critically aware of the metaphysical presumptions of his or
her own reading.

At any rate, Derrida's reading of "Mimique" calls attention to a point
Mallarmé himself likes to emphasize and endow with a symbolic meaning, namely that his writing comes out of the blank or nothingness of the
white page. The poet often speaks of writing as a play of signifiers on a
blank page, as man's "pursuit of black on white."[78] Many of his poems
play on the paradox of textuality as arising out of nothingness. His sonnet, "Surgi de la croupe et du bond [Sprung from the croup and the leap],"
may serve as a good example. To understand this poem, as Lloyd Austin
notes, it is important to follow its rhythm as the poem moves in accordance with the movement of the implied reader's eye. We first see an empty
vase with no flower to cheer up the bitter evening hour, for where a flower
should be, we find only the broken neck of a vase. But suddenly, a voice
speaks directly to us:

> Je crois bien que deux bouches n'ont
> Bu, ni son amant ni ma mère,
> Jamais à la même Chimère,
> Moi, sylphe de ce froid plafond!
>
> I believe the two mouths never drank,
> Neither my mother nor her lover,
> From the same Chimera,
> I, sylph of this cold ceiling![79]

According to Austin, the voice belongs to "none other than the inexistent
rose, a phantom hovering like a sylph beneath the cold ceiling."[80] This
phantom flower tells us that it does not exist because it was never born,

for its mother and her lover never loved each other. All there is, then, is the empty vase with nothing but "l'inexhaustible veuvage [inexhaustible widowhood]," that is, barrenness and sterility. The empty vase refuses "A rien expirer annonçant / Une rose dans les ténèbres [to breathe out anything to announce / A rose amid the darkness]." And yet, the absence of the flower gives rise to the poem; the blank at the center of the text becomes the origin of textuality, for the sonnet is telling us all about the nonexistence of its subject, the never-born rose and its never-loved mother. The central theme or paradox of this sonnet, says Austin, is that it "evokes a rose that just cannot be born," and so he sees the poem as "one of anguish, expressing a desperate effort towards some impossible creation," which may be linked up with "the great problem of Mallarmé's life, the creation of the Great Work he dreamed of and which proved impossible."[81]

We know that Mallarmé conceives of a Great Book as the very *telos* of the universe, claiming that "everything in the world exists to end up in a book."[82] All his life he was obsessed with the idea of accomplishing this impersonal *Grand Oeuvre*, of writing this Great Book, and he was convinced, he told Verlaine, "that basically there is only one, attempted unknowingly by whoever has written, even the Geniuses."[83] Since Mallarmé speaks of the poet's Orphic explication of the Earth in relation to the writing of this Great Book, it seems that the confidence in the magic power of language celebrated in the Orphic myth underlies his vision of the *Grand Oeuvre*. Ironically, however, Mallarmé's Great Book was never written, and the anguish of the absent rose, as Austin argues, reveals Mallarmé's anxiety of the impossibility of creation. Perhaps that may explain why Mallarmé sees all his finished works as mere fragments, "studies with a view of something better, like one tries out the nibs of one's pen before starting on the work."[84] In Mallarmé, therefore, we seem to find something like the mystic aspiration for the ineffable, which inspires and urges the poet to write but never allows him to attain to his final goal. For Mallarmé, what he has written seems less significant, nothing but preliminary *études*, while the nonexistent, unwritten Book constitutes the truly important part of his grand project. This forms an interesting comparison with a remark Wittgenstein makes concerning his own work on the supremacy of the silent word, the word that is never verbalized. Like Mallarmé whose Great Book was never written, Wittgenstein told a friend that he originally intended to put in his preface to the *Tractatus Logico-Philosophicus* the following statement: "My work consists of two parts:

the one presented here plus all that I have *not* written. And *it is precisely this second part that is the important one.*"[85]

Given the importance of the unwritten and unspoken word, we can understand Mallarmé's emphasis on the blank and the absent, and we can characterize his poetics as a poetics of silence. For him, poetry is a silent music, residing in "the unspoken part of discourse," like some "air or song underneath the text."[86] His aspiration for the unspoken and the inexpressible provides the theoretical premises for his emphasis on indirect suggestion, and in this respect, Mallarmé's influence on the symbolist movement cannot be overestimated. Silence for Mallarmé, however, does not mean the negation of language. On the contrary, it has the infinite possibilities of speaking and singing, or as Rilke has it, it contains "the roots of speech." The nonexistent rose in the sonnet becomes a perfect symbol of the great potential of such silence, and it is possible to see the poem, *pace* Austin, not as "one of anguish, expressing a desperate effort towards some impossible creation" but as allegorical of its own creation —the birth of poetry out of absence, blank, or nothingness. Instead of expressing an anxiety of language, the poem symbolizes the magic power of language to evoke and create things otherwise nonexistent and inaccessible. We may recall that this is precisely the meaning of poetic mystery that Mallarmé speaks about—namely, the creation of a richly suggestive atmosphere immersed in a mystery, a deliberate obscurity or indecision. The famous "L'Après-midi d'un faune" can serve as a wonderful example.[87] The sultry air of a summer afternoon, the uncertainty of the entire scene —whether this is the faun's memory of what actually happened or only his fantasy of capturing two nymphs on the borders of a quiet Sicilian marsh—the drowsy music that flows from his reed like "Une sonore, vaine et monotone ligne [a sonorous and vain, monotonous line]," his amorous ambition of seizing Venus herself on the top of Etna, his ensuing sense of guilt and fear of punishment, and finally the hushing of all sounds when the faun falls asleep again, succumbing "au fier silence de midi [unto the noon's haughty silence]"—all these combine to create an atmosphere of drowsiness, dream, and fantasy, which is perfectly suited to the theme of this poem and to symbolist poetry in general. The uncertainty of illusion or reality admirably illustrates Mallarmé's poetic principles, for in this poem as a whole, as Robert Greer Cohn remarks, "the unsureness itself is the theme."[88]

Moreover, the faun may be seen as a symbol of the poet who creates *ex nihilo*, out of his dream, memory, and imagination. Though he realizes that those nymphs may be creatures of his own desire and fantasy, that their kiss is but "ce doux rien [this sweet nothing]," the faun plays on, trying to evoke their beautiful figures by means of a song. And it is his song, like the Orphic song in Rilke, that calls into being the trees and flowers and the whole woody scenery, through which, says the faun,

> Ne murmure point d'eau que ne verse ma flûte
> Au bosquet arrosé d'accords; et le seul vent
> Hors des deux tuyaux prompt à s'exhaler avant
> Qu'il disperse le son dans une pluie aride,
> C'est, à l'horizon pas remué d'une ride,
> Le visible et serein souffle artificiel
> De l'inspiration, qui regagne le ciel.

> murmurs no water but that poured from my flute
> on the grove sprinkled with harmonies; the only wind
> prompt to exhale from the twin-pipes before
> it can disperse the sound in an arid rain,
> is, on the horizon unstirred by a wrinkle,
> the visible and serene artificial breath
> of inspiration, which regains the sky.

Here the flow of music from the flute becomes water gushing in the woods, and the breath from the mouth turns into the wind; natural scenery is thus superimposed on the image of poetry making, and the scene described comes into being by the incantation of verse, the rhythmic movement of inhaling and exhaling. In this poem, as in Rilke's sonnet quoted earlier, poetry or song makes things happen in an imaginative world, where poetry is "the only wind," the "artificial breath / of inspiration." Mallarmé's metaphor admirably anticipates Rilke's depiction of poetry as "a different breath, about / nothing. A gust inside the god. A wind." Or it may recall another of Rilke's Orphic sonnets: "Atmen, du unsichtbares Gedicht! . . . in dem ich mich rhythmisch ereigne [Breathing: you invisible poem! . . . in which I rhythmically happen]" (2, 1). In a short poem, "Sainte," the importance of nothingness and blank for the creation of a poetic world, or the significance of silence for the music of poetry, is expressed in a beautiful image. In that poem, Mallarmé describes his muse, St. Cecilia, the great patron saint of music, as the patron of poetry that speaks more in silent implication than explicit language, because running her fingers in the soft plumage of an angel's wing, the muse is portrayed as playing on a soundless instrument, as the great "Musicienne du silence."

Tao Qian: The Challenge of Simplicity

If the dialectic movement of the spirit as envisioned and described in
Hegel's *Aesthetics* unavoidably leads up to the split of an inward vision
and an outward expression, it does not, after all, create the problem of
language but merely intensifies it from a philosophical perspective. The
examples of Homer, Shakespeare, and Schiller in the previous chapter all
remind us that the difficulty of poetic articulation is not just a crisis with
modern poets like T. S. Eliot, Mallarmé, and Rilke but a problem that has
always inhabited the Western literary tradition, while Lu Ji, a third-century
Chinese poet, provides yet another example with his "Rhymeprose on
Literature," which clearly shows that the anxiety of articulation is a perennial concern in Chinese poetics as well. Already evident in Lu Ji's poetic
essay, a strong sense of the complexity of language and interpretation was
later brought to a more conscious level and materialized in Chinese poetry
in one way or another. This poetic sensibility, or what I would call the
hermeneutic sense in the Chinese tradition, manifests itself in the works
of a great poet in fourth-century China, Tao Qian (365–427), also known
as Tao Yuanming. His poetry and prose often speak of the difficulty of
speaking, and his uniquely plain style embodies a rather sophisticated
understanding of the nature of language as well as a subtle use of language to overcome its inherent limitations.

We may recall that Lu Ji characterizes the problem of poetic language
as a constant "anxiety that meaning does not match with things, and
writing does not convey meaning. And this results not so much from the
difficulty of knowing as from the limitation of one's ability."[89] Chinese
poetry before and in Tao Qian's time can be seen as largely responding to
this problem, trying desperately to counterbalance the incompetence of
words by an extremely prodigal use of words. The *fu* or rhymeprose at
that time became especially extravagant with elaborate ornaments, and
poetry in the so-called Six Dynasties period is notorious for its flamboyant
and ornate style. In their effort to overcome the inadequacy of language,
poets in Tao Qian's time seemed to have forgotten that the problem, as Lu
Ji put it astutely, "results not so much from the difficulty of knowing as
from the limitation of one's ability," which could not be solved by piling
up words into a sort of verbal monstrosity. Against such a background,
the poetry of Tao Qian appeared as a startlingly new phenomenon because
it differed from the poetry of his contemporaries precisely in its extreme
frugality of words and a style noted for its unadorned simplicity. To the

language problem Lu Ji raised, Tao Qian offered a solution that differed so drastically from the one his contemporaries sought, producing a poetry so alien to their ears and minds, that he was not at all taken seriously as a poet in his own time or immediately after. Of course, he has since been celebrated as one of the four or five most important poets in the entire history of China, but unlike the other poets who may be considered his equals in literary excellence—Du Fu (712–770), Li Bai (701–62), or Qu Yuan (c. 340–c. 278 B.C.), who were all quickly recognized and honored as poets of great merits—the canonical status of Tao Qian in classical Chinese literature was not firmly established until some five hundred years after his death. "Yuanming's literary fame reached its summit in the Song (960–1279)," as Qian Zhongshu observes in examining the vicissitudes of Tao Qian's literary fame from the Jin period to the late Tang.[90] The very belatedness in the recognition of the value of Tao Qian's poetry raises a question of immense hermeneutic interest.

In looking at possible patterns of the reception of a new literary work, Hans Robert Jauss observes that the response the first audience may have is likely to be determined by the distance or disparity between the given "horizon of expectations" at the time and the demand a new work makes on the aesthetic sensibility of its audience. In the case of a truly original work that disappoints or refutes the expectations of its audience and challenges their sensibility, the value of the work may take a long time to be recognized and appreciated. "It can thereby happen," says Jauss, "that a virtual significance of the work remains long unrecognized until the 'literary evolution,' through the actualization of a newer form, reaches the horizon that now for the first time allows one to find access to the understanding of the misunderstood older form."[91] The reception of Tao Qian in the history of Chinese literature is a good case in point. The dramatic change in the evaluation of Tao Qian in traditional criticism is significant not only because it tells us something about the mutability of aesthetic taste and judgment but also because it shows, when Tao Qian was finally canonized, what forms of expression were accepted as of paramount value and importance and what stylistic features became part of the familiar horizon of expectations in reading Chinese poetry.

From the very beginning, Tao Qian's plain and simple language poses a problem for readers and critics alike, for its very transparency tends to obscure its value and significance. When Yan Yanzhi (384–456), himself a poet much admired at the time for his elaborate style, composed a eulogy on Tao Qian, he praised Tao's moral virtues but practically ignored his literary merits, only mentioning that in his writings Tao "intended to get to the point."[92] To be sure, this was meant as a commendation, for Yan Yanzhi was alluding to Confucius' remark on the proper use of language: "So far as words can get to the point, that is enough."[93] In doing so, however, he tacitly dismissed Tao Qian's writing for lacking the elaborate embellishment and rhetorical fireworks he and his contemporaries so highly valued in poetry. To most readers of his time, then, Tao Qian's writing must have appeared rather crude and colorless, marked by its reserve, reticence, and artless simplicity—so much so that none of his contemporaries ever held him in high regard as a poet. This may account for the rather peculiar negligence of two important works of criticism written within one hundred years after his death, Liu Xie's (465?–522) *Wenxin diaolong* [The Literary Mind or the Carving of Dragons] and Zhong Rong's (459–518) *Shi pin* [Ranking of Poetry], for both fail to do him justice: the former does not mention Tao Qian at all, whereas the latter classifies him as belonging to the "middle rank," that is, as being of only secondary importance, though it honors him as "the paragon of all hermit poets, past and present."[94] In all likelihood, Tao Qian was simply out of tune with his time, for he neither wrote the kind of wooden "metaphysical poetry" (*xuanyan shi*) which was the literary fashion when he was young nor followed the ornate style that became increasingly the predominant mode of writing for his contemporaries. "He was all alone," as Kang-i Sun Chang observes, "for he lived in a period of transition, and was judged by a set of poetic criteria directly opposed to his own literary taste."[95] It was the verdict of earlier critics that Tao Qian gave at best a lackluster performance in writing and that his language was too simple and flat to be really poetic. Even Du Fu, the great poet of the High Tang period, despite his deep respect for Tao, still found it difficult to appreciate his insipidly "dry" language:

> Old Tao Qian who shunned the world
> May not have attained the *tao* thereby.
> Reading his poems, I feel it a pity:
> His language is so seared and dry.[96]

The question is, why would Tao Qian use a "seared and dry" language that many poets considered inadequate for poetic expression? Why would he choose to write in a sort of zero degree style when flowery language was the accepted norm of his time? When we read his poetry and prose, it soon becomes clear that Tao Qian was never bent on following the trend of his time—in life as well as in writing poetry. For more than fifteen hundred years, he has been justly famous for his moral integrity, and people love the story of Tao Qian's refusing to humble himself before his superiors and protesting, "How can I bow to a country boor just for five pecks of rice!"[97] With these proud words he quit the minor official post he had held and, like an ancestral Candide, withdrew to tend his own garden and live a farmer's life. There was a certain stubbornness and a great deal of courage in Tao Qian that made him a solitary traveler on the path he chose, and the same unyielding, independent spirit made him what he was both as a man and as a poet. *Le style est l'homme* may be a deceptive cliché, but in the case of Tao Qian, there is a close relationship between his style of living and style of writing, for both are the result of a well-thought-out choice, and both have simplicity as the definitive feature. Traditional criticism has exalted Tao Qian's moral integrity as a man and the edifying effect of his poetry, but it has largely failed to notice that the same principled adherence to what he believed to be true in nature and life has also determined his use of language. Though somewhat oversimplified, Zhong Rong's capsule characterization, "the paragon of all hermit poets, past and present," does mark out the most salient features of Tao's poetry and personality: his aversion to the insincerity and pretentiousness of officialdom, his awareness of the perils lurking at every corner of a political career, his appreciation of the simple joys of his home and his garden, his love of nature, and the purity of spirit revealed in the purity of his language. Nevertheless, many critics have overlooked his search for stylistic features that could express the simplicity he held so dear in a form that was congenial to it. Artificial ornaments are incompatible with natural spontaneity as he understood it, and that sense of incompatibility was the essential cause of his refusal to adopt the flowery style of contemporary writing. That he thus shunned all artificiality may also explain why so few of his imitators could succeed in achieving the effect of his style, since they tried to imitate the idealized simplicity of a farmer's life, while Tao Qian *lived* such a life. His life and personality are so closely interwoven into the text of his poetry that to understand his poetry and its stylistic features is also to understand his life as presented in his poetry, and in this sense it becomes possible to read his works as a sort of poetic autobiography. His poetry is an *autobiography* in the sense that in most of his poems, the poet becomes the subject of his own writing, which speaks about his life in the fields and comments on the meaning of such a life. But more importantly, his autobiography is *poetic* because what we know of his life and personality is mainly the result of reading his poems, and the image of Tao Qian as a farmer and hermit is created in and by his own writing. Thus our reading of Tao Qian ought to attend both to the words of his text and to those elements that are extended, as it were, from his text—namely, the lived experience that shaped his poetry and was given a shape by it. Only in the ontological sense of the poetic word, can we speak of Tao Qian's writing as a poetic autobiography.

Two recent studies have clearly recognized the complicated relationship between Tao Qian's life and his works, and regarded his poetry as consciously engaged in the making of his self-image. In her book on the poetry of the Six Dynasties, Kang-i Sun Chang has a whole section devoted to Tao Qian's writing as poetic autobiography, which, she argues, demonstrates "a consistent desire to define his ultimate self-realization in life."[98] Reading Tao Qian in his literary ambience, Chang especially notices Tao's unique sense of the self and individuality, maintaining that his personal voice makes his poetry at once a restoration of "ancient lyricism" and a "departure from the discursive mode of poetry that dominated the literary scene for over a century."[99] Tao Qian's plain style, a poetic originality in his time, is thus in itself "an expression of his individuality," "a sign of self-expression."[100] The emphasis on individuality offers a helpful frame of reference for understanding the challenge Tao Qian's language and style posed to his contemporary readers as well as the difficulty they experienced in meeting that challenge. In Tao Qian's poetry, Chang argues, the distinction between imaginative self-realization and autobiographical reflection is often blurred, and the poet "seems to see no necessary conflict between fiction and autobiography."[101] Of course, when applied to Tao Qian's works, the term *autobiography* is used in a broad, extended sense, for his poetry is not a consistent account of his life and therefore lends full legitimation to fictionality in his writings. Kang-i Sun Chang aptly acknowledges this when she remarks that Tao's poetry is "poised between the poles of factuality and fiction" and that its power lies "precisely in this dual function."[102]

In an essay on the presentation of self-image in Chinese poetry, Stephen Owen also sees Tao Qian as "the first great poetic autobiographer," one who is conscious of the problem of truth and representation.[103] "Authenticity," says Owen, "must be autobiography's first concern," but it is constantly vitiated by the author's presentation of himself not as what he is but what he wishes to be; the self-image created in an autobiography is thus always suspicious, implicated by the author's desire of presentation, in which "the human ceases to be an innocent unity of nature and action; he is now a doubleness, an outward appearance concealing, dimming, or distorting some true and hidden nature."[104] In reading Tao Qian's poetry as "autobiography," therefore, Owen undertakes to question its authenticity and to disclose Tao's self-image, that of a farmer-recluse, as inevitably containing "a doubleness—a true self and a surface role."[105] In the light of such a reading, Tao Qian's language is seen not at all as simple and transparent but as a device of the surface that conceals, dims, or distorts the poet's true and hidden nature. To read Tao Qian, then, is to penetrate the surface simplicity so as to reach the poet's true self in all its complex multifariousness. For example, in a group of poems entitled "Returning to Dwell in My Fields and Gardens," Tao Qian's first poem can be read as posing the problem of a "double self." Owen presumes that we are likely to take the speaker in the poem as a "mere peasant," only to find that the peasant is in fact Tao Qian, a sophisticated and self-conscious poet, who distances himself from us as the "common" herd:

> In youth, nothing in me followed the common rhythm,
> It is my nature always to love hills and mountains.
> By mischance I fell into the net of dust,
> And kept away from home for so many years.
> A fastened bird longs for its familiar grove,
> A fish in the pool remembers old deep waters.
> I've tilled some soil at the edge of southern moor,
> With simplicity intact, I return to farm my land.
> My homestead extends to a couple of acres,
> And eight or nine rooms with thatched roof.
> Elms and willows shade my back eaves,
> Rows of peach and plum grow before my hall.
> Half-hidden is the village of secluded people,
> Slowly wispy smoke arises from their houses.
> A dog barks in the depth of a small lane,
> A cock crows on top of a mulberry tree.
> No dust soils the pure air within my doors,
> In my bare rooms I find plenty of leisure.
> Too long I have been caged like a prisoner,
> Now at last, I come back to nature.[106]

Despite the poet's claim to the unity of self and role in coming back to nature with "simplicity intact," the text of the poem, Owen argues, betrays its own doubleness, the inevitable discrepancy between the poet's appearance of being a farmer and his desire to be a farmer, and the desire already bears evidence of the lack of a farmer's rustic simplicity. The poem becomes attractive, however, precisely for showing this "complex desire for simplicity rather than simplicity itself."[107] In this poem, Owen goes on to argue, the complex desire is carefully concealed by a facade of simple language, but a good reader should be able to see through the facade. "It should be said, once and for all," he declares, that Tao Qian "is not the naive and straightforward poet he claims to be."[108] He is suspicious not only of the poet's claim to simplicity but especially of our credulity vis-à-vis the poem's disarming plainness. Since Tao Qian is conscious of his complex self beneath the surface, a sophisticated reader of his poetry should learn to distrust that surface and question the authenticity of the image that emerges from his text. Those who believe that Tao Qian is a farmer are likely to be fooled or shocked. "We made a mistake," Owen admits on behalf of such readers, "we thought this was a farmer, and it turned out to be T'ao Ch'ien."[109]

To be sure, a skeptical reader will probably be able to probe deeper into psychological and textual substructures, but on opening a volume of Tao Qian's poetry, who would imagine that those poems were written by a "mere peasant"? Most Chinese critics and commentators see Tao Qian as a hermit poet who kept himself far from the madding crowd: an image espoused by Tao's own writings; some have argued that in spite of his professed love of hills and mountains, Tao was in fact deeply concerned about the political situation of his time—a view that is also supported by some textual evidence in his poetry. In the history of Chinese criticism, however, nobody has ever taken Tao Qian for an ordinary farmer. Perhaps at this point, we may realize that the presumed naivete of an unsophisticated reader is a rhetorical strategy Owen uses to make a case for his own skeptical attitude, his distrust of Tao Qian's simplicity. But Owen's skepticism is never skeptical of its own presumptions: it never subjects the concept of "doubleness" to the same rigorous questioning it applies to Tao Qian's poetry; it does not ask whether this "doubleness," the discrepancy between an "outward appearance" and a "true and hidden nature," presupposes a concept of representation as the correspondence of copy and original—or whether this "doubleness" does not predicate itself on a peculiar idea of Chinese poetry as a literally true record of life experience without the intervention of fictionality. Owen is evidently aware of these problems; so he declares that the poet's surface role "is not independent of the self, but is an organic dimension of it; role is desire, the surface of the self as it wishes to be known; role is the entelechy of a process of self-definition."[110] Nevertheless, the basis for his argument—the idea of "doubleness" identified as the central issue in Tao Qian's poetry—cannot escape the implications of an inside/outside opposition which also posits skepticism as a prerequisite for reading. The image of Tao Qian as a farmer-recluse is presumably not the Tao Qian we would have known had we lived in Xunyang some fifteen hundred years ago and known him as a next-door neighbor. The farmer-recluse is, however, the only Tao Qian we can ever know; what the "true self" of Tao Qian is outside any textual construction is an immaterial and impertinent question, since all we know are the texts by or about him, and he is known to us only through the mediation of those texts and our interpretation of them. The identity of Tao Qian, to use Gadamer's term, is a "hermeneutic identity," an identity not outside but within his text, which "asks to be understood" and presents itself as a question that "requires an answer."[111] To penetrate the simple language of the text in search of the poet's "true and hidden nature," therefore, seems a misguided effort that risks losing sight of a hermeneutically more relevant issue—namely, how does Tao Qian's simple language succeed in making the richness and complexity of his life experiences manifest in poetry?

Owen's advice to look for doubleness can be helpful, however, not because it reveals a discrepancy between the surface role and the true self but because it calls attention to the way Tao Qian's poems are structured around different sets of values. In the poem quoted above, for instance, we can see the tension between two opposed ways of life: life in the countryside that accommodates one's basic needs while unfolding the beauty and regenerating power of nature, and life confined to an official post, controlled by formalities, rigid regulations, and etiquette. The opposition is set up in the text by two sets of images: on the one hand, there are the "net of dust," the fastened bird, the fish stranded in a pool, the cage and prison; and on the other, hills and mountains, the lovely country house, and the quiet, secluded village with light smoke rising over the chimneys. It is interesting to note that Tao Qian does not say that he has made a discovery of nature but that it has always been his "nature" to love hills and mountains; thus his return "back to nature" must be understood as a return both to the outward natural world and to his inner nature, his own self. And yet, returning to the self already implies a distance—that one has, at least for some time, been alienated from one's own nature. For Tao

Qian, that self-alienation, a momentary separation from his true nature, is his fall into "the net of dust," his brief entanglement in officialdom, which he now admits to be a mistake and contrasts with the purity of his private life, unsoiled by dust of any kind. The regret of a momentary *faux pas*, the recantation of his briefly held official post, indeed appears again and again as one of the central themes in Tao Qian's writing from poems on nature and farming to his well-known rhymeprose, "Returning Home."

Given his love of the purity and freedom in nature, the stylistic simplicity of Tao Qian's poetry becomes thematically significant, as it implies his acceptance of life in the "fields and gardens," his preference for the "pure air" in his "bare rooms," and his rejection of the pomposity and formality of officialdom. His sketch of the village scene is remarkably new and fresh, for the picture of a dog barking in a deep lane and a cock crowing on top of a mulberry tree, with its simple vocabulary and natural rhythm, virtually cannot be found in earlier poetry. A few folk songs in the ancient *Book of Poetry* may be comparable, but the language of those songs was archaic even in Tao Qian's time and could not have the same refreshing effect as his simple diction. Of course, as Owen reminds us, Tao Qian's simple language is never simple, for his words always point away from themselves, and simplicity as a stylistic feature is not something that comes naturally without the poet's conscious effort. To write poetry at all necessarily involves composition and arrangement of materials taken from the poet's life experiences, and the complexity of Tao Qian's style is recognized by many scholars. In a discussion of Tao Qian's use of allusion, for example, James Hightower shows how Tao's poetry "can be as mannered, erudite, and allusion-laden as that of any Six Dynasties poet."[112] It seems that most of Tao Qian's contemporaries failed to recognize this complexity, and in Tao's works we often find intimations of a sense of loneliness, his desire for a fit audience, frequently expressed as a wish to find *zhiyin* or "the one who knows the sound." Frustrated in his effort to fulfil this wish, the poet imaginatively travels back in time to converse with men of his own caliber in past history. Each of the seven poems in the group entitled "On Poor Gentlemen" is addressed to a historical figure the poet admires. The first poem in the group clearly shows Tao's yearning for understanding:

> The ten thousand creatures have their reliance,
> Only the solitary cloud floats without support.
> Fainter and fainter, it dissolves in the sky,

When is the time we see its last glimmer?
The morning glow breaks the lingering mists,
Flocks of birds start their flight together.
Slowly, slowly, a bird soars out of the woods,
And comes back again before it is dark.
Knowing its strength, it keeps the old route,
How can it escape from cold and hunger?
When no one is here to know the sound,
What use is there to strike a sad note?[113]

The solitary cloud that vanishes without a trace and the bird that keeps its old route despite all hardships call to mind the image of our lonely poet, whose solitude is made explicit in the last two lines, where the sad note sounds even sadder when it dies down with no one there to take note. But because described by the poet, the sound *is* heard, for by seeking friends in the past, Tao Qian actually speaks to the future and beckons to his own audience in future generations who will know his sound. To find his fit audience, however, he had to wait for centuries, because the significance of Tao Qian's plain style was not fully recognized until the great poet Su Shi (1037–1101) made the observation that Tao's language was "dry outside but full of marrow inside, seemingly insipid but actually delectable."[114] Su Shi was of course articulating a judgment already held by some poets before him, and the fact that he was able to make that insightful remark shows that by his time, some five hundred years after Tao Qian, the stylistic simplicity of Tao's poetry was finally recognized as valuable and formed an important part of the Chinese literary tradition.

Poetics of Silence

Without going into all the details of the reception of Tao Qian's works, we may, from Yan Yanzhi's comment on Tao's writing, already get some idea as to why his poetry was not appreciated for such a long period of time. We may recall that Yan tactfully praised Tao Qian for using language in conformity with Confucius' remark on the pragmatic function of words. But in such a context, Tao Qian's plain style is bound to be misunderstood, as it is the outcome of an insight into the nature of language that has little to do with what Confucius says about using words to get to the point. Once Tao Qian was canonized as one of the great poets in the literary tradition, however, many Confucian scholars would claim him as one of their own. Lu Jiuyuan (1139–93), for instance, remarks that "Li Bai, Du Fu, and Tao Yuanming all meant to follow our [Confucian] way."[115] This raises a question which, though not quite relevant to the understanding of Tao's poetry, is nonetheless important and often debated, that is, whether Confucianism or Taoism had the greater share of influence on Tao Qian's thinking and writing—a question that keeps coming up, even today, in critical thought about Tao Qian and many other poets and writers in classical Chinese literature. In reviewing Kang-i Sun Chang's *Six Dynasties Poetry*, for example, Donald Holzman severely criticizes Chang for depicting Tao Qian as a believer in Zhuangzi's Taoist philosophy. Admittedly, it is not easy to get to the core of Tao Qian's thought, but "I firmly believe," declares Holzman with assurance, "traditional Confucian elements are at least as important in it as 'Chuang-tzu' and 'neo-Taoism.'" He enlists Tao Qian's "attitude towards life" to support his claim that Tao remained "faithful to traditional values of loyalty and respect for the social order while realizing, thanks to his poetic imagination, a new kind of fulfillment of his ambitions in retirement."[116] Instead of seeing Tao Qian's retreat from public office to a farmer's life as a free choice that the poet made to liberate himself from a cage and return to his home in the hills and mountains, critics who emphasize the influence of Confucianism tend to understand this retreat as forced upon Tao Qian when he failed to carry out the mission Confucius envisioned for every *shi* or gentleman with a strong sense of social responsibility. "With his Confucian calling deeply embedded within him," thus one critic can write in a recent essay on Tao Qian, "the poet cannot overcome his sense of frustration at being denied by his age the chance of fulfilling his duty to humanity."[117] In this critic's eyes, Tao Qian's poetry appears to be a surrogate for a failed political career, "a substitute fulfillment of the poet's public responsibility as a *shi*."[118]

There are certainly no lack of interpretations in traditional criticism that picture Tao Qian as a follower of Confucius, devoted to the study of the Confucian classics and loyal to the last emperor of the Jin dynasty—in a word, as Holzman puts it, "faithful to traditional values of loyalty and respect for the social order." Commenting on the "Drinking Wine" poems, the eighteenth-century critic Shen Deqian (1673–1769) claims that "Tao exclusively uses the *Analects*. After the Han and before the Song scholars, Yuanming can be regarded as a true disciple in the Confucian school."[119] "Yuanming's knowledge comes from the study of the classics," declares another critic Fang Dongshu (1772–1851), who constantly reads Tao

Qian's poetry with reference to Confucian writings.[120] But although he makes many references or allusions to Confucius and the Confucian classics, Tao Qian in his writings refers even more frequently to Zhuangzi the Taoist philosopher.[121] Zhu Xi (1130−1200), himself a great Confucian scholar, realizes that "Yuanming speaks mostly of Zhuangzi and Laozi, and yet his language is elegantly simple."[122] To be sure, a greater frequency of reference to Zhuangzi does not make the poet a Taoist, and Tao Qian is, after all, not a philosopher. Put in the historical context of the Wei-Jin period, however, one must admit that Tao Qian's thinking is closer to Taoist than to Confucian philosophy. As the historian Chen Yinke (1890−1969) observes, Chinese literati in that period either advocated the "doctrine of names" or upheld the principle of "following nature," the former being based on the Confucian philosophy of a strictly observed hierarchy of social relationships while the latter was related to Taoist naturalism. The two views translate into very different attitudes in political life: the Confucians were concerned about social reality and actively sought official appointments, while those influenced by Taoist philosophy retired to nature and passively defied the government by a gesture of noncooperation.[123] These very different views, however, coexisted not just in one social environment but within the outlook of one and the same person. Since Confucianism is not a religion incompatible with Taoism or Buddhism, says Chen, "those who outwardly observe Confucian norms may inwardly follow the principles of Buddhism or cultivate themselves according to the way of Taoism; there is no conflict between them."[124] Tao Qian, according to Chen Yinke, is "Confucian outside but Taoist inside," a great thinker in medieval China who created a "new naturalism."[125] The historical interpretation sheds a great deal of light on Tao Qian's life and works, providing a framework within which we can understand why he chose to quit the official post for a simple life in the country and to write the poetry that few of his contemporaries could really appreciate.

It is interesting to see how Confucianism is treated in Tao Qian's own works. When we examine his use of the *Analects*, for example, it becomes clear that Tao has positioned himself in an extremely subtle way with regard to Confucius, and sometimes his allusion to passages from the *Analects* is humorous and ironic, with potentially subversive implications. About the important Confucian concepts of benevolence, rites, and the like, Tao Qian has very little to say, and from all the passages in the *Analects*, he chooses the most lyrical moment to express his admiration of Confucius and his disciples. That moment occurs when the Master endorses his student Zeng Dian's wish to put on light clothes in late spring and go bathing in the Yi River, enjoy the gentle wind on the Rain Altar, and return home chanting poetry.[126] It is Confucius and his students in such a lovely setting that Tao Qian remembers and admires in "The Progression of Seasons":

> Casting my eyes on the mid-stream,
> Wistfully I recall the clear waters of Yi.
> Their study finished, the boys and youths
> Are coming back home, singing leisurely.
> I admire and love their quietness,
> Awake or asleep, I long to join them.
> But, alas, our times are set apart,
> Too far for me ever to pursue them.[127]

In this poem, we do not find Confucius and his disciples engaged in the immense task of constructing a perfect social order but enjoying what nature has to offer on a late spring morning. The *quietness* the poet admires and loves is not quite the most obvious term one would choose to characterize the Confucian scholars but a term of significance for Tao Qian and his life.

Those who see Tao Qian as a Confucian usually point to the sixteenth poem in "Drinking Wine" as textual evidence, where the poet recalls that "In youth I had no interest in worldly things, / But devoted myself to studying the six classics."[128] The poet goes on to say, however, that all his diligent studies have come to nothing, and it is difficult not to notice the implication that his youthful studies and ambitions seem rather pointless in his mature eyes when he decides to give up the office of the magistrate of Pengze and to live in the country as a farmer. The choice of a farmer's life needs some justification, since Confucius does not see farming as the proper way of life for a scholar, but Tao Qian's apology, presented in a group of poems entitled "Exhortation to Farmers," eventually turns into an ingenious retort. Having paid tribute to legendary sage-kings in antiquity who invented the art of husbandry, Tao Qian turns, in the last poem of this group, to Confucius and Dong Zhongshu (c. 179–93 B.C.), the renowned Confucian scholar of the Han Dynasty. The poet writes ironically about these lofty paragons of virtue:

> Confucius was obsessed with morality,
> And thought Fan Xu a vulgar man.

Dong delighted in lute and books,
And would not step into the fields.
If I could reach that loftiness
And tread on their noble path,
How could I not tidy myself up
And praise their virtue in all respect?[129]

The use of allusion here is truly remarkable, for the poet obviously identifies himself with Fan Xu, one of Confucius' less inspired students, who displeased the Master and incurred a sneering comment from him by asking about the techniques of growing crops and tending gardens. Confucius flatly refused to answer him, suggesting that he might as well go to ask an old peasant or gardener. This is a rather comic moment in the *Analects*:

> When Fan Xu left, the Master said: "What a petty fellow Fan Xu is! When the ruler loves the rites, none of his subjects would dare to be irreverent; when he loves the principle of doing what is right, none of his subjects would dare to be disobedient; and when he loves trustworthiness, none of his subjects would dare to be insincere. In such a situation, people would come from all the four quarters, carrying their children on their backs. Who needs to talk about crops?"[130]

But Tao Qian talks a lot about crops in his poetry, and he knows that he would probably also be thought a vulgar man by Confucius if he had had the chance to study with him. Dong Zhongshu is also known to have despised husbandry, for one legend has it that he kept reading the Confucian classics for three years in his study with all the blinds down and never set foot in the fields and gardens. In the last few lines of the poem, Tao Qian seems to apologize that he cannot do better than Fan Xu, but the irony is obvious, especially when read together with other poems in the same group, which have already exalted farming as noble and indispensable work worthy of such great "sage-philosophers" as Hou Ji, Shun, and Yu.

Confucianism, Taoism, and Buddhism, as Chen Yinke reminds us, are not incompatible with one another in Chinese culture, and it would be pointless to argue that Tao Qian's thinking is exclusively Confucian or Taoist. He never had to choose between those different schools of thought but was able to incorporate, as so many Chinese intellectuals have done throughout the centuries, the various elements into a healthily eclectic outlook. In that very eclecticism the Chinese mind is able to keep itself open to the different possibilities of thinking. But insofar as his understanding of language is concerned, there can be no doubt that Tao Qian is very much influenced by Zhuangzi and his reflections on the whole problem of meaning, expression, and silence. Zhuangzi's influence is clearly visible in the best of Tao Qian's poems, of which a good example is the well-known fifth poem of "Drinking Wine":

> I built my humble house in this world of men,
> But there is no noise of carriages and horses.
> You may ask, sir, how is it possible?
> With the mind aloof, the place will be remote.
> Picking chrysanthemums under the eastern hedge,
> Unawares I catch sight of the southern hills.
> The mountain air is fair in the lovely sunset,
> And flocks of birds are returning to their nests.
> There is a true meaning in all of these,
> But when I try to explain, I forget my words.[131]

The first two lines of this poem set up a structural and thematic opposition between the poet's private world and the "world of men" with its "noise of carriages and horses," an opposition that reappears time and again in Tao Qian's poetry. In the second poem of "Returning to Dwell in My Fields and Gardens," for example, we find a variation on the same theme: "In the wild country, I have little to do with men, / In these poor lanes, wheels and harness are rare."[132] In Chinese antiquity, only the emperor and his ministers had the privilege of riding in horse-drawn carriages; so the images of "carriages and horses" or "wheels and harness" do not refer to the ordinary people but metonymically stand for courtiers and high-ranking officials, and the poet's preference for poor lanes that admit no big carriages does not indicate the coldness of a misanthrope but his contempt for pomposity and haughtiness. The phrase "carriages and horses" may allude to Zhuangzi's use of "carriages and caps" as symbols of transient political power, which the philosopher dismisses as external things that "the body uses, but [that are] not part of one's inborn nature."[133] According to Zhu Ziqing (1898–1948), the first four lines may allude to a phrase in the *Zhuangzi* where the Prince Mu of Zhongshan feels dismayed that "though my body is by the river and the sea, my mind still resides under the gate of the Wei palace."[134] The prince finds it difficult to completely abandon the life at court and face the austere life in the wilderness with the tranquil mind of a hermit. If Tao Qian is alluding to the *Zhuangzi*, his use of this phrase is a reversal of the original meaning, because the poet has tranquility of mind, the bliss of solitude at heart, even though he still dwells in the world of men.[135] It seems to me that the idea expressed in the first four lines, that the inner tranquility of the mind can turn the noisy world into a quiet dwelling place, may also allude to what Zhuangzi calls *xin zhai* or the emptying of the mind, the idea that the mind is capable of coping with anything once it is devoid of worldly ambitions and concerns.[136] The next few lines beautifully portray this inner tranquility with which the poet retires to his own garden, picking chrysanthemums under the eastern hedge, and catching sight of a splendid scene of mountains and forests without conscious effort. But the most famous lines of this poem, also the most relevant to our discussion of the hermeneutic sense, are the last two lines that bring the poem not so much to a close as to an open ending, in which the poet tells us that he forgets all words the very moment he tries to explain the true meaning he perceives in the beautiful scenery. Intimated by the natural beauty of the southern hills in the lovely sunset, the true meaning of nature is there, but it is unexplained and therefore forever awaits the mediation of a new interpretation.

Tao Qian is of course alluding to the passage from the *Zhuangzi* which states that words exist for the meaning, as the trap exists for the fish: "Once you've got the fish, you forget the trap," and "once you've got the meaning, you forget the word."[137] For Zhuangzi the philosopher, meaning is something that one may grasp intuitively and keep in knowing silence but be unable to put in words. For Tao Qian as a poet, however, he must articulate what he has grasped in silence. The forgetting of words may thus suggest frustration in his effort to speak, the anxiety that he can never put the true meaning of nature in words. In a way, the poet is not unlike Mad Crank, an allegorical figure in the *Zhuangzi*, who mumbles, when asked about the meaning of *tao*, "'Ah, I know it and will tell you.' But at the moment when he wants to say it, he forgets what word it is that he wants to say."[138] For Zhuangzi, Mad Crank's forgetting signals his true knowledge of the *tao*, since *tao* is unsayable. He insists that "to explain is not as good as to keep silent, for *tao* cannot be heard."[139] But silence or the absence of explicit speech, as we have seen in Mallarmé and Rilke, is precisely what makes poetry possible and contains the great power of evocation. In such a context, then, the forgetting of words not only indicates the poet's inability to speak but also points to a superior way of conveying meaning in a negative mode of expression, in suggestive silence. That is exactly how the true meaning of nature is implied in this poem, which first affirms that there *is* a true meaning and then leaves that meaning unexplained. Here the philosophical premise for Tao Qian's choice of stylistic simplicity becomes clear: if the experience of meaning is beyond language, it is better to leave it unexpressed than to give it an inadequate expression. As Yu-kung Kao argues in discussing this poem, any articulation will destroy the poet's intuitive understanding, and therefore Tao Qian's "sudden forgetfulness of expression is the only way to assure his possession of this knowledge."[140]

Resounding with so many intertextual echoes of the *Zhuangzi*, Tao Qian's poem clearly shows his awareness of the complicated nature of language as well as the way to overcome the difficulty of poetic articulation. No explicit expression but indirect suggestion—that is the principle of this poetics of silence. What is remarkable about poetry is not that it has meaning but that its meaning always exceeds the boundaries of the text. Tao Qian's poem thematizes this excess and thereby becomes allegorical of its own generation of meaning. Instead of making a statement about meaning and precluding further exploration, he simply affirms the presence of meaning and invites each reader to interpret it in his or her own way. Meaning is infinite, and it is made manifest only in our finite interpretations. By refusing to give a finite presentation of meaning in the poem, Tao Qian keeps the possibility of meaning intact in his suggestive silence. The true meaning of nature is thus not diminished by the poet's confession of inability to explain but enriched by the infinite possibility of interpretation. That is essentially the strength of Tao Qian's poetry, the charm and legitimation of his stylistic simplicity; that is also what later poets and critics accepted from Tao Qian as an important legacy in the tradition of Chinese poetry and poetics.

The indeterminacy of meaning and the rich possibility of interpretation are evidently related to the very nature of poetic language. In the Chinese tradition, the inadequacy of language and the limitation of finite interpretations are readily recognized, and it is widely assumed that a poem may be read in different ways and have different interpretations. It is again Tao Qian who gave this theoretical principle a literary expression in his playful *Biography of Mr. Five Willows*, which has long been recognized as his autobiography.[141] The following is the first part of the *Biography*:

We do not know where this gentleman came from, nor are we sure of his real name. Around his house were five willow trees, and he took his name from them. He was a quiet man of few words, having no interest in seeking glory or fortune. He liked to read books, but did not try to have a thorough understanding of them. And yet, whenever he did grasp something, he would be so happy that he would forget about his meals.[142]

The portrait of Mr. Five Willows is rather sketchy, but it comes out alive with a few masterly strokes. The first thing that strikes us in this text is the negative mode of speaking: we do *not* know the man's origin or his name, he does *not* seek fame or fortune, he likes to read but does *not* try to understand, and so forth. As Qian Zhongshu comments, in the *Biography*, the word *no* or *not* [*bu*] is "the key [*yanmu*, literally, the 'eye'] to the whole text."[143] We have seen how the absence at the center of poetic text becomes the source of presence in Mallarmé's sonnet on the empty vase and how the negative mode of speaking works to present what is absent in Rilke's "Archaic Torso of Apollo." Here again, we have a text in which the negative mode prevails and bears directly on the meaning of the whole work. We do not know the origin or name of this gentleman, for Mr. Five Willows is just a provisional name, a name arbitrarily taken from the willow trees that happen to grow around his house. The negation of name may be an indication of Tao Qian's reaction against the social prejudice of his time, which is notorious for the snobbish vanity of the aristocrats who took great pride in their family names. But there is something more to it, for the poet may suggest that the essence of the man, like that of all things, cannot be named. The anonymity of Mr. Five Willows may thus allude to the beginning of the *Laozi*: "The name that can be named is not the constant name." The true nature of a person, like the true meaning of nature, is unnameable, and a provisional name like Mr. Five Willows is just as adequate as any other name. Or better still, because it is not a real name, it may leave the true nature of the person intact. In his biography of Tao Qian, Shen Yue recorded an interesting legend, repeated by later biographers, that Tao Qian, though not particularly talented in music, strangely kept a lute with no strings and liked to play on it when he had drunk wine and was in the right mood.[144] We read in the *Laozi* that "the great note is without sound. The great image has no shape. The *tao* hides itself in being nameless."[145] Zhuangzi also maintains that truly great music is beyond sound and form: "Listening to it, you hear no sound; looking at it, you see no shape. Yet it fills heaven and earth, and enwraps the whole universe."[146] By calling himself Mr. Five Willows, like playing a silent music on a stringless lute, the poet is thus making a meaning-gesture which implies not only his awareness of the difficulty of articulation but also his strategy to overcome it—that by keeping silent, he will be able to touch the roots of speech. One of Mr. Five Willows' eccentricities is that he likes to read but never bothers to reach a thorough understanding. This does not mean, however, that he is too lazy or too foolish to understand, for we know that whenever he does grasp something, he is so overjoyed that he forgets to eat. Giving up thorough understanding may indicate Tao Qian's reaction against the farfetched scholastic interpretations of Confucian classics, but it may also demonstrate his hermeneutic sense —namely, his awareness that meaning cannot be determined once and for all in one particular reading and that therefore one should keep one's mind open to the possibility of different interpretations. Dramatized by Tao's writing, the openness of the mind offers a decisive insight that recognizes all interpretations as valuable but no interpretation as final.

In Tao Qian's writings, the hermeneutic sense finds a literary formulation on both sides of the aesthetic experience, that is, from the author's and the reader's perspectives. When the poet claims that he knows the presence of meaning but forgets how to put it in words, he discloses the inadequacy of language and the difficulty of poetic articulation; and when he claims that he does not seek thorough understanding, he points out the indeterminacy of meaning and the open-ended orientation of all interpretations. Like most Chinese poets, Tao Qian never formulates his views as a systematic theory, but the invaluable moments of insight in his poetry and prose should enable us to catch a glimpse of the larger context of a Chinese hermeneutic theory. In such matters, Zhuangzi's influence is extremely important not only because Tao often refers to Zhuangzi's writings but also because his use of Zhuangzi turns the linguistic skepticism of a mystic-philosopher into a positive solution to the problem of language. Both sides of the signifying word, its limitation and its suggestiveness, are memorably expressed in the poet's forgetting of words. It is a moment that at once indicates the difficulty of articulation and the poet's skillful use of silence to overcome that difficulty. In the midst of speech, silence can be more expressive than words. Perhaps that is why in great works of literature, as in great music, we often find that the climactic moment is one of pause or silence. Bai Juyi, a famous Tang poet of the late eighth and early ninth centuries, thus describes the effect of such pause: "At this moment, silence excels all sounds."[147] The adverbial phrase "at this moment" is very important, for it puts silence in a frame of music and words. Perhaps this is also what Tao Qian tries to imply by playing on that stringless lute. Like forgetting words or forgetting the real name of Mr. Five Willows, it is a kind of mystic gesture for capturing the true meaning and expressing it in suggestive silence. Mallarmé's muse, the great "Musicienne du silence," naturally comes to mind. So do Rilke's wonderful lines: "Be silent. Who keeps silent inside / touches the roots of speech." In such moments, the helpless, passive silence unfolds itself as meaningful, active silence, and what cannot be said because of the limitation of language becomes what is deliberately left unsaid when the poet discovers the magic of suggestive silence, the evocative power of language. Eventually, the limitation and the suggestiveness of language must be seen not as contradictory but as complementary to each other, for they are the two sides of the same symbolic function. In this connection, we may understand why Tao Qian's unadorned simplicity impresses us much more powerfully than the poetry of most of his contemporaries. His simple language is powerful by virtue of its very simplicity. When we have read Tao Qian and the other poets of his time, we feel that while other writers in their ornateness and verbosity have said very little, Tao Qian with his simple words, his reticence, and his use of silence, has said infinitely more.

4

Author,

Text,

Reader

There are as many points of view
From which to regard her
As there are sides to a round bottle.
—Wallace Stevens, "Three Travelers
  Watch a Sunrise"

*Der wahre Leser muss der erweiterte
Autor seyn. Er ist die höhere Instanz,
die die Sache von der niedern Instanz
schon vorgearbeitet erhält.*
The true reader must be the extended
author. He is the superior court that
takes the case already prepared by the
lower court.
—Novalis, *Paralipomena
  zum Blütenstaub*

The Illusion of Identity

n one of the ancient Chinese classics, the *Book of Documents*, it is recorded that the legendary sage-king Shun (traditionally dated twenty-first century B.C.) initiated Chinese poetics with these three words: "Shi [poetry] yan [verbalizes] zhi [intention]." Shun ordered his minister Kui to be in charge of the education of royal princes, for which music and poetry were essential items in the curriculum because they were considered to be effective for securing harmonious relationship between gods and men and perfect ways to put things in perfect order. Almost like Orpheus, whose music has the power to charm savage beasts and even inanimate things, when Kui struck the stone instrument and when poetry was chanted to the melody, so we read in the *Book of Documents*, "all the hundred animals would dance to it accordingly."[1] Although these words may have been coined much later than the time of Shun and ascribed to him in order to acquire some hallowed authority, they do record a very ancient idea current at least in the sixth century B.C. and form one of the oldest tenets in Chinese theories of literature. In contrast to the Greek notion of divine inspiration, which locates the origin of poetry beyond the reach of the poet and his conscious language, the Chinese concept defines both the provenance and function of poetry within the range of human faculties as an activity motivated and governed by the poet's intention, an activity that gives the authorial intention a verbal form. As James Liu argues in *Chinese Theories of Literature*, traditional Chinese poetics is dominated by this expressive theory of poetry, which is quite different from the Greek theory of imitation. The emphasis on intention as the origin of poetic expression is further elaborated in the influential "Great Preface" to the *Book of Poetry*, in which we find one of the most cited definitions of poetry in Chinese criticism: "Poetry is that toward which intention moves. While at heart it is intention, coming out in words, it becomes poetry."[2] Through the mediation of language, poetry is here specified as the outer expression of what is intended to be its inner substance. Whether it is understood as an intellectual or emotional state, an ambition or a strong desire, a real or imagined experience, the Chinese concept of *zhi*, here translated as intention, inevitably presupposes the presence of a human agent, the operation of an intending subject. Unlike the divinely inspired Greek poet who does not understand the meaning of his own work, the Chinese poet, according to this definition, is clearly the creator of meaning because his *zhi* or intention, what he conceives of in the mind or experiences at heart, constitutes the origin of his poetry. It seems only natural, then, that the meaning of a poem should be what the poet intends it to be and that the authorial intention, the pretextual *mens auctoris*, should be the ultimate point of reference, the goal of all interpretations.

This tendency of intentionalist hermeneutics finds a powerful endorsement in the works of Mencius (371?–289? B.C.), who is regarded as a great sage and important thinker in the Confucian tradition, second only to Confucius himself. In his conversations with Xianqiu Meng, Mencius objects to rigid literalism in the interpretation of the *Book of Poetry* and proposes that the intention of the poet should be the highest authority in interpretation, the unfailing guide to the sense of poetic lines that may otherwise seem absurd or unintelligible. Having demonstrated to his interlocutor how to understand difficult lines by attending to their intended meaning in the context of their historical origin, Mencius thus sums up his exegetical method:

> So the interpreter of a poem should not let the words obscure the text, or the text obscure the intention. To trace back to the original intention with sympathetic understanding: that is the way to do it. If one should merely understand the text literally, then consider these lines from the poem *Yun han*: "Of the remaining populace of Zhou / Not one single soul survived." Taken as literal truth, this would mean that of all the Zhou people not a single person remained alive.[3]

It is clear that Mencius does not think that the language of poetry should be understood without allowing for rhetorical extravaganza and deviations from grammatical norms. Literalism is untenable because in its mechanical reading of the words or the text, it loses hold of what the text really wants to say in its original context—its true meaning—which, according to Mencius, can be grasped only by a recovery of the historical situation or context with reference to the authorial intention. As parts of the whole, words are not allowed to obscure the text but should be understood in relation to the totality of the text. The same relationship obtains in regard to the text and the author's intention. When poetic lines seem to exaggerate a certain point to achieve some special effect, the author's intention should function as the guide to appropriate understanding. A literal reading of those hyperbolic lines Mencius quoted from *Yun han* would turn the poem into nonsense, since there were of course survivors among the suffering people of Zhou. The correct reading of the poem should therefore go beyond the literal sense and interpret the text in its original context, within which the meaning the author intended becomes intelligible. In the lines quoted above, the poet's intended meaning is not and cannot be that every single subject of Zhou is dead, and the use of hyperbole is meant to emphasize the devastation that befell the kingdom of Zhou: the dire situation when famine following drought was taking a heavy toll of the kingdom's population. Mencius is of course aware of the hermeneutic distance between the reader and a text from the past, between present understanding and a past intention, but in the hermeneutic effort to bridge over that distance, the present condition of the reader is conceived only negatively as an obstacle to true understanding. He urges the interpreter to go back to the past and reconstruct the poet's intention in order to understand the poem. Ultimately, even the correct understanding of the written text is not in itself the end, but a means to the end, which is to lead from the text to the author, and to know the author as a living person. "Chanting the poems of the ancients and reading their books," says Mencius, "how can we be ignorant of what the authors were as real people? Therefore, we study the age in which they lived. We should indeed make friends with the ancients."[4] Because of the tremendous influence Mencius has exerted in the Confucian tradition, the intentionalist concepts of understanding and interpretation dominate the discourse of many Chinese critics, whose interpretive activity is often determined teleologically as the recovery of the authorial meaning and methodologically as the contextualization of a poem in past history, in a moment of the poet's lived experience. Traditional Chinese criticism, as James Liu observes, is heavily influenced by a "combination of Confucian moralism and Mencian intentionalism"; it tends to read poetry as all biographical or autobiographical and attempts to "pin every poem down to a precise date," looking for "hidden references to contemporary political events or to the poet's personal circumstances."[5] The interpretation of a poem thus becomes largely an effort to restore the text to its origin in the poet's life experience or to uncover a hidden reference the poet conceals for certain political reasons. In both cases, the authorial intention becomes the key to appropriate understanding, the source of meaning, and the final frame of reference.

In one of the most important works of Chinese criticism, *The Literary Mind or the Carving of Dragons*, Liu Xie devotes a whole chapter to the problem of true understanding, formulated in terms of a quest for *zhiyin* or "the one who knows the sound." The chapter begins with an emphatic note of difficulty, claiming, no doubt hyperbolically, that probably in every thousand years there may appear one ideal reader who truly understands what the poet means. The main obstacles to true and sympathetic understanding, according to Liu Xie, are the diversity of individual tastes and the intolerance of different opinions, for people are likely to "lavish praise on whatever is to their own taste but discard whatever they find alien and strange; each of them sticks to a narrow interpretation, never accommodating it to any change. This is indeed like 'looking eastward but not seeing western walls.'" Despite such ubiquitous parochialism, Liu Xie goes on to say, true understanding is nevertheless attainable if readers are willing to abandon their own opinions in search of what the poet has intended to say in the original context:

> When his feelings are moved, the author of a literary work allows them to come out in words, and by opening up the literary text, the reader can enter those feelings, just as in tracing the waves back to their fountainhead, he can surely discover it, however secluded it may be. When an author lived in the remote past, one cannot see his face, but by viewing his writings, one can always see his mind. Therefore, what we should be concerned about is not that the text is too obscurely deep, but that our own knowledge and experiences are too shallow to penetrate its depth.[6]

The relationship between writing and reading as Liu Xie understood it is reified in this passage by the images of water and river, for the written text, like the water or waves in a river, is conceived of as issuing forth from the author's feelings, forming a current of certain depth and a flowing movement. The reader can penetrate and enter the text as one dives into the river, and trace its flow back to the fountainhead, which is the author's thoughts or feelings. To read a poem is thus an empathetic attempt to retrace the steps the author took in writing the poem and to relive the original moment the author experienced. Liu Xie is confident that such a goal of interpretation can be achieved despite all the difficulties he has so emphatically pointed out. Even in music, which does not have a visible form, he argues, the musician's intention can be fully revealed to the one who is able to know the sound. Then how can the author's intention or idea be hidden and lost when he has given it a graphic form with his writing brush, a permanently fixed form to which the reader can come back again and again? "Thus the mind sees the idea as in a mirror, like the eye sees the form; to a sharp eye no form will remain undifferentiated, and to a quick mind no idea will fail to communicate."[7] Here the parallelism in Liu Xie's text, which is a syntactic feature pervasive in classical Chinese writing, makes almost irresistible the analogy between the comprehensibility of the author's idea in the mind's eye and the visibility of a physical form in the natural eye. The analogy presents the transition from mind to language as such a facile process that understanding seems not to be or should not be a problem. However, much of this chapter in Liu Xie's work is speaking precisely of the difficulty of understanding, even though the hermeneutic process of true understanding is described as simply a retrogression from the text to its pretextual authorial intention.

The essential notion on which the edifice of the Chinese intentionalist hermeneutics stands—namely, the idea of *zhiyin* or "the one who knows the sound"—comes from an ancient legend about Bo Ya the musician and his friend Zhong Ziqi. The legend has it that when Bo Ya played a tune on his zither and thought about the Tai Mountains, Zhong Ziqi knew exactly what he intended to convey in the music and said to Bo Ya, "How wonderfully you play the zither! The music sounds sublimely high as the Tai Mountains." Then Bo Ya played another tune intended to express his ideas about great rivers, and again Zhong understood perfectly, saying, "How wonderfully you play the zither! It strikes one as the broad expanse of great rivers." Unfortunately, such perfect communication was soon disrupted by death, and when Zhong Ziqi died, Bo Ya "broke his zither, tore off the strings, and never played the zither again for the rest of his life, for he thought that the world no longer had anyone for whom he would play the music."[8] It seems that perfect understanding can be achieved only in such legendary stories, and the point of this story is precisely how rare a chance there is, if there is any chance at all, that such perfect understanding can ever be attained. In traditional Chinese criticism, the relationship between Bo Ya the musician and Zhong Ziqi who knows the sound becomes the symbol of ideal friendship and perfect understanding. To find a *zhiyin* or an ideal reader with the capability to understand even the inmost feelings the author wants to express, has always been the dream of all Chinese poets. When Tao Qian wistfully asks with a sigh, "When no one is here to know the sound, / What use is there to strike a sad note?" he is alluding to the story of Bo Ya and Zhong Ziqi and revealing his desire for true understanding.[9] To be a *zhiyin* or ideal friend to the poet is also the goal of many Chinese critics, who try, in their scholarly annotations, exegeses, and commentaries, to go back to the author's time and recover his original intention. This can be seen, for example, in the following remarks made by Qiu Zhao-ao, a well-known seventeenth-century critic of Du Fu's poems, when he gives a definition of the task of a commentator:

> Anyone who undertakes to annotate Du's poetry must repeatedly immerse himself in it to find out its final destination. Moreover, he must go over it line by line and word by word so that hopefully he may get what the author intended in his mind across the gap of hundreds or even thousands of years, as though he were living in the author's world and seeing him in person, emotionally affected by the same sorrows and quietly contemplating the same thoughts.[10]

This may be seen as one of the classic formulations of intentionalist hermeneutics in the Chinese tradition. The process of understanding is again described metaphorically as an immersion in the text as in water, and as tracing the flow of words to their "final destination." The commentator's repeated immersion in the poetic work, his "line by line and word by word" negotiations of meaning, vividly portray his mental activity as moving back and forth within a hermeneutic circle of parts and whole, while his imaginary rendezvous with the poet in a temporally remote world, his reexperiencing of the author's emotions and thoughts, discloses the commentator's strong desire for a psychological identification with the author.

The Chinese notion of understanding as tracing the text back to the author's mind and entering his world of lived experiences has direct bearing on the issue of meaning and intention, which is also an important and much-debated issue in contemporary Western literary theory. E. D. Hirsch is probably the most eloquent and certainly the most well known of the modern advocates of an intentionalist hermeneutics. Facing what he calls the "Babel of interpretations" or the danger of radical relativism in both philosophical hermeneutics and literary criticism, he undertakes to establish a theoretical foundation for validating interpretations, a "norm that can be universally compelling and generally sharable." And that norm, he claims, can be nothing other than "the author's meaning."[11] Of course, interpretations of a poem or a novel can, and often do, differ from one another, but Hirsch maintains that all the differences are due to changes in the work's significance, not to any modification of its meaning, which remains self-identical and reproducible—that is, always the same as the author intended at the moment of composition. *"Meaning,"* says Hirsch, "is that which is represented by a text; it is what the author meant by his use of a particular sign sequence; it is what the signs represent. *Significance*, on the other hand, names a relationship between that meaning and a person, or a conception, or a situation, or indeed anything imaginable."[12] The distinction between meaning and significance makes it possible for Hirsch to differentiate understanding, by which he means "a perception or construction of the author's verbal meaning, nothing more, nothing less," from interpretation or criticism, by which he refers to commentaries that "are concerned with significance as well as meaning."[13] The distinction also provides the necessary theoretical justification for his claim that the authorial meaning remains self-identical in the face of all the changing situations and interpretations, since all the differences in interpretation can be seen simply as different commentaries on the variable significance of a literary work, while the task of true understanding, according to Hirsch, should be the reconstruction of the author's intended meaning, which is the only invariable factor and thus the only one that can yield the proper interpretation.

If the Chinese intentionalist critic quoted above aims at a psychological identification with the author, Hirsch is concerned first and foremost with the philological problem of textual meaning. He admits that no one can ever get inside the author's head and compare the meaning the author intends with the meaning one understands, but for him that is not the real issue: "The only question that can relevantly be at issue is whether the *verbal* meaning which an author intends is accessible to the interpreter of his text." Drawing on Husserl's phenomenological concept of intentionality, Hirsch gives a positive answer to the question and argues that *"an unlimited number of different intentional acts can intend the same verbal meaning."*[14] That is to say, the intentional acts of different readers can produce or reproduce an identical intentional object, namely, the author's meaning. The circularity of this argument, however, obviously creates a problem, because the statement that different people can have the same understanding of the same verbal meaning that the author originally intended is precisely what is at issue here; it could be the conclusion drawn at the end of a rigorous argument, but it cannot be posited as a premise for the argument. Gerald Graff observes in his discussion of this rather complicated issue that when we talk about the intentions of other people, we are only "drawing *inferences* about those intentions"; we are trying to determine the relevant context of an utterance, and that is "a process just as dependent on inference as any other part of the interpretive process, and therefore just as open to dispute. We can always disagree about what the proper context is of any utterance, and this disagreement creates the possibility of indeterminacy."[15] Strictly speaking, the indeterminacy of meaning is not so much a theoretical concept as a phenomenon in the reality of practical criticism, for there will always be different inferences about the original intention or the original context of an utterance, and consequently there will always be different interpretations of the same text, the same linguistic structure, the "same verbal meaning." To declare that meaning remains self-identical and only significance changes does not really solve the problem; it only posits an invariable meaning as a theoretical construct that transcends the practice of literary criticism, assuming a sort of transcendental thing-in-itself that exists out there but cannot be known in real situations of literary interpretation.

Hirsch, of course, would be the last to argue for a hermeneutic agnosticism, since he is confident that the author's meaning not only exists as a thing-in-itself but is also knowable, and that meaning as a type can be shared by different people in different places and at different times. Accordingly, the only valid interpretation is the one that recovers the same *type* of meaning as the author intends. One example he provides is the interpretation of *Hamlet*. Hirsch rejects the psychoanalytic interpretation of this play on the grounds that the Freudian reading does not belong to the same type of meaning Shakespeare intended: "In the example of *Hamlet*, we rejected the implication that Hamlet wished to sleep with his mother because we posited that such an implication did not belong to the type of meaning Shakespeare willed. . . . We rejected the implication because it was not, on our premises, the kind of trait that belonged to the type of character Shakespeare imagined."[16] One may not agree with Freud when he asserts that sublimation of the Oedipus complex is what *Hamlet* is all about, but to reject the psychoanalytic interpretation by appealing to the type of meaning Shakespeare could have willed only incurs an unnecessary burden of proof, for no one can ever really know what Shakespeare's intention was. We may notice the significant words Hirsch uses here, for what he recognizes as the Shakespearean type of meaning is "posited" by Hirsch himself as interpretive "premises." This type of meaning thus belongs more to Hirsch than to Shakespeare, and it provides a frame of reference for the critic to use in piecing together the details of the play into a coherent account. Theoretically, this posited type of meaning is only different from but not necessarily superior to, or more authentically Shakespearean than, the Freudian type which guides the psychoanalytic critic in his interpretation. At a closer look, then, one may see that in Hirsch's hermeneutic paradigm, the author's type of meaning is in fact determined by the critic, who has already formed a certain preliminary understanding of the author and his world. In other words, the intentionalist hermeneutics contains an element of subjectivity contributed by the critic and therefore cannot be presented as the kind of "objective criticism" Hirsch claims it to be.

The same applies to the Chinese version of intentionalist hermeneutics that Qiu Zhao-ao proposes. Though he claims to have Du Fu's own feelings and thoughts as guidance, he already has a very strong view of what kind of feelings and thoughts the poet Du Fu could have in the first place, for he reads Du's poetry from a definitely Confucian perspective, arguing that the greatness of Du Fu's works lies in transcending "mere letters" to become a powerful social commentary and a strong political commitment, with "not one single idea detached from the situation at Court, and not one single moment unconcerned with the sufferings of the people."[17] The task of the commentator, Qiu Zhao-ao declares, is to "interpret Du in accordance with Confucius' and Mencius' comments on poetry," reading most of the poems as political allegories or topical pieces alluding to some political event of the time.[18] As a result, what the critic presents as Du Fu's intention turns out to be the outcome of a particularly tendentious interpretation, strongly influenced by and contingent upon the critic's historical condition and his ideological principles and personal beliefs, as well as the exegetical history of Du Fu's poetry.

Hirsch admits that "no one can establish another's meaning with certainty. The interpreter's goal is simply this—to show that a given reading is more probable than others. In hermeneutics, verification is a process of establishing relative probabilities."[19] Insofar as Hirsch speaks of interpretation in terms of probability and does not insist on a single correct reading, his hermeneutic theory is very different from the kind of psychological identification we have seen in Qiu Zhao-ao's definition of critical commentary. For Hirsch, however, all the criteria used in verifying interpretations ultimately refer to a "psychological reconstruction." Here he proves to be not so different, after all, from the Chinese intentionalist critic in tracing the text back to its origin in the author's mind. "The interpreter's primary task," says Hirsch, "is to reproduce in himself the author's 'logic,' his attitudes, his cultural givens, in short, his world. Even though the process of verification is highly complex and difficult, the ultimate verificative principle is very simple—the imaginative reconstruction of the speaking subject."[20] In this respect, Hirsch's source is Dilthey, especially his emphasis on the importance of reexperiencing (*Nacherleben*) the author's original state of mind. According to Dilthey, the ability to leave behind marks or traces of their experiences in life, or what he calls life-expressions (*Lebensäusserungen*), is the unique ability that distinguishes humans from all other creatures, and the art of understanding involves an imaginative reliving of the author's experiences as he or she has permanently recorded them in the work.[21] A general human nature provides the basis for communication among different individuals; thus the interpreter is able to understand the workings of an alien mind when he "projects his own sense of life into another historical milieu," entering a different state of mind, "thus making possible within himself a re-experiencing of an alien form of life."[22] Hirsch has fully adopted these ideas in his theory, and his entire argument, as he himself declares, "may be regarded as an attempt to ground some of Dilthey's hermeneutic principles in Husserl's epistemology and Saussure's linguistics."[23]

Some scholars have argued, however, that Dilthey's hermeneutics cannot be reduced to a project for the psychological reconstruction of the authorial intention. Rudolf Makkreel, for instance, strongly objects to such a simplistic misunderstanding by calling our attention to the fact that Dilthey, following Schleiermacher, defines the task of hermeneutics as "to understand the author better than he understood himself."[24] Borrowed from Schleiermacher, this motto of Dilthey's hermeneutics clearly shows that "re-experiencing can no longer be conceived in terms of reproducing either the actual process of creation or the actual state of mind of the author," who is now "no longer a privileged interpreter of his work. This is the significance of Dilthey's claim that disinterestedness is a property of the lived experience of the creative artist."[25] Hirsch's use of Dilthey, Makkreel argues, goes against this very definition of the hermeneutic task and "ignores Dilthey's own methodological ground rules which do not permit the validity of interpretation to depend on the reproduction of the meaning intended by an author."[26] If Dilthey's hermeneutics aims at a higher level of understanding than the author's, its aim is also higher than what Hirsch demands. Moreover, since the meaning of a work cannot be separated either from a sense of its original context or from its present significance, Hirsch's differentiation of meaning from significance is also dubious. According to Makkreel, "It is a mistake to think that we can first fix its meaning and then determine its historical significance as a mere application."[27] Once we cease to posit meaning as something isolated from practical criticism and interpretation, we immediately realize that meaning is not self-identical but changes just as much as significance. I have mentioned earlier that the indeterminacy of meaning is not a theoretical construct but the reality of practical criticism, because no interpretive method or strategy can bring two readers to exactly the same understanding of a literary work, and the meaning one understands cannot be divorced from one's own knowledge and cultivation, which are largely determined by one's historical conditions. This is also the point Gadamer makes when he argues that the hermeneutic circle, which results from the fact that one always approaches a text with the anticipatory movement of fore-understanding, "is not a 'methodological' circle, but describes an element of the ontological structure of understanding."[28]

That one's ability to understand is already historically constituted is what Gadamer tries to indicate by the concept of historicity, which fully recognizes the changeability of meaning in time and variable situations. In order to maintain the invariability of meaning, Hirsch proposes a directly opposite concept of historicality. He writes:

> We may set against this principle of historicity the principle of *historicality*, which asserts that a historical event, that is to say, an original communicative intent, can determine forever the permanent, unchanging features of meaning. The doctrine of historicality has a different scope from that of historicity. Gadamer's historicity implies that meaning *must* change over time; but historicality maintains that meaning can stay the same if we choose to regard meaning as a historically determined object.[29]

There is no question that the author's act of composing a literary work, like all other acts and events that happen in real life, is a historical event with all its definite givens. It does not follow, however, that the meaning of the work is also always historically determinate. On the contrary, as Barbara Herrnstein Smith argues, there is a crucial difference between natural and fictive discourses. A literary work as fictive utterance, that is, as a verbal structure that "was not 'performed' and did not 'occur' in the historical universe," is not itself a historical act or event, and its meaning or meanings are "*historically indeterminate* and therefore not even theoretically ascertainable on the basis of historical evidence." This is not to deny the meaning of a literary work its historical relevancy but to recognize that its indeterminacy is itself historically determined by its nature as fictive utterance. "In other words," Smith continues, "to speak of the meanings of a fictive utterance as historically indeterminate is not to override—ignore, mistake, or betray—something that is *there*, but to acknowledge the fact that something is *not* there."[30]

Perhaps we can see a connection between Smith's distinction of natural and fictive discourses and a similar distinction that Roman Ingarden makes between real and represented objects with regard to determinacy and indeterminacy. Based on Husserl's epistemology, Ingarden observes that the essential characteristic of a real object is that it is "*unequivocally, universally* (i.e., in *every* respect) *determined*," while an intentional object as represented in language has an infinite number of "spots of indeterminacy," which "in principle cannot be entirely removed by any finite enrichment of the content of a nominal expression."[31] If a story begins with a descriptive sentence like "An old man was sitting at a table," says Ingarden, though the represented table has its range of meaning, many of the determinate aspects of a real table (its shape, size, color, material, etc.) are "left quite unsaid and therefore—this being a purely intentional object—*not determined*."[32] Ingarden's assimilation of Husserl is obviously very different from that of Hirsch, and for Ingarden the meaning of a represented object is not at all permanently fixed by the author's intention or intentional act. Indeterminacy, according to Ingarden, is a property, an ontological attribute of intentional objects, including all the objects and events represented in a work of literature. That is to say, indeterminacy in literary works is not a theoretical hypothesis but a fact every reader encounters. One of Ingarden's contributions to literary theory is precisely a seminal study of the schematic nature of a literary text, of how an indeterminate meaning is enriched and *concretized* in one way or another in the process of reading.

At this point, we may notice that indeterminacy as a concept developed in phenomenological criticism and hermeneutics has implications for literary studies that are totally different from those of indeterminacy as understood in deconstructive criticism. Here the difference again pivots on the problem of meaning, or the lack of it. According to Graff, who relies on Timothy Bahti as a deconstructive critic, deconstruction has made indeterminacy a pervasive property that "enters into and infects the interpretation of the text, so that it is not just literature but also the *interpretation* of literature that is fraught with uncertainty."[33] But if we consider the issue in reference to the works of Derrida and Paul de Man, we can see that deconstruction takes a resolutely antihermeneutical stance and ignores the question of meaning altogether, whereas indeterminacy in Ingarden's and Gadamer's sense is always a property of the text and meaning, as well as that of interpretation. As we have seen in de Man's discussion of Rilke, it is not semantic indeterminacy but syntactic figuration, an askesis which brings nothing but the acoustic effects of Rilke's "phonocentric poetics" to the foreground, that is of interest and significance for a deconstructive reading.

What Ingarden calls meaning and recognizes as indeterminate and changeable becomes, in Hirsch's terminology, "significance," while he reserves the word "meaning" for a hypothetically invariable element of the text, identical with the author's original intention. Hirsch seems to acknowledge the hypothetical nature of this invariable meaning when he admits that his argument is "unabashedly and . . . necessarily theoretical."[34] Apparently, theory here refers to a conceptual realm distinct from the practice of literary criticism, and yet it provides criticism with an authoritative guidance from above or outside, offering critics an Archimedean fulcrum in hermeneutics that will finally solve all the problems of conflict in interpretation. It is interesting to note that yet another contention for intentionalist hermeneutics, advanced by Steven Knapp and Walter Benn Michaels, professes to be unabashedly antitheoretical rather than theoretical, and goes one step further than Hirsch in asserting that not only does a text mean what the author intends but meaning and authorial intention are always one and the same thing. To differentiate meaning from intention, the two critics argue, already errs in making an unnecessary theoretical move that splits apart terms that are in fact inseparable. The main point of their argument is "not that there *need* be no gulf between intention and the meaning of its expression but that there *can* be no gulf. Not only in serious literal speech but in *all* speech what is intended and what is meant are identical."[35] Since meaning *is* intention, so they argue, to choose intention over other things to get meaning is simply falling into the trap of theory. "But as soon as we recognize that there are no theoretical choices to be made," Knapp and Michaels claim, "then the point of theory vanishes. Theory loses."[36] Their essay is provocatively entitled

"Against Theory," and the two critics seem to argue that once theory stops, practical criticism will happily reach the correct understanding of the meaning of literature, which has always been the same as the author's intention. Not surprisingly, their essay has incited many to rise in defense of theory, as the collection of articles in a special *Critical Inquiry* book clearly shows. It is not necessary to advance yet another theoretical argument against this antitheoretical, "pragmatist argument," but it may be helpful to look instead at practical criticism, to examine some exemplary cases and see how a literary text is actually interpreted, and to see how the interpretations demonstrate the necessary hermeneutic difference that arises from the historicity of critics of different positions and different times, even if they all appeal to the authorial intention as exegetical guidance.

The Testimony of Praxis

Among the critics who contributed to the collection of essays written in response to Knapp's and Michaels' intentionalist argument, Hershel Parker contends from a textual scholar's practical point of view that a literary text is not an immutable arrangement of words and that its meaning is much more complicated than Hirsch, Knapp, and Michaels have taken it to be. Parker cites as evidence alterations in the novels by Herman Melville, Mark Twain, Stephen Crane, Theodore Dreiser, Norman Mailer, and others to show that sometimes, because of authorial revision or editorial patching, a passage in a text may embody "two different and contradictory authorial intentions rather than one," and that "nonmeanings, partially authorial meanings, and inadvertent, intentionless meanings coexist in standard literary texts with genuine authorial meanings."[37] Such empirical evidence should make it clear that a text does not always mean what its author intends, but the intentionalist critic might argue that the very purpose of textual criticism, the effort to establish a good, "authoritative" edition of a literary text, is precisely to recover authorial intention. What the intentionalist tends to ignore, however, is the fact that authorial intention as established in textual criticism is itself an outcome of scholarship and interpretation.

Perhaps the most compelling argument that demonstrates the necessary constructive nature of all interpretations is advanced by Stanley Fish in many of his brilliantly polemic essays. A case in point is his discussion of the difference in editorial opinions as revealed in the Variorum edition of Milton's poetry. One of the textual cruxes appears in Milton's sonnet, "Lawrence of virtuous Father virtuous Son," of which the last two lines—"He who of those delights can judge, and spare / To interpose them oft, is not unwise"—may be read in very different ways. The two editors, A. S. P. Woodhouse and Douglas Bush, cannot agree upon the exact meaning of "spare," that is, whether the word here means "leave time for" or "refrain from." Consequently, two different readings are proposed. In one reading, Milton appears to recommend to the reader "those delights"—he who can leave time for them is not unwise—but in the other reading, the poet seems to admonish the reader against indulgence in such delights—he who knows when to refrain from them is not unwise. Proponents of the two contrary readings all appeal to formal features of the text and Milton's "known attitudes" to support a particular interpretation, but the fact that they can all do so to promote mutually exclusive readings suggests that what is considered as verification is in fact interpretation shaped by the interpreter's preliminary understanding. From the same evidence, Woodhouse and Bush come to exactly the opposite conclusions, and therefore it becomes possible for Fish to argue that "evidence brought to bear in the course of formalist analyses—that is, analyses generated by the assumption that meaning is embedded in the artifact—will always point in as many directions as there are interpreters; that is, not only will it prove something, it will prove anything."[38] Fish maintains that both formal features and intention, which are often considered the basis for interpretation, are in fact created by interpretation: "Rather than intention and its formal realization producing interpretation (the 'normal' picture), interpretation creates intention and its formal realization by creating the conditions in which it becomes possible to pick them out." The verification process is therefore an obvious hermeneutic circle, though Fish does not use that term: "I 'saw' what my interpretive principles permitted or directed me to see, and then I turned around and attributed what I had 'seen' to a text and an intention."[39] The circularity inhabits not just the philological circle of individual words and the totality of the text, but also the cognitive circle of preliminary understanding and the very formal features that are recognized and understood.

Another example Fish discusses in great detail is Milton's *L'Allegro*, lines 45–46: "Then to come in spite of sorrow, / And at my window bid good-morrow." The question here is, Who comes to the window? Critics have debated the appropriate answer and have recommended a number of candidates: Mirth, the Lark, the Cheerful Man, Dawn, and others. The pattern of verification is again circular. As Fish notes:

(1) The proponent of each reading makes concessions, usually by acknowledging that there *is* evidence for the readings he opposes.
(2) Each critic is able to point to details which do in fact support his position.
(3) But in order fully to support his respective position every one of the critics is moved to make *sense* of the lines by supplying connections more firm and delimiting than the connections available in the text.
(4) This making of sense always involves an attempt to arrange the images and events of the passage into a sequence of logical action.[40]

In other words, each critic is able to support his or her reading of the whole passage by pointing to the logical coherence of the details, and yet the critic is able to arrange the details in a coherent structure only because he or she already has some preliminary understanding of what the whole passage is about. Assumptions about the meaning of the whole text form the enabling perspective from which the critic can arrange the details of the text in a certain sequence, and the sequence of details so arranged can in turn support the interpretation of the text as a whole. In fact, this circularity of understanding becomes especially visible wherever a controversy on textual cruxes brings the verification process to the foreground.

In Chinese literature, one of the most enigmatic works and one that seems to invite critical controversy is a famous poem by the late Tang poet Li Shangyin (813?–58), whose works are typically fraught with semantic and syntactic indeterminacies, and admit of very different interpretations. The poem we shall discuss presently is conventionally referred to as "Jin se [The Patterned Lute]"; *jin* or brocade is used here as an adjective, meaning "richly adorned," "embellished," or "ornamented," and *se* is a musical instrument, similar to a lute or zither. The title of a poem, like that of program music, usually provides an important clue to the theme or content of its text, but in this case "Jin se" does not constitute the real title, which would implicitly mark out the contour of the meaning of the poem, because it is just the first two characters of the first line conveniently taken to be its title. In this case, then, the title as clue is missing, and the whole text becomes a puzzling maze of elegant words and phrases, a labyrinth of alluring yet evasive imagery. The poem is virtually untranslatable, but in order to present the different readings that have all been attempted to make sense of it by making connections in a hermeneutic circle, I have prepared the following fairly literal translation:

> The patterned lute, for no reason, has fifty strings;
> Each string, each fret, recalls the prime years.
> Zhuangzi in his morning dream was puzzled by the butterfly;
> Emperor Wang entrusted to the cuckoo his spring passion;
> Over the vast sea the moon shines, pearls are shedding tears;
> On Blue Fields the sun warms, a smoke rises from the jade.
> This mood might have been a thing to be remembered;
> But even then, it was already vague and lost.[41]

Before we examine several of the interpretations Chinese critics have proposed in answering the questions the poem asks in almost every line, let us first look into some of the allusions embedded in the text. As Chinese poems are usually very short and the form of a "regulated verse" (*lü shi*, which is the form used here) contains only eight lines, references and allusions are perhaps the most frequently used rhetorical devices by means of which Chinese poets try to augment the possibility of meaning beyond the textual limitation that the brevity of the poetic form necessarily imposes. In the poem quoted above, Li Shangyin characteristically makes a number of philosophical and literary allusions, some less obvious than others, whose complexity adds to the difficulty in comprehending the poem's total meaning. Commentators have traced Li's use of allusions to several sources from which the poet may have drawn the image of the patterned lute, but they cannot come to a general agreement upon whether the number of strings originally on the lute should be twenty-five or fifty. The question is, Why "for no reason" does the lute have fifty strings? As we shall see, to know the exact number is crucial for the critics in deciding the age of the person whose "prime years" correspond to the number of strings and frets. In line 3, the reference is to a famous passage in the *Zhuangzi*, in which the philosopher (referred to as Zhuang Zhou) talks about a strange dream he once had that reveals his idea of the equality and transformation of all things in their initial, undifferentiated condition. The dream is a fascinating fable of identity, or rather the illusion of identity, as it puts into question the very boundaries between dream and reality, Self and Other, being and becoming:

Once Zhuang Zhou dreamed of himself being a butterfly; he was really a butterfly fluttering around, happy and comfortable, knowing not that he was Zhou. After a while, he woke up, and he was surprisingly Zhuang Zhou himself. It is not clear whether it was Zhou who had dreamed of being a butterfly or it was the butterfly who had dreamed of being Zhou. Yet there must be differentiation between Zhou and the butterfly, and this is called the transformation of things.[42]

This dream and its dreamy uncertainty have always caught the imagination of poets, and whoever reads this passage cannot help noticing its poetic appeal as well as its philosophical questioning. In an interview with Roberto Alifano, Jorge Luis Borges compares Zhuangzi's dream with some well-known poetic expressions of the relation between dream and life, and finds Zhuangzi's version the most poetic. "Life is a dream" is a plain statement with no metaphorical embellishment or imagery and is too abstract to be poetry. Shakespeare's line, "We are such stuff as dreams are made on," says Borges, is closer to poetry. When Walther von der Vogelweide cries out, "I have dreamed my life, was it real?" the poetic condition reaches further than in Calderón or Shakespeare, but it is for Zhuangzi that Borges reserves his highest praise: "There is poetry in that brief text. The choice of the butterfly is felicitous, since the butterfly has a tenuous quality that is fitting for the stuff of dreams."[43] In referring to Zhuangzi's dream of the butterfly, Li Shangyin could have meant to imply the transformation of things, the uncertainty of one's identity or reality, or some other aspect of the passage that has relevance to the poem as a whole, but the fact that one can hardly pinpoint the exact meaning in Li's use of Zhuangzi adds to the general effect of vagueness that prevails in the entire text.

The next line of Li Shangyin's poem turns to a totally unrelated story about the legendary Emperor Wang of Shu. According to one version of the legend, Emperor Wang seduced his prime minister's wife and felt ashamed of himself. He abdicated the state to his minister and went into self-imposed exile. When the emperor died, his spirit was transformed into a cuckoo. Lines 3 and 4 may thus share the idea of transformation as a common theme, but one may still wonder what this allusion really means: what is the nature of the Emperor's "spring passion," and what feeling is implied here—remorse, sorrow, amorous desire, or some other emotional effect? The pearls shedding tears in line 5 may be a variation on an old legend about the mermaids at sea. According to the legend, when these mermaids weep, their tears change into shining pearls while falling down their cheeks to the sea. In this line, however, it is not the mermaids but the pearls that are shedding tears. The Blue Fields in line 6 is a mountain famous for its fine jade, and the entire line may allude to a remark made by the poet Dai Shulun (732–89) that the scene represented in poetry is a sort of metaphorical mirage which, like the smoke rising from fine jade when the sun warms up the Blue Fields, can only be seen from afar but cannot be put in front of one's eyes; in other words, it is vague, alluring, beautiful, but unreal.

Equipped with at least the minimum of necessary information about allusions, the critic can now set about fulfilling the task of interpretation and begin making sense of the whole poem by linking together the various lines and images. But where is the starting point? Where should he begin to make connections and put the disparate elements together in an intelligible pattern? Evidently, the critic must somehow have a preliminary intelligible shape in his mind before he can put the scattered images and allusions into that frame of intelligibility. That is to say, the critic must begin with the concept of genre and have some idea of what the poem as a whole is about before he can connect the images, allusions, and all the other textual elements into a coherent whole. As we shall see, Chinese commentators on "The Patterned Lute" all begin their interpretation by making a guess at the idea of the whole poem with reference to the authorial intention and by locating it in the map of poetic types or genres, which will then guide them in correlating all the lines, images, and their associations. A generic conception of the literary work is where interpretation starts. "All understanding of verbal meaning," as Hirsch rightly observes, "is necessarily genre-bound."[44] For Hirsch, the type of poetry should be the type the author intends, but practical criticism does not seem always to work out that way. The Chinese commentators would be most willing to accept Hirsch's view, as they indeed tried to form a generic conception with regard to authorial intention, but the outcome of their very different readings is nonetheless a testimony to the indeterminacy of meaning and the poem's susceptibility to different interpretations.

Of the more or less plausible readings of this poem, I would choose just a few to demonstrate how all the commentaries work in a hermeneutic circle. Let us first look at the exegesis advanced by Zhu Yizun (1629–1709), who begins his interpretation by relating the poem to a particular moment in Li Shangyin's biography and decides that this is an elegy the poet wrote in memory of his deceased wife:

> The lute originally has twenty-five strings, which are now broken into fifty; "for no reason" emphasizes the breaking of strings [which is an euphemistic expression for the death of one's wife]. "Each string, each fret," followed by "recalls the prime years," suggests that she died at the age of twenty-five. The butterfly and the cuckoo refer to her transformation into other forms of life. The pearls are shedding tears for her, and the smoke of fine jade implies her interment, as the familiar saying goes, "burying her fragrance and entombing the fine jade."[45]

Once Zhu Yizun puts the poem and its various formal features into the generic frame of an elegy, all the details seem to fall in place in a coherent explanation. Insofar as it makes connections and accounts for the various textual elements, his interpretation is valid, persuasive, and probably the most influential among all the traditional readings. But it in no way prevents other critics from proposing totally different readings. Another commentator on the poem, He Zhuo (1661–1722), understands the poetic genre and the various images altogether differently:

> This piece expresses the poet's self-pity in the style of Qu Yuan who writes about his own sorrow allegorically as a lady's lament over her fading beauty. The line about Zhuangzi implies that all has been an empty dream, and the line about Emperor Wang entertains some hope for the next cycle of life. The vast sea and the Blue Fields indicate his being buried in obscurity without due recognition, while the shining moon and the warm sun suggest that he is all the more unfortunate in being the only one not appreciated in a time of fair opportunities.

The two readings differ from the very start in their generic assumptions, which let the two critics see things differently and make different connections. Given the fact that self-pity and lament over one's obscurity in the form of a social or political allegory are indeed quite common in Chinese poetry, He Zhuo's interpretation is persuasive in its own way. For Zhu Yizun, the poem is about Li Shangyin's deceased wife who died at the age of twenty-five, which is suggested by the strings on the lute suddenly broken into fifty. He Zhuo reads the poem as the poet's lament over his own fate; thus the gender of the person memorialized in the poem, as the result of different generic assumptions, becomes different in the two interpreta-tions. The most important thing about the reference to Zhuangzi, for example, in Zhu's interpretation is said to be the "transformation into other forms of life," but in He Zhuo's it is the idea of dream as empty nothingness, a waste of one's talent. Even though both critics understand the jade in the Blue Fields as referring to something buried, for Zhu Yizun it is a metaphor for the poet's wife buried in her tomb, but for He Zhuo it is the poet himself metaphorically buried in obscurity. What comes out clearly from this interesting conflict in interpretation is the neutrality of the text, that the poem neither firmly supports nor absolutely rejects these very different generic assumptions and interpretations. In the light of such a conflict, we can see clearly that interpretations are shaped in a step-by-step negotiation of meaning between the text's claim and the critic's understanding.

But the two critics have by no means exhausted the possibility of inter-pretation. In yet another reading, a totally different view arises from yet another conception based on genre. The poet Huang Tingjian (1045–1105) recalls that his friend the great poet Su Shi told him that Li Shangyin's poem "has its source in *Gujin yuezhi* [The Record of Music, Past and Present], where it is said that the patterned lute is an instrument with fifty strings and the same number of frets. Its sound can evoke the feelings of comfort, sorrow, serenity, and harmony." According to Su Shi, then, the poem is rather straightforwardly about the musical instrument the poem explicitly describes in so many ways. Huang Tingjian adds that "the line about Zhuangzi in Li's poem indeed suggests comfort; that of Emperor Wang, sorrow; pearls shedding tears in the moonlit sea, seren-ity; and smoke rising from fine jade on the Blue Fields, harmony."[46] Such a reading takes the four lines in the middle of the poem as representing four different kinds of mood expressed in music, and figuratively four kinds of mood or emotion expressed in poetry. Therefore, when read liter-ally, the poem is about music, but metaphorically it speaks of poetry itself, since music and poetry are in any case never far from each other. Interestingly, such an interpretation seems to adumbrate what Jonathan Culler proposes as one of the conventions or expectations for making sense of "obscure or minimal poems," that is, "the rule that poems are significant if they can be read as reflections on or explorations of the problems of poetry itself."[47] In fact, this is also the point Qian Zhongshu makes in his reading of this famous but enigmatic poem. In an earlier edition of Li Shangyin's poetry, "The Patterned Lute" is put at the beginning of his collected works and may thus be understood as the poet's comment on his own writing, a kind of poetic preface to his works. Qian Zhongshu takes this point, which was noticed by an earlier critic, and further develops it. Strikingly modern and yet grounded in solid traditional scholarship, his interpretation merits to be quoted in full, but as it contains many references and allusions that presuppose a certain amount of specific knowledge of Chinese literature and criticism, I have omitted some lines and translated only the main argument:

> The poet can make "patterned lute" as well as "jade zither" into metaphors for poetry. Du Fu does this in his own first poem of the *Xi ge* [Western Tower] group: "The red seal tinsel resembles a recluse's satin cap; / New poems have the sound of a fine jade zither." The patterned lute and the jade zither are indeed comparable. . . . When the poet sees the fifty strings of the lute, he is made aware of his aging years, that he is near fifty. . . . The first two lines of Li's poem suggest that his prime years are gone but his works remain, that the energy and effort of a lifetime, all his joys and sorrows, are all presented here, in tunes either happy or sad, serene or harmonious. . . . Lines 3 and 4 speak of his method of making poetry. Whatever he has thought or felt is expressed in metaphors and images, as Zhuangzi's pleasure is seen in the flying butterfly, or Emperor Wang's remorse is embodied in the crying cuckoo: all are figuratively put but never said directly. Meaning is "entrusted" because it is manifest in things other than itself, and one is likely to be "puzzled" because the intention is hidden in metaphorical language. . . . Lines 5 and 6 speak of his poetic style or the world his poetry creates. . . . Instead of "pearls are tears," he says "pearls are shedding tears," suggesting that what have turned into pearls are still warm as tears, valuable as treasure but still quivering with human bitterness. . . . The same is true with the smoke from warm jade, which is not hard and cold as ordinary jade. This implies that even though his poems are highly refined, they have real life and genuine emotions, totally different from the kind of overwrought and lifeless poetry that fails not because it does not shine like pearls or jade, but because its tears are already dry and its smoke has vanished. Hofmannsthal describes Heine's poems as brighter and more enduring than pearls, but with light and moisture as living things (*unverweslicher als Perlen / Und leuchtender, zuweilen ein Gebild: / Das traget am lebendigen Leib, und nie / Verliert es*

seinen innern feuchten Glanz ["Zu Heinrich Heines Gedächtnis"]).
Isn't this pearls shedding tears?. . . . Lines 7 and 8 conclude the poem
in response to the first two lines. Looking back, the poet is filled with
sorrow; recalling the time of past pleasure, he has a strong sense of
the mutability of things and the passing of time, feeling sad that one
so easily wakes up from a beautiful dream, that every feast must have
an end. He realizes that whatever pleasure he once had, "even then,
it was already vague and lost."[48]

Qian Zhongshu's reading of the poem takes more details into consideration than any of the others quoted above, makes a most convincing argument, and therefore presents a most probable interpretation. Following
his argument and accepting the assumption that Li Shangyin's poem is
indeed about poetry itself, the last couplet — "This mood might have been
a thing to be remembered; / But even then, it was already vague and
lost" — seems to suggest that whatever the poet intends to preserve in his
work, whatever mood he wants to remember by enshrining it in a fixed
form, is already vague in its origin and even more so in verbal representation. If we may indeed take "The Patterned Lute" as Li Shangyin's poetic
preface to his own works, then it gives us a fairly good indication of the
kind of poetry we can expect of him: poetry that is highly personal, suggestive, atmospheric, full of associations and possibilities, guiding its readers to a world of intense beauty and pleasure, where every word, every
image, speaks of itself and at the same time of something else. If we try to
look for an equivalent or similar kind of poetry in the West, it would
probably be the kind advocated in symbolist poetics, the ideal poetry Paul
Verlaine hopes for and describes as "la chanson grise / Où l'Indécis au
Précis se joint [the tipsy song / where the Undefined and Exact combine]."[49]
With such poetic gems, Li Shangyin has secured his reputation of being
the most suggestive of all poets in the history of classical Chinese literature.

In reading Li Shangyin's "The Patterned Lute" as a poem about poems,
we turn all its difficulties in structure and imagery into characteristics
of the poetic language itself. That is to say, the very difficulties in interpretation become hermeneutically significant as enactments of the operation
of poetic language, the function of symbolic representation. Such a reading is especially engaging and persuasive in modern times, when problems of language and representation come to occupy an essential place in
our thinking about literature, but we must admit that the other, more
traditional interpretations mentioned above also have their persuasive

power insofar as they offer a coherent account of the whole poem and its
textual elements with regard to a different set of problems and concerns,
and insofar as their generic assumption can find endorsement in other
poems which, like Bai Juyi's "The Pipa Player's Song," speak as much of
the poet's life as of music and poetry. Of the various plausible interpretations, each reader may privilege one over the others, as we all have our
own judgment and preference, but it is often impossible to claim that one
interpretation has absolute validity while all others are invalid or simply
wrong. In the interpretation of poetry, it is often easier to discern the
weakness of a particular reading than to specify what constitutes the perfect interpretation. The appeal of a particular interpretation is to a large
extent a matter of individual taste and personal choice, partly shaped or
determined by social and aesthetic norms of the time, rather than a conclusion reached by following objective laws or based on factual evidence.
There are of course many ways to expose and exclude misunderstanding
and inadequate interpretations from the pool of plausible and acceptable
ones. For example, philologically incompetent understanding of words,
anachronistic interpretation of the context or content of a literary work,
the misapplication of one set of cultural values and criteria to a work
from a totally different cultural background—any of these may disqualify
a certain interpretation from being considered as plausible. The difficult
problem in hermeneutics, however, is not the exclusion of inadequate
interpretation but the establishment of validity in interpretation, and it is
indeed much easier to disprove an interpretation than to prove it as the
absolutely valid one. As the critical controversy on "The Patterned Lute"
shows, all interpretations work in a hermeneutic circle between the whole
and parts, between the generic assumption and explication of textual
details, and the circularity of the process casts doubt on any claim to
absolute interpretive validity. To appeal to the author's intention can hardly
solve the problem, for what the author intends is itself often the outcome
of interpretation and therefore not uncontaminated by the circularity of
argument. As Dilthey observes, the hermeneutic circle not only inhabits
the relationship between the whole of a work and the individual words
but is "reduplicated in the relationship between the individual work itself
and the spiritual tendencies of its creator, and it returns again in the relationship between the work and its literary genre." Even the philological
circle alone is already sufficient to undermine any claim to absolute validity, since no interpretation can prove its objectivity outside the circle. "Theoretically," says Dilthey in acknowledgment of this central difficulty in all

hermeneutic practice, "we here reach the limits of all exegesis, which is able to realize its task only up to a certain point. For all understanding remains partial and can never be terminated. *Individuum est ineffabile.*"[50]

In addition to the difficulty of circularity on a purely philological level, the temporal factor further complicates the problem of validation. Not only does the semantic value of words gradually shift in time, but so do social and aesthetic norms which make the present interpretation of a text differ from the way it was interpreted in the past. For Schleiermacher, such temporal distance between past and present understanding constitutes the main reason that hermeneutics as a rigorous practice is necessary, for the less rigorous hermeneutic practice takes understanding for granted, assuming that "the speaker and hearer share a common language and a common way of formulating thoughts," but taking temporal distance into consideration, the more rigorous hermeneutics assumes that "the speaker and hearer differ in their use of language and in their ways of formulating thoughts, although to be sure there is an underlying unity between them."[51] Temporal distance between the moment of creation of a text and that of its reading, as Schleiermacher sees it, tends to give rise to misunderstanding, which the interpreter must try to eliminate by putting himself "both objectively and subjectively in the position of the author."[52] Schleiermacher argues that the circular movement of understanding runs from the whole of the text to the individual parts and from the parts back to the whole, until it leads to a moment when the text is perfectly understood and nothing therein remains strange or unintelligible. At that moment, the hermeneutic circle dissolves in perfect understanding as the interpreter has not only put himself in the position of the author but has also gained conscious knowledge of what the author created unconsciously, and therefore reaches a level of understanding higher than the author's.

In romantic hermeneutics, temporal distance and the circularity of understanding are all negatively conceived as factors to be eventually eliminated in a perfect understanding, but how to overcome the circularity of individual understanding to reach a universally true interpretation is a question that remains unanswered. As Gadamer observes, romantic historicism contradicts its own recognition of everyone's finitude and historical limitation by arguing for the possibility of achieving an infinite, perfect understanding. It is only in Heidegger's existential analysis of being as *Dasein*, being imbedded in its specific time and place, that the positive hermeneutic significance of temporal distance and our own historicity are fully recognized. Gadamer speaks emphatically of the changed perception of the value of temporal distance: "Time is no longer primarily a gulf to be bridged because it separates; it is actually the supportive ground of the course of events in which the present is rooted. . . . It is not a yawning abyss but is filled with the continuity of custom and tradition, in the light of which everything handed down presents itself to us."[53] With his emphasis on cultural tradition as the necessary ground for understanding, Gadamer rehabilitates the concept of "prejudice" in the Heideggerian sense of the fore-structure of understanding—that is, the linguistic and cultural knowledge with which the interpreter approaches a text, the horizon of expectations which allows that reader to listen to the language of the text and understand what the text has to say. In this new light, the hermeneutic circle is not seen as a vicious circle but as the description of an ontologically structural element in understanding; the circle does not disappear when the text is understood: it is not "dissolved in perfect understanding but, on the contrary, is most fully realized."[54]

The changed emphasis in hermeneutic theory has profound implications for practical criticism. The interpreter now no longer needs to eliminate his own historicity as a negative prejudice. Being fully conscious of both his own position and the claim of the text, he can now allow his prejudice—in the positive sense of the fore-structure of understanding—to be challenged, tested, and modified by the text in the reading process. With the realization that understanding is an infinite process of inquiry—a dialogue between the author, the text, and the reader in the constant exchange of questions and answers—the interpreter no longer needs to attempt to close the text with a definitive answer but can keep the critical dialogue open. "The essence of the *question*," as Gadamer remarks, "is to open up possibilities and keep them open."[55] If Schleiermacher claims that present understanding is superior to the original production on the grounds that conscious knowledge places the interpreter on a higher level than the author as unconscious genius, Gadamer now sees the better position of the interpreter mainly in the light of the positive significance of temporal distance, which makes understanding not merely a reproductive but always a productive attitude. Once it is realized that understanding is an infinite process and open to various possibilities, it is then no longer necessary to seek the definitive perfect interpretation, nor is it appropriate to think of the present understanding as superior either as more informed knowledge or as more conscious than an unconscious production. "It is enough to say," as Gadamer puts it straightforwardly, "that we understand in a *different* way, *if we understand at all*."[56] Gadamer has extensively discussed the hermeneutically positive value of the temporal distance between the present understanding and a text from the past. It remains the task of literary hermeneutics to look into the matter more concretely in terms of the production and the reception of a literary work, that is, the structuring of poetic imagery and its subsequent realizations.

Textual Schema and Indeterminacy

In his famous book *Mimesis*, which investigates the various ways of representing reality in Western literature from antiquity to the twentieth century, Erich Auerbach begins his discussion of this enormous subject with a stylistic comparison between the Homeric epics and biblical narrative, the two great fountainheads of Western literature and culture. According to Auerbach, every object, every episode in Homer is fully externalized, meticulously described to the last detail, and presented to the reader almost as fully realized as reality itself. In Homer's narrative, Auerbach observes, "a continuous rhythmic procession of phenomena passes by, and never is there a form left fragmentary or half-illuminated, never a lacuna, never a gap, never a glimpse of unplumbed depths," because "the Homeric style knows only a foreground, only a uniformly illuminated, uniformly objective present."[57] In sharp contrast to such a fully externalized style, the biblical text in the Old Testament appears to be extremely concise and austerely sketchy. It supplies the reader with only enough information to follow a minimal narrative, while leaving everything else in obscurity: "Time and place are undefined and call for interpretation; thoughts and feeling remain unexpressed, and only suggested by the silence and the fragmentary speeches; the whole, permeated with the most unrelieved suspense and directed toward a single goal (and to that extent far more of a unity), remains mysterious and 'fraught with background.'"[58] In Auerbach's view, the Homeric text seems self-evident and leaves no gap whatsoever for the interpreter to fill in, whereas the obscurity of the Old Testament gives rise, of necessity, to endless exegeses. In the light of our discussion of the nature of language with regard to the symbolic representation in poetry and the emphasis in traditional Chinese poetics on implicitness and suggestiveness, it is clear that the style of the Homeric epics is more akin to the discourse of artistic prose, as it indeed leads to the development of prose fiction in Western literature, while the biblical style has a much greater structural resemblance and rhetorical affinity to the language of poetry.

The very obscurity of biblical narrative, which has given rise to a great deal of commentary and interpretation and which may seem opaque and undesirable when measured with the yardstick of Homeric perspicuity, becomes a virtue rather than a defect in the eyes of St. Augustine, who sees it as the welcome veil over divine truth and relates it with the aesthetic pleasure in deciphering the meaning of a mystery. "Aesthetic pleasure derives, according to Augustine, from the very discovery of hidden meanings," observes Bernard Huppé; "the quality of the pleasure has a direct relation to the difficulty of the ambiguities to be resolved."[59] Indeed, Augustine admits that many things in the Old Testament are obscured by rhetorical tropes, but he argues that "the more these things seem to be obscured by figurative words, the sweeter they become when they are explained."[60] Such an argument for the value of stylistic obscurity may have been motivated by Augustine's religious feeling and his faith in the superiority of the Bible to pagan literature, but for him as for the medieval sensibility under his dominating influence, beauty and aesthetic pleasure are inseparable from the contemplation of a deeper meaning in all creation, and the greater the challenge to interpret things where interpretation seems difficult, the more satisfactory it is when ingenious connections are made which make sense in a symbolic interpretation. For the medieval mind, symbolic interpretation was the characteristic way of thinking. "The formation of symbols was artistic," as Umberto Eco remarks. "To decipher them was to experience them aesthetically. It was a type of aesthetic expression in which the Medievals took great pleasure in deciphering puzzles, in spotting the daring analogy, in feeling that they were involved in adventure and discovery."[61] In a way, the medieval mode of thinking was a mode of reading which converted the whole world into a big book to be deciphered, seeing it as a universal allegory and "perceiving the world as a divine work of art, of such a kind that everything in it possesses moral, allegorical, and anagogical meanings in addition to its literal meaning."[62] Not only was the Bible allegorically interpreted, but works of pagan literature were also read for deeper meanings. When texts of all kinds were thought to be symbols and allegories, textual obscurity that challenged the mind was inevitably privileged as the source of intellectual as well as aesthetic pleasure. Both the Bible and classical literature suggested to the medieval writer, says Huppé, "that the enigmatic, the difficult, the ambiguous, were part of the grand style of serious literature. The Christian understanding of the Bible and of pagan literature made almost inevitable the development of a theory that serious poetry should be allusive, enigmatic, periphrastic."[63]

In this connection, we may recall Mallarmé's claim that art, like religion, should envelop itself in mystery if it wants to retain its sacredness. Paul Valéry also observes that "what is clear and comprehensible and corresponds to an exact idea never produces an impression of the divine." "All that's 'noble,' lofty, and heroic," he declares, "is founded on obscurity."[64] Augustine's preference for stylistic obscurity has indeed many echoes not only in the Middle Ages but all along the tunnel of history.[65] In modern literature especially, textual difficulty and even obscurity become significant features partly as a reaction against the nineteenth-century tradition of realism and naturalism. In his pioneering work on the theory of the avant-garde, Renato Poggioli sees the deliberate obscurity in much of modern poetry as a gesture of antagonism to social and aesthetic norms as well as a device to achieve a new effect in language. Obscurity is the poet's "necessary reaction to the flat, opaque, and prosaic nature of our public speech, where the practical end of quantitative communication spoils the quality of expressive means."[66] This idea of obscurity or stylistic difficulty as a device to call attention to the means of expression itself obviously resembles the critical notion of poetic language, or the poetic function of language, as developed by the Russian formalists; indeed, Poggioli himself has pointed out that there were close ties binding Russian formalism and the avant-garde movement together.[67] From Victor Shklovsky's concept of "defamiliarization," the idea that "art is to make objects 'unfamiliar,' to make forms difficult, to increase the difficulty and length of perception," to Jan Mukařovský's concept of "deautomatization," the notion of poetic language as "foregrounding" of the utterance, "the intentional violation of the norm of the standard"—modern literary theory tends to define the function of poetic language as distinct from that of daily speech and to identify the ambiguous, the difficult, and the enigmatic as characteristic of poetic language.[68] Shklovsky's concept of "defamiliarization," as Jurij Striedter observes, "already contained hints pointing further," that is, to the Czech structuralist notion of the work of art as "a sign in an aesthetic function," thus marking the first phase of the evolutionary series from Russian formalism to Czech structuralism.[69] Surely it is not just the modern avant-garde poets who defamiliarize the representation of objects and events; the Russian formalists themselves often use literary works of earlier times to illustrate the point of their theory, which they do not believe should be understood as merely a theoretical legitimation of modern avant-garde literature. For Shklovsky, defamiliarization may be seen as the determinant factor not only for the birth of a new work or a new genre but also for the rise of a new literary movement. Writing in opposition to the hackneyed poetic diction of neoclassicism, the romantic poets already advocated the idea of poetic language as new and unfamiliar. Wordsworth warns those readers who have been "accustomed to the gaudiness and inane phraseology of many modern writers" that they will, should they read his poetry with the usual kind of expectations, "no doubt, frequently have to struggle with feelings of strangeness and awkwardness."[70] The principal object in writing his poems, he continues, is to adopt in poetry the "language really used by men" and to add a certain coloring of imagination, "whereby ordinary things should be presented to the mind in an unusual way."[71] Shelley makes a similar point that remarkably anticipates the concept of defamiliarization. Poetry, Shelley remarks, "awakens and enlarges the mind itself by rendering it the receptacle of a thousand unapprehended combinations of thought. Poetry lifts the veil from the hidden beauty of the world, and makes familiar objects be as if they were not familiar."[72] The poets themselves, however, never fully explored the theoretical implications of this concept of defamiliarization in the same manner as the Russian formalists did later. More important, as Striedter argues, "it was not sufficient to point up general defamiliarizing devices and to erect a theory of literature on them. What also had to be shown was why, under different conditions, the same devices achieve different effects." And that is of course the direction the Czech structuralists took in extending the formalist concept of defamiliarization "to the identification of these devices as factors of construction, and thereby to the description of concrete work structures as the organization of elements and devices in specific functions."[73]

The defamiliarized text—that is, a text of which the form is made difficult and somewhat obscure—forces the reader to attend to the linguistic signs themselves and perceive things represented in language with a new and awakened sensibility. It is not only in poetry but also in prose fiction that modern literature privileges such stylistic difficulty. Roland Barthes' distinction, in his book *S/Z*, between the "readerly" and the "writerly" texts—that is, the classical and the avant-garde—is a well-known example of theorizing on this modern tendency. The text he favors, the kind of text that gives readers an intense, orgasmic pleasure or bliss (*jouissance*), is the more difficult type of text, "the untenable text, the impossible text."[74] It is the type of text that leaves a lot of things unexplained and unexpressed, or to borrow Auerbach's phrase, a text that is "fraught with background." Barthes speaks of the aesthetics of reading figuratively in terms of an erotics of reading, which is for him the only possible way to speak of the unspeakable experience of bliss. "Is not the most erotic portion of a body *where the garment gapes?*" he asks; "it is intermittence, as psychoanalysis has so rightly stated, which is erotic: the intermittence of skin flashing between two articles of clothing . . . it is this flash itself which seduces, or rather: the staging of an appearance-as-disappearance."[75] The idea of erotic seduction is used here to convey the idea of textual suggestiveness. The phrase Barthes chooses to characterize textuality, "appearance-as-disappearance," is truly felicitous because language at once conceals and reveals, with endless joy and pleasure promised in the gaps and between the lines, forever beckoning to the reader and appealing to his or her sensibility and imagination. Such seductive intermittence exists not just in avant-garde texts but in all texts, and interestingly it is a very "readerly" classical text, Balzac's *Sarrasine*, that Barthes selects to be the object for his semiotic analysis in *S/Z*.

Is then the ultimate classical text, the text of Homer's epics written in a fully externalized style, totally without gaps or intermittence, and altogether resistent to interpretation? "Homer can be analyzed, but he cannot be interpreted," Auerbach claims assuredly. "Later allegorizing trends have tried their arts of interpretation upon him, but to no avail. He resists any such treatment; the interpretations are forced and foreign, they do not crystallize into a unified doctrine."[76] No matter how we want to characterize the allegorical interpretations of Homer, the fact that Homer was read for moral and spiritual meanings by the Greek allegorists testifies that the Homeric text is by no means closed to interpretation. Despite Homer's fully externalized style, allegoresis, or the mode of interpretation that finds deeper meanings where such meanings are not obvious, first arose precisely in the reading of Homer. It was then transferred to the reading of the Old Testament and gradually became the basis of all textual interpretation in the Middle Ages.[77] Of course, the validity of allegorical interpretation can be questioned, but the possibility of interpretation itself is beyond question. Let us recall Roman Ingarden's notion of the literary work as a multilayered schematic structure. According to Ingarden, insofar as they attempt to represent objects or events in language, all literary texts are stratified or schematic, with an indefinite number of spots of indeterminacy which are subsequently concretized in the reading process. In this sense, Homer's epics are also schematic, and no matter how uniformly illuminated they may be, they are neither destitute of spots of indeterminacy nor of what Barthes calls seductive intermittence. For example, Helen, the most beautiful woman in all classical literature, is hardly portrayed in Homer's *Iliad* in any detail. In book 3, when "white-armed Helen" goes to the wall of Troy to see the duel between Menelaus and Paris, Homer does not pause to give a detailed description of Helen as he does later in book 18 of the magnificent shield Hephaestus made for Achilles. The great beauty of Helen is not "seen" by the reader but "overheard" in the reactions of the Trojan elders. "Who on earth," the Trojans ask one another in a low voice when they see Helen coming to the tower, "could blame the Trojan and Achaean men-at-arms for suffering so long for such a woman's sake?"[78] Not a single word in the Homeric text describes her face or figure, her clothing or ornament, but a strong sense of Helen's immortal beauty is conveyed to the reader by the awed whispers of the Trojan elders. We may even say that it is precisely this lack of description, this "appearance-as-disappearance," or this blank, that has made Helen what she is, for properly framed in elaborate descriptions of war and suggestive whispering admiration, Helen's beauty, which is the cause of all these, remains in the background and, once concretized and made alive in the reader's imagination, becomes infinitely more vivid and more impressive than any verbal description could have been.

From this we may see that both textual types discussed by Auerbach, the Homeric and the biblical, the illuminated and the obscure, are inevitably schematic in structure. Even with the fully externalized and uniformly illuminated Homeric text, the complete realization of the fictional world that the poet has constructed in the narrative still requires the reader's active participation. Moreover, it is always possible to interpret the text in terms of its spiritual or metaphysical meanings beyond the literal sense and therefore to find what is absent from the text no less significant in interpretation, if not more, than what is literally there. With the biblical type of text, which has a higher degree of stylistic difficulty and uncertainty, the possibility of interpretation indeed increases remarkably on every level. In fact, structural schema is a feature of textuality shared by all works of literature, and that may account for the rich possibilities of meaning and interpretation. As we have seen, the beauty of Helen in Homer's text is suggested but not explicitly described; it owes much to the reader's imagination and emerges, as it were, from the gaps or blanks in the Homeric text. In his discussion of aesthetic experience as anticipatory imagination, Hans Robert Jauss mentions "the *amor de lonh*, the 'love from afar' which inspires Jaufre Rudel to become the poet of that purest longing which finds its fulfillment in nonfulfillment," and Don Quixote whose "love for Dulcinea remains perfect because he never finds her," as examples of the function of imaginative creation of things not given in the text.[79] By not fulfilling the reader's usual expectations, the text remains open and powerfully alluring, offering an opportunity for the reader to bring his or her imagination into full play.

In an ancient Chinese song, "The Mulberry Trees on the Road," we can find the use of a rhetorical device similar to the one of Homer's that we have just discussed above, a device which indirectly conveys to the reader a sense of the beauty of Luofu of Qin, the young lady the poem praises. Again, the most effective lines of this poem speak of her beauty without describing her features. The poetic eye turns, as it were, to those around her and scans their reactions:

> When the passers-by see her, they put down
> carrying-poles and stroke their beards.
> The young man sees her,
> and takes off his hat.
> The ploughman forgets his plough;
> the spadesman forgets his spade.
> Returning home marital strife ensues,
> all for a glimpse at Luofu the fair.[80]

Unlike the Trojan war, the "marital strife" in this poem is not a protracted ten-year struggle, but its origin, like that of the Trojan war, is likewise the beauty of a woman, which is nonetheless not fully described in the text. Perhaps with the awareness that great beauty can never be satisfactorily portrayed in words, the Chinese poet chooses to reveal the beauty of Luofu indirectly, not through other people's eyes but through the actions that reflect what other people see in their eyes. This doubly distancing reflection seems to put the object of seeing in the distance, but by the same token, it serves to activate the reader's imagination to visualize what is only suggested by the text. The use of such a device is of course not limited to speaking of superior beauty but serves to evoke whatever is inexpressible and to say whatever is unsayable. Thus, we may appreciate the tacit but powerfully suggestive expression of sorrow in a short lyric (*ci*) by the Chinese poet Xin Qiji (1140–1207), whose use of the same suggestive device is meant to achieve a very different purpose:

In my youth I didn't know
What sorrow tastes like.
Climbing up high,
Up the towers high,
To make lovely new lyrics,
I spoke of sorrow and dismay.

In old age too well I know
What sorrow tastes like.
Whenever I'd talk,
I'd rather not talk;
"What a nice cool day"
Is all I can say.[81]

For the young man who does not yet know sorrow, melancholy is nothing more than a rhetorical game, a gesture or mannerism, a mere convention with no substance. But when he is old and weathered in adversity, when he has drunk sorrow to the lees, he loses all interest in rhetorical maneuver and does not speak of sorrow, of which the depth of his knowledge can be measured only by the degree of his reticence and silence. Now the poet has learned, as Wordsworth says of his own adulthood experience, "To look on nature, not as in the hour / Of thoughtless youth; but hearing oftentimes / The still, sad music of humanity."[82] For Xin Qiji, "the still, sad music of humanity" and the knowledge of such music are all beyond language, and the way he points to that inexpressible experience is an indirect speech, a seemingly irrelevant comment that speaks of something contrary to sorrow—the comfort of the cool autumn weather. In this poem, articulated sorrow is only artificial sentimentality, and the knowledge of the taste of sorrow, acquired through long and embittered life experience, is not talked about but kept in knowing silence. Perhaps this may remind us once again of Laozi's paradox of the mutual exclusion of knowing and speaking, but by saying that he no longer talks about sorrow, the poet puts the pregnant moment of silence in a frame of evocative language. This framing of silence is of vital importance in poetry, because it is only against this verbal frame as presence that the silent and the absent become charged with meaning. We can appreciate the significance of what Barthes calls "appearance-as-disappearance" as the textual strategy of framing silence in language. In Xin Qiji's lyric poem, as in the works of Rilke, Mallarmé, Tao Qian, and others, what is absent from the text is called into being by the act of naming and evocation, but once evoked, it becomes a more effective way of expression than explicit speech. In this respect, the famous lines of Keats' "Ode on a Grecian Urn"—"Heard melodies are sweet, but those unheard / Are sweeter"—may be said to articulate a similar poetic principle.[83] In the Chinese poem, what is said in the text invites the reader to imagine what is unsaid, and the old man's seemingly irrelevant understatement—"What a nice cool day"—impresses us as a powerful expression of his sense of bitterness and resignation.

The appreciation of suggestiveness and the sense of its superiority to explicit speech inform much of Chinese poetry and poetics. This is evident in the Chinese emphasis on *hanxu* or fruitful implicitness—the idea that the meaning of a poem should extend beyond the text, aiming for the maximum effect in the minimum of words. The extreme thrift of words is essential to Chinese poems, which are usually short and concise, and great Chinese poets are always masters of verbal economy. The works of Wang Wei (701–61), like those of Tao Qian, are acclaimed especially for effect of this kind. He can build up a certain mood or atmosphere in a few words, while pointing to many things outside the text, which the reader must bring into the picture. For example, homesickness is a topic almost every Chinese poet writes about, but Wang Wei's treatment of this subject stands out from all others because of its typical understatement, its subdued voice that speaks of some small, familiar things which, once remembered, symbolize and personalize the abstract idea of home. The poem below, the second in a group of three poems entitled "Za shi" [Miscellaneous Poems], is quite exemplary:

> Coming from my home village, sir,
> You must know things over there.
> The day you left, by that window,
> Did the plum tree begin to flower?[84]

Here, the speaker in the poem meets with someone from his home village, and out of a million "things over there" he wants to know, he chooses only to ask about the plum tree by a certain window. All the rest is not mentioned, and yet, through this seemingly odd choice, he unfolds his tender feelings and fond memories which are always bound to something personal and concrete—like this old plum tree at home that blossoms in very cold days in early spring—something simple yet important that reminds him perhaps of someone special, of a particular moment or event in his life. Such small objects related to one's past are intimately personal and would not mean as much to an outsider as they do to the poet. In reading this poem, however, the reader is initiated, as it were, into the world of the speaker's personal memories and emotions, and allowed to share with him the private significance of the plum tree by that particular window. It is this initiation and the intimacy the reader feels that make the poem so lovely and charming. Thus the tree and the window acquire a private meaning which the reader shares as an insider, convinced that there is something special about them. But what exactly is that private meaning? Why does the speaker in this poem choose to ask about that plum tree? What memories does it summon up? All these questions, though certainly relevant to the poem and its reading, are not even raised in the text; it is the reader who raises these questions and finds an answer, and the way the questions are raised and answered largely depends on the reader's imagination. In this sense, the meaning of the poem is as much the reader's private meaning as the poet's, for different readers will raise different questions about the poem's context and give different answers, and the tree and window will become symbols of home for each reader in a unique manner. Although each character in each line follows exactly the right sound pattern as demanded by the metrical rules, this poem as a whole is written in a casual tone, a conversational kind of language, thus adding to the effect of closeness and intimacy. With the last line posed as a question, it issues an irresistible invitation to interpretation. Indeed, the special effect of this poem depends very much on its ability to imply questions that require an answer.

The poet, however, does not have to include a question to invite the reader's participation and answer. He may simply leave out the answer to a question the poem raises or supposedly replies to. This is what we find in another Wang Wei poem, "Chou Zhang shaofu [A Reply to Assistant Magistrate Zhang]":

> In old age I value only tranquility;
> Nothing concerns my heart any more.
> For myself I have no suitable plan,
> Except for retreating to the woods I know.
> The wind in the pines blows to loosen my girdle,
> The mountain moon shines as I pluck my lute.
> You ask about the reason for life's ups and downs:
> The fisherman's song echoes back from the shore.[85]

From the title we know that the poem is written as a reply to a friend's inquiry about the philosophy of life, but the poet never really gives an explicit answer in the text. Or we may say that the poetic text does provide an answer, but it does so by enactment, not by argument—that is, by showing what the poet will do in facing life's ups and downs. He has grown old enough to know the best way to cope with life's many frustrations and disappointments in tranquility, allowing nothing to disturb his quiet life back in the woods. The "fisherman's song" in the last line alludes to an ancient work called "Yu fu" or "The Fisherman," in which the poet Qu Yuan (fourth century B.C.) meets an old fisherman on the edge of a river at a miserable moment of his life, having suffered calumny at the hands of some mean courtiers, lost favor with his king, and just been banished from the court. The fisherman tells him that a wise man should not abide by the world's conditions, that he should just let the muddy current run its course. Being a man of principle and loyalty, Qu Yuan declares that he would rather drown himself in the river than have his integrity tainted by the muddy world, but "the fisherman smiled and paddled away, singing a song as he went:

> When the waters in the Canglang are clear,
> They can wash my hat's tassel;
> When the waters in the Canglang are muddy,
> They can wash my feet.

Then he was gone and spoke no more."[86] This is of course a fable with a moral, and the fisherman is a thinly disguised philosopher of the Taoist persuasion who feels quite indifferent to the ups and downs in political life, the constantly changing news from the court: who loses and who wins, who's in, who's out. Not only does Wang Wei adopt such an attitude for himself, but he also gives it to his friends who come to him for advice.[87] By referring to the fisherman's song, the last line of his poem is a non sequitur to the question his friend asks, but it does imply a subtle answer which his friend, and by extension every reader, will have to find not only in the text but also elsewhere, outside the text. The meaning of Wang Wei's poem, as Chinese critics all agree, extends beyond the boundaries of the text.[88]

Many critics have praised Wang Wei for his skillful use of implicitness, and the idea of having meaning outgrow the limits of the text is formulated as a principle in Chinese poetics. For example, an important stylistic and structural device in writing poetry, known as *xing*, which critics find difficult to define and whose exact meaning they often debate, can nevertheless be broadly understood as a strategy for speaking of two things in terms of indirect associations rather than direct comparison. Zhong Rong's definition of *xing* as the device for expressing "a surplus of meaning where words have come to an end" is not only one of the earliest but also one of the most pertinent.[89] He does not single out this device as the most important one, but the idea of meaning as reaching out beyond the text becomes a critical commonplace in later development of Chinese poetics, since it is incorporated into a whole line of poetic theory from Sikong Tu (837–908) to Yan Yu (1195?–1245?) and Wang Shizhen (1634–1711).

Sikong Tu's *Twenty-four Moods of Poetry* is put in verse, thus exemplifying the common practice in the Chinese literary tradition of writing poetry to comment on poetry. This seems to reveal a certain attitude toward language, the author's belief that the different kinds of poetic mood or style can best be shown by examples rather than explained in discursive language. Although there are twenty-four poems, each suggesting a different mood or poetic effect, the notion of poetry as the use of symbolic language constitutes the core of Sikong Tu's brilliant reflections. For example, the image of a gentle breeze brushing against one's clothes, something that appears to have a shape but disappears as soon as one holds it in hand, is used to symbolize the idea of "lightness" (*chongdan*) as a stylistic feature or mood of poetry. "Naturalness" (*ziran*) is exemplified in something picked up at hand and not borrowed from neighbors, something not studied but created without effort, like the budding of flowers in early spring. Images expressing "tragic pathos" (*beikai*) include a strong wind tossing up waves and crushing forest trees, a warrior holding his sword in sorrow, dead leaves whirling down from the twigs, and raindrops falling on green moss.[90] The highly suggestive and ambiguous language makes the meaning or meanings of these poems highly elusive, but that in itself demonstrates precisely the kind of meaning or mood the poems try to convey and accords with the schematic, elliptical nature of poetry, which allows many different interpretations. Of Sikong Tu's twenty-four poetic dicta, the most influential is the one on "implicitness" (*hanxu*):

> Without putting down a single word,
> reap all the spirit and charm.
> Without speaking of one's self,

it already bears too much sorrow.
It has the True Master,
with him to sink or float.
Like wine overflowing the press,
or flowers at the breath of autumn.
Like dust dancing in the void,
like foam sparkling over the sea.
Shallow or deep, amassed or apart,
All things be taken in the one.[91]

The elusive and suggestive imagery in this poem admirably illustrates the mood or effect of implicitness, which is its subject, and in this sense the poem becomes a perfect enactment of the principal idea its text purports to convey. The True Master in line 5 alludes to a phrase in the *Zhuangzi*: "As though they have a True Master, but there is no trace of him."[92] The untraceable Master and the other images all point to the same idea, that of achieving the poetic effect with as few words as possible, each word a trace of something absent but of great magnitude and significance. Poetry, according to Sikong Tu, should mean more than what its actual text says, reaping all spirit and charm without "putting down" a single word. As he told his friends, the taste of poetry is "beyond the salty and the sour," allowing the reader to have "a sense beyond the taste," "an image beyond the image," "a scene beyond the scene."[93] In a word, the meaning and the beauty of poetry reside not so much in what is said as in what is implied by keeping silent. As a later critic Liu Xizai (1813–81) remarks: "All the wonder of regulated verse lies in places where there are no words. The turns and connections between two lines are all crucial spots of the poem."[94] Sikong Tu's poem on implicitness, especially the first two lines, may be said to have given the poetics of silence a most radical expression. This silence, however, is not empty but framed in language. "To keep silent does not mean to be dumb," as Heidegger argues. "Keeping silent authentically is possible only in genuine discoursing. To be able to keep silent, Dasein must have something to say—that is, it must have at its disposal an authentic and rich disclosedness of itself."[95] Considering Sikong Tu's poetic theory in the light of this Heideggerian notion of silence, Qian Zhongshu points out that Sikong Tu's phrase "without putting down" should be understood as "without putting down more" or "without putting down again," and that the moment of silence, like the idea of *blanc* in Mallarmé and Claudel or the blank space in Chinese landscape painting, is always framed in words, in lines and colors.[96] It is important to realize the close relationship between silence and its verbal frame; in fact, suggestiveness is nothing but the framing of silence, the use of words around a center of absence which contains the possibilities of meaning and interpretation.

The credit for making the theory of poetic suggestiveness most systematic and influential in the Chinese tradition should go to the twelfth-century critic Yan Yu, whose *Canglang's Remarks on Poetry* is famous for introducing the Buddhist term of Chan (Zen) into the critical discourse on poetry, though he was not the first to do so. The point of convergence between Chan and poetry, according to Yan Yu, is *miaowu* or "miraculous enlightenment," which is a moment of epiphany when one suddenly has an insight into the nature of things. Like a monk trying to grasp the meaning of Chan through meditation, one must also meditate on the best works of earlier poets and commune with the great poets before one can come to the sudden revelation of the secret of poetic art.[97] This sudden enlightenment or revelation, Yan Yu argues, does not come from the mere accumulation of knowledge but from a long and intuitive process of meditation on ancient works. "Poetry," says Yan Yu in one of the most controversial passages of his work, "requires a different kind of talent, which has nothing to do with books; poetry requires a different kind of interest, which has nothing to do with reasoning. And yet one cannot attain to its highest point unless one reads extensively and reasons exhaustively. The superior kind is that which neither involves reasoning nor falls into the trap of words." The ideal kind of poetry, he goes on to say, should be "like music in the air, color in the features, the moon in water, an image in the mirror, with meaning reaching out to infinitude when words have come to an end."[98] In differentiating poetry from bookish knowledge and rational thinking, Yan Yu is trying to grasp the essence of what makes poetry poetic, a problem with which modern Western literary theory is also much concerned. It is noteworthy that all the images and analogies Yan Yu uses to speak of poetry are intangible and inaccessible things which have traces in the text but are themselves absent from it. His concept of poetry reminds us of Sikong Tu's poetic dictum on implicitness, and his emphasis on the surplus of meaning echoes Zhong Rong's definition of *xing* as a device to generate indirect associations beyond textual boundaries. But Yan Yu is not alone in advocating the kind of poetry that does not "fall into the trap of words," with meaning "reaching out to infinitude when words have come to an end." Before him, another important poet Mei Shengyu

(1002–60), for example, already advocated a similar kind of poetry, arguing that a poet may be said to have achieved the consummation of art when he is able "to describe a scene that is extremely difficult to describe in such a way that it appears as though right in front of one's eyes, and to contain endless meaning that is perceived beyond words."[99] Yan Yu's contemporary, Jiang Kui (1155?–1221), a fine poet and musician who called himself the White-Stone Taoist, also holds that "language is valuable for its implicitness" and quotes Su Shi as saying that "the word that has an end but an endless meaning is the supreme word."[100] In some of his poems, Su Shi, like many other poets of his time, makes analogies between poetry and Chan or Buddhist ideas, as when he writes to his friend Shenliao, a Buddhist monk who also loves to write poetry:

> If you wish for subtle words in verse,
> strive tirelessly for the void and quietude;
> for the quiet comprehends all motions,
> and the void admits of ten thousand worlds.[101]

Void and quietude are all common Buddhist concepts, but used in critical discourse, they are largely secularized, and in adopting these terms, Su Shi is not just paying homage to his cenobite friend but borrowing the language of Chan to express his own ideas on the art of poetry. Like blank, nothingness, and silence, void and quietude are important to poetry because they contain, in their very emptiness and stillness, the possibility for imagination and enrichment, the great possibility of poetry. The way Chinese poets use Chan Buddhist concepts is not without equivalent or analogous cases in the West. A case in point is the way medieval aesthetic experience "tacitly adopted the Paulinian formula for the use of God's grace, 'tamquam nihil habentes, et omnia possidentes' (as having nothing, and yet possessing all things, II Corinthians 6, 10)," an attitude that can be seen, as Jauss observes, in troubadour poets' glorification of the beauty of the inaccessible beloved.[102] The same principle may be said to underlie Homer's indirect sketch of Helen, Xin Qiji's reticence about sorrow, and indeed all poetic efforts that try to evoke the inexpressible by framing the unexpressed in language.

There are numerous other statements of similar ideas throughout the history of Chinese criticism, but I shall quote just one more example from the sixteenth-century poet and dramatist Tang Xianzu (1550–1616) who, like Yan Yu and others, conceives of poetry as comparable not only with the Buddhist notion of Chan but also with the Taoist notion of *tao*. Both poetry and the religious-mystic notions, says Tang Xianzu, share the quality of mystery or obscurity: "All consider as beautiful that which appears to exist and to fade away at the same time."[103] The analogy between poetry and the mystic notion of Chan or *tao*, the intangible music or mirror image as metaphors for poetry, the concept of meaning as lurking in the blank space of poetic discourse to be generated in the reading process and reaching beyond the boundaries of the text—all these are quite common in classical Chinese poetics. They may illuminate and be illuminated by many similar ideas in Western criticism when we put them together side by side, and their mutual illumination may throw some light on both traditions, leading to a broad view that literary texts, in the tradition of Chinese poetry as well as in that of the West, are structurally open and indeterminate, invariably calling for the reader's active participation in fulfilling their potential for meaning and aesthetic enjoyment. Traditional criticism has largely ignored the function of the reader, but modern criticism acknowledges that the concretization of the schematic text has always depended on the reader's creative understanding and participation.

The Role of the Reader

In his investigation of the history of aesthetic experience, Jauss outlines the gradual transformation of what he terms *poiesis*—that is, the productive side of aesthetic experience—from its classical sense of the imitation of a model of perfection to its modern sense of creation which itself brings the perfect into being. The meaning of poiesis underwent a further and more radical change with the advent at the turn of the century of avant-garde art, which broke away from classical aesthetic concepts and values, abandoning the perfect form and the idea of beauty as the aesthetic object for disinterested, contemplative admiration. Jauss sees Paul Valéry's aesthetic theory as a clear illustration of this drastic change of the meaning of poiesis. "Beauty is a sort of corpse," thus Valéry describes the changed definition of this important concept for the modern times. "It has been supplanted by novelty, intensity, strangeness, all the *shock values*. Raw excitement is the sovereign mistress of recent minds, and works of art are at present designed to tear us away from the contemplative state, the *motionless delight*, an image of which was at one time intimately connected with the general notion of the Beautiful."[104] A direct consequence of this radical change is the convergence of poiesis with *aesthesis*, the combination of the productive and the receptive sides of aesthetic experience. Now avant-garde art, Jauss maintains, finds itself on a new course:

> And it frees aesthetic reception from its contemplative passivity by making the viewer share in the constitution of the aesthetic object: poiesis now means a process whereby the recipient becomes a participant creator of the work. This is also the simple meaning of [Valéry's] provocative, hermeneutically unjustifiably controversial phrase: *"mes vers ont le sens qu'on leur prête"* (my poetry has the meaning one gives it).[105]

The modern work of art becomes, in Valéry's term, an *objet ambigu*, which has as its essence such an indefinable nature that its status as a work of art becomes problematic. With a front wheel of a bicycle mounted on a stool, Marcel Duchamp's *Bicycle Wheel*, for example, challenges not just traditional definitions of art and beauty but the very distinction between art and extra-artistic reality. It frustrates our conventional expectations so violently that as a work of art it poses a serious problem to the very concept and name of art and brings about a crisis of its own identity. When confronted with such an ambiguous object, the viewer, Jauss observes, "must ask himself and is called upon to decide whether this can *still* or *also* claim to be art."[106] Therefore, it is not so much the intrinsic nature or value of the work as the viewer's decision that establishes the ambiguous object as a work of art: "The paradoxical identity of work and reality," Jauss observes, "places the actual poietic effort on the viewer."[107] This is happening not just in the realm of visual arts but in literature as well, for the blurring of the boundary between literature and extraliterary reality is also a strong and notable tendency in modern literature. A William Carlos Williams poem, for example, deliberately obscures the boundary between poetic and ordinary discourse by taking the form of a simple note of apology, a note perhaps left on a kitchen table: "This is just to say I have eaten the plums which were in the icebox and which you were probably saving for breakfast. Forgive me, they were delicious: so sweet and so cold." As Jonathan Culler remarks in *Structural Poetics*, when this note is set down on the page with line break, wide margin, and all the typographic paraphernalia of poetic form, it is no longer a note but demands to be read as a poem, that is, "the convention of significance comes into play."[108] In taking the note as a poem, the reader accordingly suspends its referential function as a piece of everyday language and subjects it to a set of expectations usually related to fictive discourse, assuming that it signifies something different from, and probably deeper than, what it literally says. In this case, then, the note, like Duchamp's bicycle wheel, contains an essential ambiguity with regard to its own status as literature, and it is not so much the verbal artifice itself as the reader's attitude that establishes the poem as a poem. Besides formal patterns and linguistic deviation of verse, the most important factor that contributes to the production of "the true structure or state of poetry," Culler maintains, "is that of conventional expectation, of the type of attention which poetry receives by virtue of its status within the institution of literature."[109] Commenting on several poems to illustrate his point, Culler specifies the expectations of impersonality, totality, and significance as the most important conventions in reading poetry. Once a text is read as a poem, the reader assumes that it is not addressing a particular person in a real situation but is an instance of fictive discourse that has a total structure or coherent frame within which all the elements are correlated and become intelligible. The structuralists, especially those influenced by French theories, work mostly on narrative fiction rather than poetry, but Culler's argument for a "poetics of the lyric" and a "phenomenology of reading" constitutes perhaps the most original chapter of his book and can be seen as a significant contribution to the study of poetry from the perspective of structuralism.

Having commented on the Williams poem, Culler claims that the operations of conventional expectations are not restricted to the reading of modern poetry. This simple point needs to be emphasized even more strongly because much of modern poetry, with its radical disruption of classical norms and conventions, seems so completely alienated from tradition that any critical theory dealing with its avant-gardism may appear to be limited in scope and inapplicable to other types of writing. Jauss, for example, views the traditional and the modern as though radically incommensurate in his critique of the "provocative overextension of the poietic role of the reader."[110] Such an overextension, Jauss argues, gives rise to a tendency in modern literature—ranging from Baudelaire and Flaubert to Robbe-Grillet and Samuel Beckett—to move gradually away from the classical aesthetics of representation toward the modern aesthetics of perception; at the same time such an overextension also leads to a tendency in theoretical formulations from Valéry to Shklovsky and Bertolt Brecht which "too one-sidedly emphasized the innovative achievement of techniques of alienation as the highest aesthetic value."[111] Jauss is evidently revising his own earlier theoretical position, which gives much emphasis to the role of the reader (which the alienating avant-garde text increasingly solicits), and much of his critique of contemporary avant-garde literature and theory is quite to the point. Nevertheless, it would seem at least an exaggeration to say that tradition and the avant-garde, or representation and perception, are positioned at the opposite ends of a rigid dichotomy, and it would seem rather useless to blame the "overextension" of the reader's role in modern times for the collapse of "the cognitive and communicative efficacy of aesthesis."[112]

In confronting the challenge of modern avant-garde works, we may very well seek to expand our own horizon of expectations rather than limit our aesthetic experience to either the traditional or the avant-garde. Gadamer's effort to reappropriate contemporary avant-garde art to the changed paradigms of understanding becomes particularly meaningful in this respect. As we have seen earlier, in *The Relevance of the Beautiful and Other Essays*, one of Gadamer's recurring themes is a unifying *"eidos* or perspective from which we can describe and interpret contemporary art."[113] Instead of seeing the challenge of an ambiguous object as the "identity crisis" of contemporary art, Gadamer defines the work of art—any work of art—in terms of its "hermeneutic identity" which alone, he insists, constitutes the meaning of a work. "What gives the work its identity as work? What makes this what we call a hermeneutic identity?" In answering these questions, Gadamer expounds a concept that already contains the different aspects of Jauss' aesthetic experience in the very status or identity of the work: "Obviously, this further formulation means that its identity consists precisely in there being something to 'understand,' that it asks to be understood in what it 'says' or 'intends.' The work issues a challenge which expects to be met. It requires an answer—an answer that can only be given by someone who accepted the challenge. And that answer must be his own, and given actively."[114] In other words, the reader's poietic role, his effort to interpret the meaning of the work, has always been constitutive of the very identity of the work. Using the example of different readers' different perceptions of a staircase that Dostoevsky sketches in *The Brothers Karamazov*, Gadamer demonstrates how Ingarden's notion of concretization works in the reading process; and he maintains that it works not only in literature but also in visual arts, not only in traditional arts but in avant-garde arts as well. It is not just Picasso, Braque, and the other avant-garde artists who challenge the viewer to assume the responsibility of definition, but Titian or Velazquez also require the viewer to "read" a painting till he or she sees the whole picture as resonant with meaning and understands what the picture says in its specific language. Thus "there is always some reflective and intellectual accomplishment involved," says Gadamer, "whether I am concerned with the traditional forms of art handed down to us or whether I am challenged by modern forms of art. The challenge of the work brings the constructive accomplishment of the intellect into play."[115] Jauss' differentiation of aesthetic experience into poiesis, aesthesis, and catharsis is certainly helpful in clarifying the three different aspects of our experience of art, these being the productive, receptive, and communicative efficacies respectively; for the comprehension of the aesthetic experience as a whole, however, we must reassemble these three categories, restore them to their ontological oneness, and seek to understand aesthetic experience in its totality or, to borrow Gadamer's term, its "aesthetic non-differentiation."[116] That is to say, the reader's poietic role in establishing the meaning of a work has always been part of the very concept of the work, and this concept applies to traditional as well as to avant-garde arts and literature. The status or identity of a work, as Gadamer argues, has always been hermeneutic, and this is so because the presence of meaning and the need for interpretation are already part of what we recognize as a work of art.

In the light of the hermeneutic identity of a work of art, we may appreciate what T. S. Eliot says about the music of poetry. The question here is again a question of musicality and meaning, sound and sense, and for Eliot they do not seem to form an incompatible pair. In his discussion of the music of poetry, Eliot puts much emphasis on the meaning of language, and that, he assures us, is not a contradiction, because "the music of poetry is not something which exists apart from the meaning. Otherwise, we could have poetry of great musical beauty which made no sense, and I have never come across such poetry." Even Edward Lear's deliberately nonsensical verse is not without sense, because such nonsense "is not vacuity of sense: it is a parody of sense, and that is the sense of it."[117] Language is the social institution of meaning, of which each word is recognized as a linguistic sign because it has already been assigned a meaning defined according to the rules of a particular linguistic community. Insofar as a poem is written in words, it is necessarily meaningful. On the other hand, meaning in poetry is not detached from the actual language that brings the meaning into being. In seeing the nature of the work of art as symbolic, Gadamer emphasizes the ontological status of the work of art, that it is not a shell or container to be discarded once its meaning or signified is extracted. This is where the language of art and the language of philosophy differ from one another, because the language of art, unlike that of theoretical discourse, cannot be adequately translated into any form other than its own, and "the essence of the symbolic," says Gadamer, "lies precisely in the fact that it is not related to an ultimate meaning that could be recuperated in intellectual terms."[118] From this we can come to the conclusion that a work of art is not just meaningful, calling upon the viewer or the reader to interpret what it means, but its meaning is never definitively interpreted, never exhausted by translating the language of art into a discursive paraphrase. Again as Eliot observes, "only a part of the meaning can be conveyed by paraphrase, that is because the poet is occupied with frontiers of consciousness beyond which words fail, though meanings still exist."[119] If we understand "frontiers of consciousness" as the boundaries of thinking or intellect, what Eliot says here is then quite close to Gadamer's notion of the symbolic. The meaning of what is said in a work of art, Gadamer notes, "always transcends what is expressed by what is said," and therefore in art there is always an "excess of meaning."[120]

These ideas and formulations cannot fail to remind us of many similar pronouncements with which Chinese critics express their understanding of the important features of poetry. We may recall, for example, Sikong Tu's idea of poetry as conveying a "sense beyond the taste," "an image beyond the image," "a scene beyond the scene," or Yan Yu's remark that the meaning of poetry is "reaching out to infinitude when words have come to an end." The words in a poem are put down by the author, but the meaning that extends beyond the text cannot be controlled by him. Put in this context, then, the poet's desire to find his *zhiyin* or "the one who knows the sound," which is so often articulated in Chinese poetry, can be understood as the poet's acknowledgment of the role the reader plays in bringing the meaning of the poem to its completion beyond the text. Du Fu has written these famous lines:

> Literary writing is a matter of lasting importance,
> Its gain and loss are known to the inch of heart.[121]

Du Fu probably meant to say that the value and subtle meaning of a poem is known only in the poet's own heart, but isn't it reasonable to assume that he really longed to be known in the reader's heart? After all, the desire for understanding can be found expressed in the works of poets in many different literatures and cultures. When Milton undertakes to sing of creation and the loss of Paradise, he hopes to "fit audience find, though few."[122] In such statements, there is evidently a sense of difficulty as well as the desire for understanding. Perhaps we may say that poets themselves have already realized that their works are incomplete unless they are properly understood by readers at the other far end of a communicative process. That is to say, they already have the sense that the identity of their work is necessarily hermeneutic. Thus the poet's desire for *zhiyin* or "fit audience" already inscribes the reader in the poetic structure, and it is only by gratifying that desire in concretization that a reader becomes the one whom the poet addresses.

The "excess of meaning" suggests that not only is the meaning of a literary work uncontrolled by its author, not only does it overflow the boundary of the text, but also the production of meaning partly results from the reader's contribution. T. S. Eliot, who is often thought to be a precursor of New Criticism, certainly did not confine himself to the text as isolated from both the author and the reader. On the contrary, he has a very clear sense of the role of the reader when he observes that a poem "may appear to mean very different things to different readers, and all of these meanings may be different from what the author thought he meant." Not only that, but the reader's interpretation, Eliot continues, "may differ from the author's and be equally valid — it may even be better." The emphasis on the reader's poietic function would not strike Eliot as unusual, for he believed that "there may be much more in a poem than the author was aware of. The different interpretations may all be partial formulations of one thing; the ambiguities may be due to the fact that the poem means more, not less, than ordinary speech can communicate."[123] In the light of such conscious acknowledgment of the reader's role, Valéry's critical views, especially the radical statement that his poems have whatever meaning one attributes to them, can perhaps be understood more sympathetically. That statement may indeed sound relativist and irresponsible or, as Jauss puts it, "hermeneutically unjustifiably controversial," but it may also reveal Valéry's remarkable insight into the hermeneutic identity of poetry. "It is an error contrary to the nature of poetry, and one which may even be fatal to it," Valéry maintains, "to claim that for each poem there is a corresponding true meaning, unique and conformable to, or identical with, some thought of the author's."[124] Perhaps Valéry is not a systematic theorist with a complete set of aesthetic principles, but with the experience and sensibility of a poet, he is definitely conscious of the incompleteness of the work of art and fully aware of the rich possibilities of meaning that can be realized only in the reader's mind.

It is Roman Ingarden who first systematically formulates the theory of reading as concretization, which is further developed by the Czech structuralists, notably Jan Mukařovský and Felix Vodička. Ingarden conceives of the literary work as a schematic structure with infinite spots of indeterminacy, but he insists that the structure is also at least partially objectively determined and that the reader, in filling out the spots of indeterminacy and rendering the schematic structure concretized, may often do it in a way not warranted by the text, "not in agreement with the positively determined objective moments." As a result, Ingarden insists that the literary work must be "distinguished from its respective concretizations, and not everything that is valid for the concretization of the work is equally valid for the work itself."[125] He believes that each work of literature has one correct interpretation and that even though its meaning may be obscured for centuries by falsifying concretizations, a literary work may finally find its ideal reader who "sees it adequately, and who in one way or another shows its true form to others."[126]

It is for this last point—the belief in an ideal concretization—that the Czech structuralists take issue with Ingarden. Vodička contends that "Ingarden presupposes an ideal concretization that would fully realize *all* the esthetic qualities of the work. To this, one can object that esthetic value does not have absolute validity. It is always closely related to the development of the esthetic norm, either coinciding with it or deviating from it."[127] As Jurij Striedter points out, in their semiotic understanding of the work of art as a sign composed of various signs on different levels, the Czech structuralists do not exclude any textual stratum from temporal change; on the contrary, they assume "the historic contingency of every structuring of the work as an aesthetic object on all its levels."[128] To be fair to Ingarden, however, one must admit that if he entertains the notion of an ideal concretization at all, he entertains it only briefly and knows it as an "ideal." This may be seen clearly in his remark that:

> the literary work is never *fully* grasped in *all* its strata and components but always only partially, always, so to speak, in only a *perspectival foreshortening*. These "foreshortenings" may change constantly, not only from work to work but also in one and the same work; in fact, they can be conditioned and required by the structure of the given work and its individual parts. On the whole, however, they are not so much dependent on the work itself as on the given conditions of the reading.[129]

Ingarden here obviously recognizes the historical conditions of the reader as the main reason that the same work can be concretized differently at different times. His desire for an ideal concretization, if not taken literally, could thus be seen as a desire for the appropriate balance between the subjective element of reading and the objectively determined structure of the work itself.

In traditional Chinese criticism, the incompleteness of all finite understanding is also one of the important issues often discussed, albeit briefly, by poets and critics. Ouyang Xiu (1007–72), one of the most important literary figures of his time, provides a revealing example in the form of an interesting anecdote from his personal reminiscence:

> When Mei Shengyu wrote poems, he took me as the only one who knew his sound, and I also said to myself that no one in this world could know Mei's poems better than I did. And yet when I once asked him to list his own best works, all the lines he recited for me were not those I liked. From this I know that what one appreciates in a scroll may not conform to the author's original intention.[130]

If contemporaries and close friends like Ouyang and Mei, both great poets of the same period of time, could not reach the same point in terms of intentionality and aesthetic evaluation, how can anyone across the enormous gap of time and space talk about reconstructing original intention or the horizon of original expectations with any assurance? The difference in understanding because of the change in historical condition is readily accepted in Chinese criticism, and Ouyang Xiu testifies that this hermeneutic difference exists even among contemporaries, not to mention people of different times and different places. Anecdotes like this could serve as a reminder of the tentativeness of reception theory that tries to recuperate historical understanding of a literary work and to create a vision of literary history on the basis of reconstructed horizons of expectations. What the Chinese critic emphasizes is the limitation of knowledge and perspective of each individual, the inexplicable vagaries of personal taste, and the changeability of sense and sensibility.

A famous phrase in the appendix to the *Book of Changes* that marks out the limitation of each finite apprehension of *tao*—"The benevolent sees it and calls it benevolence; the wise sees it and calls it wisdom"—may be said to have established the philosophical foundation for the Chinese sense of hermeneutic difference.[131] With the authority of the canonized ancient classic from which it comes, this phrase often becomes an endorsement of critical opinions that attempt to relativize the power of the predominant ideology in the Chinese tradition and to argue for the legitimacy of alternative views. A most delightful example of the subversive use of this phrase is Jin Shengtan's (1610?–1661) ingenious paraphrase of it in his defense of *Xixiang ji* [The West Chamber Romance], a famous play and love story which was accused of being obscene by moralistic critics when it first appeared in the early seventeenth century. In his defense of this play as a literary work, Jin Shengtan developed a radical theory of reading, taking this work as one of the greatest books ever written, equal to the best of ancient classics. "*The West Chamber* is most definitely not an obscene book, but a wonderful work of literature," he argues in a passionate contention. "The literary sees it and calls it literature; the obscene sees it and calls it obscenity."[132] No competent reader in China would miss Jin Shengtan's reference, and the phrase alluded to from the *Book of Changes* powerfully turned the accusation of obscenity around to those who made that accusation. Jin Shengtan maintains that the play is a wonderful work because it contains every human emotion and every possibility of interpretation, and it contains all of these by virtue of just a single word—*wu* or "nothingness." Because of this "nothingness," which obviously carries the implication of the Chan Buddhist concept of void, the work speaks for everyone and belongs to everyone. According to Jin Shengtan, his commentary also contains "nothingness" and belongs to whoever reads it. In his formulation of the process of reading, it is the commentator and the reader who create the text: "The text of *The West Chamber* on which Shengtan comments is Shengtan's text, not that of *The West Chamber*. And *The West Chamber* with Shengtan's commentaries which all the talented men on earth read is the text of all the talented men, not Shengtan's text."[133] Such a radical theory of reading definitely puts the reader at the very center of creation, whereas the literary text is admired for offering the space for the reader's creativity. By paraphrasing the same line from the *Book of Changes*, another critic Xue Xue also tries to justify the different perspectives that have given rise to so many different interpretations of Du Fu's poetry. "The martialists read it as the art of war," he observes, "the Taoists read it as *tao*; and those who govern the state read it as politics. None of these readings is invalid."[134] Statements like this, which are rather common in traditional Chinese criticism, indicate how Chinese poets and critics share a remarkable sense of the hermeneutic identity of the literary work, and how they all realize the inevitable plurality of meaning and interpretation.

In the Western critical tradition, the reader's role in concretizing and actually shaping the text always poses a problem of relativism or subjectivism, or is at least often perceived as posing such a problem. By holding onto the "positively determined objective moments" in the schematic text, which is otherwise rather indeterminate, Ingarden shows this concern and tries to free his theory from the charge of subjectivism. Wolfgang Iser, who adopts Ingarden's view as the starting point for his own theory of aesthetic response, also maintains that "however individual may be the meaning realized in each case, the act of composing it will always have intersubjectively verifiable characteristics."[135] Iser, in other words, remains committed to the objectively defined givens of textual schema, which serve to mark out the boundaries of legitimate individual readings from invalid misreadings. It is precisely on this point that Stanley Fish takes issue with him in an interesting critical debate. Fish argues that the very distinction Iser makes between textual givens and the reader's contribution is itself an assumption, that everything in Iser's account of the reading process — "the determinacies or textual segments, the indeterminacies or gaps, and the adventures of the reader's 'wandering viewpoint'—will be the product of an interpretive strategy that demands them, and therefore no one of those components can constitute the independent given which serves to ground the interpretive process."[136] Fish does not, however, just remove intersubjectively verifiable characteristics from the text and make the reader the sole creator of formal features of the text, he also proposes the concept of "interpretive community" as a sort of safeguard against the danger of subjectivism. In his theory, all textual features are made by the reader's interpretive strategies, but what seems to be "the rankest subjectivism," Fish argues, "is qualified almost immediately when the reader is identified not as a free agent, making literature in any old way, but as a member of a community whose assumptions about literature determine the kind of attention he pays and thus the kind of literature 'he' 'makes.'" The last word, therefore, does not belong to the reader but to the interpretive community which makes "a collective decision as to what will count as literature, a decision that will be in force only so long as a community of readers or believers continues to abide by it."[137] The idea of interpretive community presumably helps disengage the critic from the burden of the subject-object dichotomy because, Fish notes, the problem no longer exists once we realize that the meanings a reader confers onto the text "will not be objective because they will always have been the product of a point of view rather than having been simply 'read off'; and they will not be subjective because that point of view will always be social or institutional."[138] In this respect, Fish's view is to some extent similar to that of the Czech structuralists.[139] Rejecting Ingarden's concept of textual schema as independent of various concretizations, Mukařovský and Vodička regard not only the concretization but also the aesthetic object itself as always changing and changeable, yet they also avoid the charge of subjectivism by positing collective social relations as the condition binding on all individual concretizations. For Mukařovský, recognition of the reader's role does not lead to subjectivism, since the aesthetic object is placed in "the collective consciousness," which puts individual aesthetic experience into a collective social context. With regard to individual evaluation and the aesthetic object, as Striedter notes, "Mukařovský emphasizes the dependence of the individual reader (as well as the individual author) on norms and values shared by social collectives."[140]

The collective, social, institutional interpretive community does indeed offer a competent explanation for both the agreement and disagreement in interpretation; it works as a necessary constraint, at least theoretically, in reader-response criticism and absolves the critic from the charge of subjectivism. In American reader-response criticism, especially in the model of interpretation that Fish proposes, the author and the text fade out; everything is determined by the reader, but everything the reader does is in turn determined by the norms and assumptions of the interpretive community. In calling our attention to the social and institutional background of each individual's understanding, the notion of the interpretive community is extremely helpful. In a peculiar way, however, this later development in Fish's theory may remind us of the interpretive model he proposes in his earlier work, *Surprised by Sin*; there Fish argues that the experience of reading *Paradise Lost* is a reenactment of the fall of man, because the reader is likely to be led astray by Satan's specious rhetoric but will soon be rectified by Milton's epic voice or by the text itself. The reading experience is therefore also a process of the reader's education, a process of learning God's—and Milton's—teaching.[141] Now the readers in an interpretive community, like the prelapsarian Adam and Eve in the Garden of Eden, are free to make whatever choice their interpretive strategies allow them to make, but they are free only to the extent that they are created or determined so by the interpretive community as the highest, final authority —which, like God, holds the true and only omniscience. The sinister side of this analogy is that God, of course, also holds the power to expel Adam and Eve from paradise when He decides that they have made a wrong choice. If this analogy is not unreasonable, the problem of the concept of interpretive community should also become alarmingly obvious, for the individual will soon find that he or she does not really have much of a choice, since whatever individual choice is made is already predetermined by a higher power in the name of collectivity. Whoever does not accept God's foreknowledge and His predetermination of every human act will have the same doubt about the tenability of the concept of interpretive community, and whoever believes in the individual's right to make free choices will find this concept teeming with dangerous political implications. Steven Mailloux, for example, finds Fish's idea of the interpretive community analogous to the nightmarish totalitarian society of Oceania that George Orwell describes in *1984*, namely, a collective community under a tight ideological control by the Party. He compares Fish with O'Brien, the Party's spokesman: "In the same way that O'Brien claims that the Party's collective mind creates reality," says Mailloux, "Fish argues that interpretive communities create what they claim merely to be discovering or describing."[142] In addition to the compelling issue of ideological control or what has been called the politics of interpretation, there are two theoretical questions that are not yet satisfactorily solved by positing the presence of an interpretive community. First, simply transferring the decisive power from the individual to the communal agency does not clarify the nature of interpretation, and second, neither the individual reader nor the interpretive community can simply decide what counts as literature at random, because there must be a reason for both individual and communal decisions, and that reason cannot be the reason if it is not independent of the decision. There is also the problem of change in socially defined aesthetic norms and hermeneutic horizons, which cannot be adequately explained internally without taking into consideration those challenges that come from outside the community and its collective mind. If the New Critics and the formalists are often blamed for taking the literary text as a self-contained autonomous entity in isolation from its social and historical milieu, it would be equally questionable for the reader-oriented critic to assume that the reader or the interpretive community can be a self-contained autonomous entity. If the reader is to respond at all, there must be something prior to and outside his or her interpretive conventions and strategies, something to which the reader can respond and of which the community is engaged in the act of interpreting. Fish's polemical essays are collected in a book provocatively entitled *Is There a Text in This Class?* For him, the question is rhetorical, and the answer is given in his many essays. For literary hermeneutics in general, however, that question, like all truly hermeneutic questions, still remains open and asks to be further explored.

Epilogue: Toward Interpretive Pluralism

Literature is valuable for its richness
and variety. Why should all comments
and appreciations be unified as if
coming out of one mouth?
—Ge Hong, *Baopuzi*

The person who understands must not
reject the possibility of changing or
even abandoning his already prepared
viewpoints and positions. In the act
of understanding a struggle occurs
which results in mutual change and
enrichment.
—Mikhail Bakhtin, "Notes (1970–1971)"

This book has argued for the recognition of the shared, the common, and the same in the literary and critical traditions of the East and the West beyond their cultural and historical differences, and yet what is recognized as the same is the presence of difference in all understanding and interpretation, the hermeneutic difference in aesthetic experience and literary criticism. The realization that meaning is always changing, that it is not determined once and for all by the author who permanently inscribes it in the text but is contingent upon the reader in a personal confrontation with the literary work, inevitably leads to the acknowledgment of the plurality of meaning and interpretation and to an appreciation of the principles of interpretive pluralism. In other words, the search for the same in this intercultural study has arrived at the sameness by way of difference, for it has come to emphasize the presence of hermeneutic difference and the necessity of opening up one's mind to different views and different positions. In contemporary Western literary theory, difference is certainly very much emphasized, but this very emphasis on difference, as Steven Conner argues, often ironically turns Western postmodernist theory into a totalizing discourse of consensus, a discourse that "closes off the very world of cultural difference and plurality which it allegedly brings to visibility," because this emphasis on difference tends to preclude the possibility of the same and thus results in a total "consensus in postmodernist discourse that there is no longer any possibility of consensus, the authoritative announcements of the disappearance of final authority and the promotion and recirculation of a total and comprehensive narrative of a cultural condition in which totality is no longer thinkable."[1] In contemporary literary theory, this totalizing tendency often manifests itself as attachment to one particular concept, term, or critical method as the exclusively valid or correct one; and it manifests itself first and foremost in the claim that the recognition of difference is of the highest value in criticism. Each of the various "schools" of critical theory obstinately insists on the value of one view, one opinion, one approach, or one way—its own way—of reading the literary text. For Wimsatt and Beardsley, the text is the only thing that matters; considerations of the author and the reader are all irrelevant fallacies. For E. D. Hirsch, every interpretation must conform to the authorial intention as the only objective criterion for its validity. For Stanley Fish, the reader or the interpretive community is the sole arbitrator of meaning, while "the objectivity of the text is an illusion."[2] In recognizing the indeterminacy of meaning and the importance of cultural, ethnic, gender, or other differences, modern critics are often rather determinate about their own interpretation. But why do we have to choose just one of the many different factors and approaches that contribute to the production of meaning and the understanding of a literary work? Why must the birth of the reader be at the cost of the death of the author? Why is the value of literary criticism said to lie in promoting a single view or method at the cost of a more balanced and sensible view of the hermeneutic process? Of course, we do not have to make such a limiting choice. We do not have to eliminate the text and its formal features to recognize the role of the reader, nor do we have to conceive of the reader as locked up in a prison of communal, collective thinking. Indeed, nothing needs to be excluded from contributing to the understanding of literature: the author, the text, and the reader all have their claims and specific ways of affecting the formation of meaning, and a deeper understanding of literature results from the synthesis of all these claims, a tentative agreement or balance of such competing forces, a moment of learning and cultivation in the fusion of horizons.

Contrary to the totalizing discourse in much of contemporary theory and criticism, literary hermeneutics as we have understood it has as its inevitable consequence the advocacy of interpretive pluralism, the emphasis on the importance of an open-ended and truly reciprocal dialogue as the paradigm of communication. Of course, there are different kinds of pluralism; the very form or formulation of pluralism is in itself pluralistic. An essay by Richard McKeon articulates one view of interpretive or critical pluralism. Taking his example from the different readings of Aristotle in the history of the interpretation of Aristotle's works, McKeon acknowledges that some interpretations are sound and suggestive whereas others are less sound and less suggestive but that the important task is not so much to identify the true interpretation as to be open to the plurality of interpretations, "to read interpretations of Aristotle which depart from one's own in the expectation that they may bring to attention insights into neglected facts, or thoughts that might be borrowed, or that they might suggest methods and principles that go beyond either interpretation or either critical method. Critical pluralism opens the way to a continuing history of interpretation which will enrich our understanding of works which have undetermined and indefinite potentialities of meanings and values in successive readings."[3] In pursuit of fruitful and suggestive interpretations, critical pluralism thus requires the willingness to engage other views and interpretations and to let one's own prepared viewpoints be challenged, tested, and modified by the Other. Interpretive pluralism thus formulated is surely not without its discontents, and one complaint against it is the skeptic's view that pluralism is too naively idealistic, that in reality "we are all dogmatists in one way or another," and that, worse still, pluralism may serve as "a strategy of 'repressive toleration.'"[4] Pluralism can be insincere, says another critic; it may claim "to encourage multiplicity while in fact championing the opposite."[5] Still another complains from an antipluralist point of view that pluralism is "a polemic for inclusion coupled with a programmatic commitment to exclusions," and specifically the exclusion of Marxism.[6]

The doubt of the practicality or sincerity of critical pluralism, however, does not in itself discredit its principle, nor does it invalidate the open orientation of literary hermeneutics. As for the charge of exclusion, one may answer that exclusion is not inherently an attribute of interpretive pluralism; rather, interpretation becomes pluralistic at the very moment when it engages opposing views and positions. Gadamer speaks of "a potentiality for being other [*Andersseins*]" in the experience of a true dialogue, the necessity "to expose oneself and to risk oneself."[7] Dialogue or conversation characterizes the hermeneutic process of coming to an understanding, and it involves the willingness to accept the challenges of the Other: "Thus it belongs to every true conversation that each person opens himself to the other, truly accepts his point of view as valid and transposes himself into the other to such an extent that he understands not the particular individual but what he says."[8] In reading a literary work, therefore, it is important to be aware of interpretations or critical views that are different from one's own. This means that one does not commit oneself to a particular interpretation or a particular approach to the work of literature but critically examines the very interpretation and approach that seem to make sense in one's reading. We can begin by examining the critical views that are generally accepted or predominant in contemporary literary theory and criticism.

The reader, for example, gets much attention and emphasis that he richly deserves in contemporary critical theory, but there is a related tendency to see the text as of less and less importance. In this connection, it is helpful to remember that the text as the object of aesthetic experience and interpretation offers the space for the fusion of horizons. It has its own voice and claim that must enter into the hermeneutic process and become the ground on which the reader builds up his or her individual concretization. "Literary art can be understood," as Gadamer argues, "only from the ontology of the work of art, and not from the aesthetic experiences that occur in the course of the reading." This is, however, not simply going back to the ontological text as advocated in New Criticism, for Gadamer goes on to say: "But this has a further consequence. The concept of literature is not unrelated to the reader. Literature does not exist as the dead remnant of an alienated being, left over for a later time as simultaneous with its experiential reality. Literature is a function of being intellectually preserved and handed down, and therefore brings its hidden history into every age."[9] In reading Gadamer's work, one often feels that a tension seems to exist between his emphasis on the interpreter's historicity and his effort to ground interpretation in the ontology of the work of art. Gadamer has most eloquently argued for the excess of meaning, the "inexhaustibility" of interpretation, and the positive value of "prejudice," understood as each individual's fore-structure of understanding, but at the same time he firmly rejects what he calls "an untenable hermeneutic nihilism"—namely, the view that there is no criterion of an appropriate reaction, that one understanding is just as legitimate as any other.[10] Such a tension, however, is not so much a critical self-contradiction in theory as a sign of a healthy fluidity of thinking, determined by the essential open-ended orientation of the hermeneutic process itself. In literary hermeneutics, therefore, the plurality of meaning and interpretation are well balanced by the ontology of the work of art, its specific mode of existence; and the emphasis of one element does not exclude the contribution of the other or others.

The author of a literary work, though largely neglected in contemporary theory, remains an important factor in understanding and interpretation. Annabel Patterson shows convincingly how the discredit of the authorial intention in New Criticism comes as a result of "an emergent new discipline, the academic and professionalized study of English Literature,"

in which the evaluative function and the interpretive authority are transferred from the author to the critic.[11] The authorial intention then falls
further into "a new and potent form of disesteem, as a result of the convergence of a number of disparate attacks on the related ideas of human
subjectivity, of selfhood, of the individual as a locus of subjectivity or an
(even partially) free agent capable of having intentions, and hence on the
very idea of authorship."[12] The disintegration of the self into different
psychic functions in Freudian psychoanalysis, the critique of the individual as a product of bourgeois false consciousness in classical and especially structuralist Marxism, and finally the promotion of an impersonal
and anonymous discourse in Foucault and Derrida, Patterson argues, have
all contributed not so much to the solution of the problem of intention as
to the denial or elimination of this problem. However, the problem of
intention keeps coming back to haunt even the most anti-intentionalist
and antihermeneutic readings of literature. For example, says Patterson,
"by deconstructing Proust's text de Man was only, by his own admission,
'trying to come closer to being as rigorous a reader as the author had to
be in order to write the sentence in the first place.'"[13] To put the disesteem
of the authorial intention in historical perspective is then to understand
the complexity of the problem and to avoid a simplistic elimination of
intention. "It is undeniable," as Patterson remarks, "that literary critics
and theorists do not publish their essays anonymously, and that their own
intentions are part of the complex structure of professional practice that
contributes to the meaning of the positions they take."[14] It certainly takes
an author to make the authoritative announcement of the death of the
author, and in thinking critically about literature and literary theory, we
must bear in mind not just the problematic nature of the author's intention but the critic's or the theorist's intention as well. From the perspective of interpretive pluralism, then, the author and his intention need not
be ignored in order to arrive at an appropriately creative understanding.
Understanding is always a teleological process toward the resolution of
textual difficulties and inconsistencies, the falling in place of the disparate
textual elements that otherwise seem to cancel one another out and block
the formation of meaning. The resolution of such hermeneutic problems,
however, is never final and fixed, but only temporarily allows us to construct a coherent frame of reference within which the meaning of the
work emerges. The validity in interpretation is therefore not absolute but
temporary and contingent, and the best interpretation is the one that
accounts for the most elements in the process of reading, offers the most

coherent explanation of the text, and simply makes the best sense of the literary work as a whole.

In the Chinese tradition, differing means of understanding and interpretation appear to have been more readily acknowledged than in the West and accepted with greater tolerance; relativism does not seem to be the bugbear that every critic holds in absolute abhorrence. Despite their moralistic tendency and intentionalist hermeneutics, even the Confucian scholars recognize the arbitrary nature of language and readily acknowledge the basic plurality of meaning. Their very effort to "rectify names [*zhengming*]," that is, to fix the correspondence between the sign and the object it signifies, already testifies to their awareness of the radical dissonance of verbal expression. They also advocate a suggestive style and economy of expression. As Mencius puts it: "Words that speak of things near at hand but with far-reaching import are good words."[15] *The Book of Changes*, which the Confucians adopted as one of the canonical classics, is praised for its conciseness, as it "names the small but implies the great; its import is far-reaching, its style is elegant, and its words are indirect but right to the point."[16] If the nature of language is recognized as inherently metaphorical, its way of expression indirect and symbolic, and its meaning always exceeding the boundaries of the text, it is then only logical to infer that interpretation must be varied and flexible. Dong Zhongshu (176–104 B.C.), who was instrumental in establishing Confucianism as the predominant orthodoxy in early imperial China, declared that "[*The Book of*] *Poetry* has no direct interpretation."[17] He made that claim at a time when Confucian scholars were trying hard to reinterpret ancient writings to achieve a synthesis of ancient thoughts in the framework of Confucianism, which in itself constitutes a fascinating episode in the history of Chinese hermeneutic thinking. What Dong Zhongshu meant by that phrase was no more than a denial of the more straightforward, literal interpretation of *The Book of Poetry*, and he thereby justifies and sets up the ground for allegorical interpretation of ancient verse in terms of Confucian ethical and political philosophy.

Nevertheless, once it is admitted that poetic language is not to be taken literally, a door is opened to various divergent interpretations. The famous pronouncement in *The Book of Changes* that the benevolent and the wise will have different visions of the *tao* already serves to legitimize hermeneutic differences, and critics always refer to it as authorization of their different interpretations. By the same token, Dong Zhongshu's phrase can also be used to justify an interpretive plurality in reading poetry, though

originally Dong was speaking of a specific work, *The Book of Poetry*.
This is apparently how Shen Deqian (1673–1769) understands Dong's
phrase when he argues that readers of poetry should just immerse themselves in reading and not seek "a forced uniformity" in understanding
and making an aesthetic judgment. Moreover, he goes on to say, "the
words of the ancients contain an infinitude of meaning, which is then
experienced by posterity in various ways as according to their different
dispositions, shallow or deep, high or low. . . . This is what Master Dong
meant when he said that poetry has no direct interpretation."[18] The infinite
possibility of meaning is finitely and temporarily realized by each reader
in his or her own way; thus the reading of poetry may yield many interpretations that cannot be leveled into one by imposing a forced uniformity. In the works of Wang Fuzhi (1619–92), the role of the reader and
the plurality of interpretation are even more clearly acknowledged. By
citing different readings of some ancient verses as interpretive models, he
virtually argues for the legitimacy of hermeneutic difference and emphasizes the importance of emotion and aesthetic pleasure. "Readers find in
the author's one single intent whatever is in keeping with their own dispositions," says Wang. "There is no limit to the possible permutations of
human emotion, but each reader can find in poetry what suits his own
emotion; and that is precisely why poetry is so valuable."[19] The idea underlying all such critical opinions in the Chinese tradition is an open-minded
acceptance of different readings so long as they come from real enjoyment, as a result of the pleasure of the text. Speaking of reading and
understanding in a tone reminiscent of Tao Qian's Mr. Five Willows, the
critic Xie Zhen (1495–1575) declares boldly: "Of poems some can be
understood, some cannot, and some need not be. They are like the moon
in water or flowers in a mirror; so don't trace every line too doggedly."[20]
This statement does not of course mean to abandon critical discrimina-
tion or responsibility, but it does express the spirit of tolerance and enjoyment, the spirit of interpretive pluralism, which accepts and even celebrates the divergence of meaning as a matter of course. What is implied in
this statement is not only the realization that nothing should be excluded
from understanding and interpretation, that the reader should be free to
choose whatever is available to him or her, but more radically that the
reader should also be free *not* to choose but to declare his enjoyment
without thorough understanding.

In agreement with this pluralistic spirit of the pleasure of reading, it
should be noted that the emphasis on silence and the blank as the source

of textuality, which forms the centerpiece of the argument in this book, should also be taken as one approach among many to the study of hermeneutic problems in the reading of literature, and that the kinds of texts discussed in this book are by no means the only kinds that merit extensive critical inquiry. If the hermeneutic phenomenon is an ontological given rather than a purely theoretical issue, then hermeneutics, which promises to bring what is experienced to the level of conscious understanding and thereby enlarge and enrich the potential of aesthetic experience, ultimately teaches nothing that is not already experienced in life; and all that is discussed here, following the advice of Mauthner and Wittgenstein, can be discarded like the ladder after its proper use. Gadamer's notorious suspicion of any systematic approach or method can also be understood in this connection. The point is that we should not feel constrained by any theoretical concept or approach but should take all relevant factors into consideration in the reading and enjoyment of literature. Both the reading of literature for enjoyment and the scholarship of literary studies are essentially personal pursuits, which should not be constrained to one fixed perspective or one methodology. Perhaps this may sound incredibly syncretic or represent a typically Chinese eclectic attitude, but by virtue of its very open-mindedness and common sense, and in the context of many debated issues about author, text, and reader in contemporary Western literary theory, this eclecticism may open a new vista on the critical scene and promise some new insights into the nature of literary hermeneutics.

Notes

Preface

1 Hans-Georg Gadamer, *Truth and Method*, 2d rev. ed., English translation revised by Joel Weinsheimer and Donald G. Marshall (New York: Crossroad, 1991), p. 259.

2 Hans Robert Jauss, "Literature and Hermeneutics," trans. Timothy Bahti, in *What Is Criticism?* ed. Paul Hernadi (Bloomington: Indiana University Press, 1981), p. 137; and Jauss, *Toward an Aesthetic of Reception*, trans. T. Bahti (Minneapolis: University of Minnesota Press, 1982), p. 28.

3 James J. Y. Liu's posthumously published book, *Language-Paradox-Poetics: A Chinese Perspective*, ed. Richard John Lynn (Princeton: Princeton University Press, 1988), is an admirable pioneering work that attempts to highlight the hermeneutic significance of poetic language in the Chinese tradition. Despite the author's wish to mark the "possible points of convergence" between Chinese and Western literary theories, however, the book as a whole seems to fall short of its aspiration to offer an insightful study of hermeneutics from the perspective of comparative poetics. For a discussion of both the strengths and weaknesses this book contains, see my review in *Chinese Literature: Essays, Articles, Reviews* 10 (July 1988): 190–94.

4 René Wellek, "The Crisis of Comparative Literature," in *Concepts of Criticism*, ed. Stephen Nichols (New Haven: Yale University Press, 1963), p. 283.

5 Hans-Georg Gadamer, "The Relevance of the Beautiful," in *The Relevance of the Beautiful and Other Essays*, ed. Robert Bernasconi, trans. Nicholas Walker (Cambridge: Cambridge University Press, 1966), p. 12.

6 Martin Heidegger, ". . . Poetically Man Dwells . . . ," in *Poetry, Language, Thought*, trans. Albert Hofstadter (New York: Harper & Row, 1975), p. 218.

7 Ibid., pp. 218–19.

8 Jean-François Lyotard, *The Postmodern Condition: A Report on Knowledge*, trans. Geoff Bennington and Brian Massumi (Minneapolis: University of Minnesota Press, 1984), p. 82.

9 Michel Foucault, *The Order of Things: An Archaeology of the Human Sciences* (New York: Vintage, 1973), p. xv.

10 Steven Conner, *Postmodernist Culture: An Introduction to Theories of the Contemporary* (Oxford: Basil Blackwell, 1989), p. 9.

11 See Zhang Longxi, "The Myth of the Other: China in the Eyes of the West," *Critical Inquiry* 15 (Autumn 1988): 108–31.

12 Conner, *Postmodernist Culture*, p. 9.

13 The title, literally "Pipe-Awl Chapters," alludes to a phrase in the *Zhuangzi*, "to peep at the sky through a pipe and to point at the earth with an awl," which can of course never give one any idea of the breadth of the sky or the depth of the earth. The four volumes of Qian Zhongshu's *Guan zhui bian* (Beijing: Zhonghua shuju, 1979), written in elegant classical Chinese interspersed with quotations in English, French, German, Italian, Spanish, and Latin, form an immense work of commentaries on ten of the classic works in the Chinese tradition. It is a monumental work of modern scholarship that evinces its author's great learning and his sustained effort to bring the ancient and the modern, Chinese and Western, into mutual illumination.

14 Zhang Longxi, "Shi wu da gu" [Poetry Has No Direct Interpretation], *Wenyi yanjiu* [Literature and Art Studies], no. 4 (1983): 13–17.

1 The Debasement of Writing

1 Plato, *Apology* 22b, *The Collected Dialogues, Including the Letters*, ed. Edith Hamilton and Huntington Cairns (Princeton: Princeton University Press, 1963), p. 8.

2 Plato, *Ion* 534c, in *Collected Dialogues*, p. 220.

3 No wonder that W. K. Wimsatt and Monroe C. Beardsley would quote, in their famous essay "The Intentional Fallacy," the passage from Socrates' *Apology* to support their attack on intentionalism. See William K. Wimsatt, *The Verbal Icon* (Lexington: University of Kentucky Press, 1954), p. 7.

4 Plato, *Apology* 22c, in *Collected Dialogues*, p. 8.

5 M. H. Abrams, *The Mirror and the Lamp: Romantic Theory and the Critical Tradition* (Oxford: Oxford University Press, 1953), p. 210.

6 Friedrich von Schelling, Conclusion to *System of Transcendental Idealism*, trans. Albert Hofstadter, in David Simpson, ed., *German Aesthetic and Literary Criticism: Kant, Fichte, Schelling, Schopenhauer, Hegel* (Cambridge: Cambridge University Press, 1984), p. 122.

7 Ibid., p. 123.

8 Ibid., p. 124.

9 Immanuel Kant, *Critique of Judgment*, trans. Werner S. Pluhar (Indianapolis: Hackett, 1987), sec. 43, p. 170; sec. 48, p. 179.

10 Ibid., sec. 43, pp. 170–71.

11 Ibid., sec. 44, p. 173.

12 Gadamer, *Truth and Method*, pp. 53, 56.

13 Kant, *Critique of Judgment*, sec. 53, p. 196.

14 Ibid., sec. 46, p. 174.

15   Ibid., sec. 46, p. 175; sec. 47, p. 177.

16   See Gadamer, *Truth and Method*, pp. 54–60.

17   Kant, *Critique of Judgment*, sec. 50, p. 188.

18   Arthur Schopenhauer, *Parerga und Paralipomena*, sec. 57, in *Werke*, 2 vols., ed. Werner Brede (Munich: Carl Hanser, 1977), 2:304, 306.

19   René Wellek, *A History of Modern Criticism: 1750–1950* (New Haven: Yale University Press, 1955), p. 309.

20   Gadamer, *Truth and Method*, p. 59.

21   Schopenhauer, *The World as Will and Representation*, in *German Aesthetic and Literary Criticism*, ed. Simpson, p. 188.

22   Martin Redeker, *Friedrich Schleiermacher: Leben und Werk* (Berlin: Walter de Gruyter, 1968), pp. 92–93.

23   Ibid., p. 91.

24   Friedrich Schleiermacher, *Hermeneutics: The Handwritten Manuscripts*, trans. James Duke and Jack Forstman (Missoula, Mont.: Scholars Press, 1977), p. 95. See also Wilhelm Dilthey, "The Rise of Hermeneutics," trans. Fredric Jameson, *New Literary History* 3 (Winter 1972): 229–44; and Paul Ricoeur, "The Task of Hermeneutics," in *Hermeneutics and the Human Sciences*, ed. and trans. John B. Thompson (Cambridge: Cambridge University Press, 1981), pp. 45 ff.

25   Schleiermacher, *Hermeneutics*, p. 112.

26   Gadamer, *Truth and Method*, p. 192.

27   Friedrich Schleiermacher, *Introductions to the Dialogues of Plato*, trans. William Dobson (New York: Arno Press, 1973), p. 5.

28   Ibid., p. 14.

29   Schleiermacher, *Hermeneutics*, p. 50.

30   See Kurt Mueller-Vollmer's introduction to *The Hermeneutics Reader: Texts of the German Tradition from the Enlightenment to the Present* (New York: Continuum, 1985), pp. 8–12.

31   Schleiermacher, *Hermeneutics*, pp. 56, 98.

32   Ibid., p. 97.

33   Ibid., p. 110.

34   Northrop Frye, *Anatomy of Criticism: Four Essays* (Princeton: Princeton University Press, 1957), p. 5.

35   Michel de Montaigne, *Essays*, trans. J. M. Cohen (Harmondsworth: Penguin, 1958), p. 349.

36   Confucius, *Lunyu zhengyi* [The Analects with Exegesis], ed. Liu Baonan, in vol. 1 of *Zhuzi jicheng* [Collection of Classics], vii.1, p. 134.

37   Ibid., xvii.19, p. 379.

38   Ibid., xiv.4, p. 301.

39   Ibid., xv.41, p. 349.

40   This quotation is not found in the *Analects*, but in *Zuozhuan* or Zuo's commentary on the *Spring and Autumn Annals* (in *Shisan jing zhushu* [Thirteen Classics with

Annotations], ed. Ruan Yuan, 2 vols. [Beijing: Zhonghua shuju, 1980], 2:1985).
Some critics have questioned its authenticity on the grounds that it seems to jar with
Confucius' utilitarian view of language as we find it in the more reliable record of the
Analects, but we need not see the two records as being at variance, for it is possible to
interpret what Confucius says here as making a strategic point, which serves the
practical purpose of helping carry the message far enough to its destination.

41 Foucault, *The Order of Things*, pp. 41–42.
42 Michel Foucault, "Language to Infinity," *Language, Counter-Memory, Practice: Selected Essays and Interviews*, ed. Donald F. Bouchard, trans. Bouchard and Sherry Simon (Ithaca, N.Y.: Cornell University Press, 1977), p. 56.
43 Gadamer, *Truth and Method*, p. 390.
44 Plato, *Phaedrus* 275d, in *Collected Dialogues*, p. 521.
45 Confucius, *Lunyu* [The Analects], xv.8, p. 336.
46 Plato, *Phaedrus* 275a, in *Collected Dialogues*, p. 520.
47 Plato, *Philebus* 39a, in *Collected Dialogues*, p. 1119. For recollection as recovery of knowledge, see Plato, *Phaedo* 75e; *Meno* 81c; *Philebus* 34c; and *Theaetetus* 198d, all in *Collected Dialogues*.
48 Plato, *Epistle* ii, 314c, in *Collected Dialogues*, p. 1567.
49 Schleiermacher, *Introductions to the Dialogues of Plato*, p. 17.
50 Gadamer, *Truth and Method*, p. 369.
51 Georg Wilhelm Friedrich Hegel, *The Phenomenology of Mind*, 2nd rev. ed., trans. J. B. Baillie (London: George Allen & Unwin, 1949), p. 340.
52 Ibid., p. 530.
53 Richard Rorty, "Philosophy as a Kind of Writing: An Essay on Derrida," *New Literary History* 10 (Autumn 1978): 145.
54 Georg Wilhelm Friedrich Hegel, *The Philosophy of History*, rev. ed., trans. J. Sibree (New York: Willey, 1944), p. 103.
55 Ibid., p. 135
56 Georg Wilhelm Friedrich Hegel, *Science of Logic*, trans. A. V. Miller (New York: Humanities Press, 1976), p. 32.
57 Ibid., p. 107.
58 Stephen Ullman, *Principles of Semantics* (Oxford: Basil Blackwell, 1963), p. 120.
59 Sigmund Freud, "The Antithetical Sense of Primal Words," trans. M. N. Searl, in *Collected Papers*, 5 vols., authorized translation under the supervision of Joan Riviere (New York: Basic Books, 1959), 4:185.
60 Qian Zhongshu, *Guan zhui bian* [Pipe-Awl Chapters], 1:2.
61 Wilhelm Dilthey, *Entwürfe zur Kritik der historischen Vernunft*, in *Gesammelte Schriften*, 17 vols. (Stuttgart: B. G. Teubner; Göttingen: Vandenhoeck & Ruprecht, 1914–74), 7:225.
62 Jacques Derrida, *Of Grammatology*, trans. Gayatri Chakravorty Spivak (Baltimore: Johns Hopkins University Press, 1976), p. 3.
63 Ibid., p. 29.

64   Ibid., p. lxxxii.

65   Ibid., p. 90.

66   Ibid., p. 92.

67   Ibid., p. 76.

68   Ibid., p. 80.

69   Ibid., p. lxviii.

70   Ibid., p. 334 n. 44.

71   Ernest Fenollosa, *The Chinese Written Character as a Medium for Poetry*, ed. Ezra Pound (San Francisco: City Lights Books, 1969), p. 8.

72   Ezra Pound, trans., *Confucian Analects*, (London: Peter Owen, 1956), p. 9.

73   George A. Kennedy, "Fenollosa, Pound, and the Chinese Character," in *Selected Works of George A. Kennedy*, ed. Tien-yi Li (New Haven: Yale University Press, 1964), p. 462.

74   T. S. Eliot, intro. to Ezra Pound, *Selected Poems* (London: Faber & Gwyer, 1928), p. xvii.

75   Ibid., p. xvi.

76   Georg Wilhelm Friedrich Hegel, *Enzyklopädie der philosophischen Wissenschaften in Grundrisse* ([Hamburg: Meiner, 1969], sec. 459, p. 373), quoted in Derrida, *Of Grammatology*, p. 25; Fenollosa, *The Chinese Written Character*, p. 9.

77   Ernest Renan, *Oeuvres complètes* (10 vols., ed. Henriette Psichari [Paris: Calmann-Lévy, 1947–61]), *De l'origine du langage*, 8:90, quoted in Derrida, *Of Grammatology*, p. 123.

78   Joseph Riddel, " 'Neo-Nietzschean Clatter'—Speculation and/on Pound's Poetic Image," in Ian F. A. Bell, ed., *Ezra Pound: Tactics for Reading* (London: Vision, 1982), p. 211.

79   Arthur Schopenhauer, *On the Fourfold Root of the Principle of Sufficient Reason*, trans. E. F. J. Payne (La Salle, Ill.: Open Court, 1974), pp. 163–64.

80   Stephen Ullman, *Semantics: An Introduction to the Science of Meaning* (New York: Barnes & Noble, 1964), p. 173.

81   Joachim Ritter and Karlfried Gründer, eds., *Historisches Wörterbuch der Philosophie*, vol. 5 (Basel: Schwabe, 1980), s. v. "Logos."

82   Hans-Georg Gadamer, "Mensch und Sprache," in *Gesammelte Werke* (Tübingen: J. C. B. Mohr [Paul Siebeck], 1986), 2:146; also see *Philosophical Hermeneutics*, ed. and trans. David E. Linge (Berkeley: University of California Press, 1977), pp. 59, 60.

83   There are well over forty English translations of the *Laozi* or *Dao de jing*, and the key term *tao* (*dao*) is translated as "way" in many of them. See, e.g., the otherwise excellent translations by Wing-tsit Chan (*The Way of Lao Tzu* [Indianapolis: Bobbs-Merrill, 1963]) and D. C. Lau (*Tao Te Ching* [Harmondsworth: Penguin, 1963]).

84   See Qian Zhongshu, *Guan zhui bian* [Pipe-Awl Chapters], 2:403–10.

85   *Laozi zhu* [The Annotated Laozi], annotated by Wang Bi (226–49), in vol. 3 of *Zhuzi jicheng* [Collection of Classics], i.1, p. 1.

86   Ibid., i.3a, p. 1; xxv.56, p. 14; xxxii.72, p. 18; lvi.128, p. 34.

87   Sima Qian, *Life of Laozi*, quoted in Wei Yuan, *Laozi benyi* [The Original Meaning of

the Laozi], p. v; in vol. 3 of *Zhuzi jicheng* [Collection of Classics].

88 Wei Yuan, *Laozi benyi* [The Original Meaning of the Laozi], p. 1.

89 Plato, *Epistle* vii, 343, in *Collected Dialogues*, p. 1590.

90 Qian Zhongshu, *Guan zhui bian* [Pipe-Awl Chapters], 2:410.

91 Jacques Derrida, *Positions*, trans. Alan Bass (Chicago: University of Chicago Press, 1981), p. 41.

92 Derrida, *Of Grammatology*, p. 11.

93 *Zhouyi zhengyi* [The Book of Changes with Exegesis], 70c, in *Shisan jing zhushu* [Thirteen Classics with Annotations], ed. Ruan Yuan, 1:82.

94 Derrida, *Of Grammatology*, pp. 12–13.

95 Zhuangzi (369?–286? B.C.), *Zhuangzi jishi* [Variorum Edition of the Zhuangzi], ed. Guo Qingfan, in vol. 3 of *Zhuzi jicheng* [Collection of Classics], xiii, p. 217.

96 Ibid., xxvi, p. 407.

97 Heraclitus, *The Art and Thought of Heraclitus: An Edition of the Fragments with Translation and Commentary*, ed. and trans. Charles H. Kahn (Cambridge: Cambridge University Press, 1979), p. 45; Ludwig Wittgenstein, *Tractatus Logico-Philosophicus*, trans. C. K. Ogden (London: Routledge & Kegan Paul, 1983), 6.54, p. 189.

98 Derrida, *Of Grammatology*, p. 24.

99 Jacques Derrida, "Différance," in *Margins of Philosophy*, trans. Alan Bass (Chicago: University of Chicago Press, 1982), p. 3.

100 Ferdinand de Saussure, *Course in General Linguistics*, trans. Wade Baskin (New York: Philosophical Library, 1959), p. 120.

101 Gadamer, *Truth and Method*, pp. 407, 408.

102 Liu An (178?–122 B.C.), *Huainanzi* [The Master of Huainan], ed. and annotated by Gao You (fl. 205–212), in vol. 7 of *Zhuzi jicheng* [Collection of Classics], pp. 116–17.

103 Kwang-chih Chang, *Art, Myth, and Ritual: The Path to Political Authority in Ancient China* (Cambridge, Mass.: Harvard University Press, 1983), p. 81.

2 Philosopher, Mystic, Poet

1 Wittgenstein, *Tractatus*, p. 27. This is reiterated in the middle and at the very end of the book. See 4.116, p. 7; 79, p. 189.

2 Ibid., p. 27.

3 Ibid., 4.112, p. 77; 6.421, p. 183. Also see Ludwig Wittgenstein, *Philosophical Investigations*, trans. G. E. M. Anscombe, 3d ed. (Oxford: Basil Blackwell, 1968), p. 36.

4 Wittgenstein, *Tractatus*, 4.11, p. 75.

5 Ibid., 4.0031, 4.003, p. 63.

6 Ibid., 6.53, p. 189.

7 Bertrand Russell's intro. to Wittgenstein, *Tractatus*, pp. 11, 22.

8   Derrida, "White Mythology," in *Margins of Philosophy*, p. 268.

9   Anatole France, *The Garden of Epicurus* (trans. Alfred Allinson [New York: Dodd, Mead, 1923], p. 214), quoted in Derrida, *Margins of Philosophy*, p. 213.

10   Kant, *Critique of Judgment*, sec. 59, p. 228.

11   *Zhuangzi*, xxxiii, p. 474.

12   Aristotle, *On Poets* 2, in *"Poetics," with ... "On Poets"*, trans. Richard Janko (Indianapolis: Hackett, 1987), p. 56. In *Poetics* 47b, Aristotle already includes "the Socratic dialogues" in the various literary genres for which there is no general term in Greek. See p. 2.

13   Sir Philip Sidney, *An Apology for Poetry*, ed. Forrest G. Robinson (Indianapolis: Bobbs-Merrill, 1970), p. 8.

14   Percy Bysshe Shelley, *A Defence of Poetry*, in *Shelley's Critical Prose*, ed. Bruce R. McElderry (Lincoln: University of Nebraska Press, 1967), p. 9.

15   Dante Alighieri, *Literary Criticism of Dante Alighieri*, trans. R. S. Haller (Lincoln: University of Nebraska Press, 1973), p. 110.

16   William Shakespeare, *A Midsummer Night's Dream*, 5.1.16. This and all further references are to *The Riverside Shakespeare*, ed. G. Blakemore Evans et al. (Boston: Houghton Mifflin, 1974).

17   *Zhuangzi*, xxvi, p. 403; xxvii, p. 409.

18   Rorty, "Philosophy as a Kind of Writing," p. 145.

19   Derrida, "White Mythology," in *Margins of Philosophy*, p. 270.

20   Giambattista Vico, *The New Science*, trans. Thomas G. Bergin and Max H. Fisch (Ithaca, N.Y.: Cornell University Press, 1976), p. 78.

21   *Zhouyi zhengyi* [The Book of Changes with Exegesis], 74b, in *Shisan jing zhushu* [Thirteen Classics with Annotations], ed. Ruan Yuan, 1:86. The hexagrams are highly abstract signs consisting of six horizontal lines in different combinations. In ancient Chinese thought, they were believed to represent all things in the universe and their relationships—signs that imply the binary relationship of the *yin* and the *yang*, the principles of the feminine and of the masculine. The notion of hexagrams originating in the patterns of trace in nature and of using the sensuous to signify the spiritual was later carried over to account for the origin of writing, the creation of Chinese ideograms.

22   Derrida, *Margins of Philosophy*, p. 252.

23   Hegel, *The Philosophy of History*, pp. 103–4.

24   Derrida, *Margins of Philosophy*, pp. 268–69.

25   Ibid., pp. 258, 271.

26   Fritz Mauthner, *Beiträge zu einer Kritik der Sprache*, 3 vols., 3d ed. (Leipzig: Felix Meiner, 1922–23), 2:463.

27   Ibid., 1:235–36.

28   Ibid., 1:704.

29   Ibid., 1:1.

30   Ibid., 1:713.

31   Ibid., 1:1–2.

32 Allan Janik and Stephen Toulmin, *Wittgenstein's Vienna* (New York: Simon & Schuster, 1973), p. 197.

33 Ibid., p. 232.

34 Gershon Weiler, *Mauthner's Critique of Language* (Cambridge: Cambridge University Press, 1970), pp. 301, 302.

35 Martin Buber, *Ecstatic Confessions*, trans. Esther Cameron (New York: Harper & Row, 1985), p. 5.

36 Weiler, *Mauthner's Critique of Language*, p. 296.

37 Fritz Mauthner, *Der Atheismus und seine Geschichte im Abendlande*, 4 vols. (Stuttgart: Deutsche Verlags-Anstalt, 1922–23), 4:447.

38 *Laozi*, lvi.128, p. 34; *Zhuangzi*, xxii, pp. 326, 330.

39 Mauthner, *Der Atheismus*, 4:444–45.

40 Fritz Mauthner, *Wörterbuch der Philosophie: Neue Beiträge zu einer Kritik der Sprache*, 2 vols. (Munich: Georg Müller, 1910), 2:468, s. v. "Tao".

41 Meister Eckhart, *Meister Eckhart: A Modern Translation*, trans. Raymond Bernard Blakney (New York: Harper & Brothers, 1941), p. 111.

42 K. Venkata Ramanan, *Nagarjuna's Philosophy as Presented in the Maha-Prajñaparamita-Sastra* (Rutland, Vt.: C. E. Tuttle, 1966), p. 128.

43 Ibid., p. 274.

44 D. T. Suzuki, *Essays in Zen Buddhism*, 1st series (London: Luzac, 1927), p. 7.

45 *Laozi*, ii.6, p. 2.

46 Ernst Cassirer, *Language and Myth*, trans. Susanne K. Langer (New York: Harper & Brothers, 1946), p. 74.

47 Mauthner, *Wörterbuch der Philosophie*, 2:131, s. v. "Mystik".

48 Buber, *Ecstatic Confessions*, pp. 7, 9, 10.

49 Ramanan, *Nagarjuna's Philosophy*, pp. 50–51.

50 Karl Vossler, *The Spirit of Language in Civilization*, trans. Oscar Oeser (New York: Harcourt, Brace & Co., 1932), p. 33.

51 *Zhuangzi*, xxii, p. 326.

52 Quoted in Qian Zhongshu, *Guan zhui bian* [Pipe-Awl Chapters], 2:457; also 1:13.

53 Qian Zhongshu, *Guan zhui bian* [Pipe-Awl Chapters], 1:14–15.

54 Wittgenstein, *Philosophical Investigations*, 531, pp. 143–44.

55 Derrida, *Margins of Philosophy*, p. 209.

56 Stanley Burnshaw, *Robert Frost Himself* (New York: George Braziller, 1986), p. 123.

57 Friedrich Schiller, "Die Götter Griechenlands" (1788), in *Werke*, 6 vols., ed. Alfred Brandstetter (Zurich: Stauffacher, 1967), 1:187.

58 Schiller, *Tabulae votivae*, "47. Sprache" (1796), in *Werke*, 1:273.

59 Shelley, *A Defence of Poetry*, in *Shelley's Critical Prose*, p. 30.

60 *Zhuangzi*, xiii, pp. 217–18.

61 Ibid., xvii, p. 253.

62 Lu Ji, preface to "Wen fu" [Rhymeprose on Literature], in *Wen xuan* [A Literary Anthology], 3 vols., ed. Xiao Tong (501–31) (Beijing: Zhonghua shuju, 1977), 1:239.

63 Ibid., 1:240.

64 Ibid., 1:242–43.

65 James J. Y. Liu, *Chinese Theories of Literature* (Chicago: University of Chicago Press, 1975), p. 31.

66 Liu Xie, *Wenxin diaolong zhushi* [The Literary Mind or the Carving of Dragons], ed. Zhou Zhenfu (Beijing: Renmin wenxue, 1981), p. 296.

67 Ibid., p. 295.

68 Xu Zhenqing, *Tan yi lu* [Discourses on Art], in *Lidai shihua* [Remarks on Poetry from Various Dynasties], 2 vols., ed. He Wenhuan (Beijing: Zhonghua shuju, 1981), 2:766.

69 Qian Zhongshu, *Guan zhui bian* [Pipe-Awl Chapters], 2:406.

70 W. J. T. Mitchell, *Iconology: Image, Text, Ideology* (Chicago: University of Chicago Press, 1986), p. 43.

71 Ibid.

72 Joel Fineman, *Shakespeare's Perjured Eye: The Invention of Poetic Subjectivity in the Sonnets* (Berkeley: University of California Press, 1986), pp. 262, 269.

73 Ibid., p. 149.

74 Barbara Herrnstein Smith, *Poetic Closure: A Study of How Poems End* (Chicago: University of Chicago Press, 1968), p. 51.

75 Ibid., pp. 141, 142.

76 Hallett Smith, *The Tension of the Lyre: Poetry in Shakespeare's Sonnets* (San Marino, Calif.: Huntington Library, 1981), p. 86.

77 Gadamer, *Truth and Method*, p. 127.

78 Gadamer, "The Relevance of the Beautiful," in *The Relevance*, pp. 46, 47.

79 Mitchell, *Iconology*, p. 43.

80 Stéphane Mallarmé, "Symphonie littéraire," in *Oeuvres complètes*, ed. Henri Mondor and G. Jean-Aubry (Paris: Gallimard, 1945), p. 261.

81 Mallarmé, "Le Tombeau d'Edgar Poe," in *Oeuvres complètes*, p. 70.

82 All quotations of T. S. Eliot are from *The Complete Poems and Plays: 1909–1950* (New York: Harcourt, Brace & World, 1971).

83 William Butler Yeats, *Collected Poems* (New York: Macmillan, 1956), p. 293.

84 Yeats, "Sailing to Byzantium," in *Collected Poems*, pp. 191, 192.

85 John Keats, "Ode on a Grecian Urn," 44–45, in *Complete Poems*, ed. Jack Stillinger (Cambridge, Mass.: Harvard University Press, 1982), p. 283.

86 David Spurr, *Conflicts in Consciousness: T. S. Eliot's Poetry and Criticism* (Urbana: University of Illinois Press, 1984), p. 80.

87 Smith, *Poetic Closure*, p. 241.

88 Spurr, *Conflicts in Consciousness*, p. 93.

89 Eliot, "The Metaphysical Poets," in *Selected Prose of T. S. Eliot*, ed. Frank Kermode (New York: Harcourt Brace Jovanovich, 1975), p. 64.

90 Helen Gardner, *The Art of T. S. Eliot* (New York: E. P. Dutton, 1950), p. 75.

91 Ibid., p. 185.

92 Spurr, *Conflicts in Consciousness*, p. 104.

93 Gardner, *The Art of T. S. Eliot*, p. 47.

94 Eliot, "In Memoriam," in *Selected Prose*, p. 243. For his comparison of Tennyson with Herbert, see "The Metaphysical Poets," pp. 64–65.

95 Harold Bloom, ed., *Modern Critical Views: T. S. Eliot* (New York: Chelsea, 1985), p. 2. For a reading of *In Memoriam* as expressing a deep-seated anxiety of language, see William A. Wilson, "Victorian Philology and the Anxiety of Language in Tennyson's *In Memoriam*," *Texas Studies in Literature and Language* 30 (Spring 1988): 28–48.

96 Eliot, "The Use of Poetry and the Use of Criticism," in *Selected Prose*, pp. 79–80.

97 Spurr, *Conflicts in Consciousness*, pp. 103, 106.

98 Ibid., p. 80.

99 Smith, *Poetic Closure*, pp. 241–42.

3 The Use of Silence

1 Stephen Spender, "Rilke and Eliot," in *Rilke: The Alchemy of Alienation*, ed. F. Baron, E. S. Dick, and W. R. Maurer (Lawrence: Regents Press of Kansas, 1980), p. 52.

2 Ibid., p. 47.

3 Ibid., p. 52.

4 Rainer Maria Rilke, "The First Elegy," 1–2. Unless otherwise indicated, German texts and English translations are from *The Selected Poetry of Rainer Maria Rilke*, ed. and trans. Stephen Mitchell (New York: Vintage, 1982). Reference will be to the number of the elegy and line numbers in the German text.

5 Rainer Maria Rilke, "To Witold Hulewicz, November 13, 1925," in *Briefe aus Muzot* ([Leipzig: Insel, 1935], p. 337), quoted in Mitchell's notes to *The Selected Poetry*, p. 317.

6 Heinrich von Kleist, "On the Marionette Theater," trans. Christian-Albrecht Gollub, in *German Romantic Criticism*, ed. A. Leslie Wilson (New York: Continuum, 1982), p. 244.

7 Kathleen L. Komar, *Transcending Angels: Rainer Maria Rilke's Duino Elegies* (Lincoln: University of Nebraska Press, 1987), p. 14.

8 In his largely unsympathetic reading of Rilke's poetry, Egon Schwarz also remarks that Rilke's thought is "so suffused with Christian elements" that "one is justified in speaking of him as a post-Christian poet (since he categorically renounced Christianity)" (*Poetry and Politics in the Works of Rainer Maria Rilke*, trans. David E. Wellbery [New York: Frederick Ungar, 1981], p. 18).

9 Ursula Franklin, "The Angel in Valéry and Rilke," *Comparative Literature* 35 (Summer 1983): 215.

10 Richard Jayne, "Rilke and the Problem of Poetic Inwardness," in *Rilke*, ed. Baron et al., p. 194.

11 Paul de Man, *Allegories of Reading: Figural Language in Rousseau, Nietzsche, Rilke, and Proust* (New Haven: Yale University Press, 1979), p. 43 passim.

12 Komar, *Transcending Angels*, p. 199.

13 E. L. Stahl, "The *Duineser Elegien*," in *Rainer Maria Rilke: Aspects of His Mind and Poetry*, ed. William Rose and G. Craig Houston (London: Sidgwick & Jackson, 1938), pp. 140–41.

14 In considering the arrangement of the *Elegies* as a whole, Kathleen Komar also notes that "The Fifth Elegy" is where the problem for the poet is "at worst," articulating his "despair of human situation" (*Transcending Angels*, p. 201).

15 Rainer Maria Rilke, "To Lev P. Struve, February 25, 1926," in Maurice Betz, *Rilke in Frankreich: Erinnerungen—Briefe—Dokumente* (Wien: Herbert Reichner, 1937), quoted in Mitchell's notes to *The Selected Poetry*, p. 329.

16 De Man, *Allegories of Reading*, pp. 26, 26–27.

17 Ibid., p. 44.

18 Rainer Maria Rilke, "Für Leonie Zacharias," in *Sämtliche Werke*, 6 vols., ed. Ernst Zinn (Wiesbaden: Insel, 1955–66), 2:249.

19 Rilke, "Magie," in *Sämtliche Werke*, 2:175.

20 Hans Egon Holthusen, *Rainer Maria Rilke: A Study of his Later Poetry*, trans. J. P. Stern (Cambridge: Bowes & Bowes, 1952), p. 32.

21 Walter A. Strauss, "Rilke and Ponge: L'Objet c'est la poétique," in *Rilke*, ed. Baron et al., p. 70.

22 Quotations are from Rainer Maria Rilke, *The Sonnets to Orpheus*, trans. Stephen Mitchell (New York: Simon & Schuster, 1986).

23 Rilke, *The Selected Poetry*, p. 91.

24 Rilke, "To Princess Marie von Thurn und Taxis-Hohenlohe, November 17, 1912," quoted in Mitchell's notes to *The Selected Poetry*, p. 337.

25 Joachim W. Storck, "Poesie und Schweigen: Zum Enigmatischen in Rilkes später Lyrik," *Blätter der Rilke-Gesellschaft* 10 (1983): 107.

26 Rilke, "Für Frau Fanette Clavel," in *Sämtliche Werke*, 2:258.

27 Gadamer, *Truth and Method*, p. 97.

28 Gadamer, "The Relevance of the Beautiful," in *The Relevance*, p. 9.

29 Ibid., pp. 38, 39.

30 Gadamer, "Composition and Interpretation," in *The Relevance*, p. 69.

31 Gadamer, "The Relevance of the Beautiful," in *The Relevance*, p. 52.

32 De Man, *Allegories of Reading*, pp. 3, 5.

33 Ibid., pp. 16, 19.

34 Ibid., p. 32.

35 Ibid., pp. 40, 41.

36 Ibid., p. 43.

37 Ibid., p. 48.

38 Ibid., p. 50.

39 Gadamer, "Composition and Interpretation," in *The Relevance*, p. 69.

40 De Man, *Allegories of Reading*, p. 49.

41 Gadamer, "On the Contribution of Poetry to the Search for Truth," in *The Relevance*,

pp. 108, 114.

42 Gadamer, "Philosophy and Poetry," in *The Relevance*, p. 134.

43 Ibid., pp. 134–35.

44 Gadamer, "Aesthetic and Religious Experience," in *The Relevance*, pp. 146, 146–47.

45 N. 15 to the editor's introduction to Gadamer, *The Relevance*, p. 172.

46 Plato, *Philebus* 39a, in *Collected Dialogues*, pp. 1118–19.

47 Mallarmé, *Oeuvres complètes*, p. 310.

48 Jacques Derrida, *Dissemination*, trans. Barbara Johnson (Chicago: University of Chicago Press, 1981), pp. 195, 191.

49 Ibid., pp. 194–95.

50 Ibid., pp. 206, 207.

51 Derrida, *Of Grammatology*, p. 92.

52 Derrida, *Dissemination*, p. 248.

53 Ibid., p. 252.

54 Ibid., p. 231.

55 Ibid., pp. 236, 262.

56 Ibid., p. 253.

57 Mallarmé, "Hérésies artistiques: L'art pour tous," in *Oeuvres complètes*, p. 257.

58 Guy Michaud, *Mallarmé*, trans. Marie Collins and Bertha Humez (New York: New York University Press, 1965), p. 15.

59 Mallarmé, "Le mystère dans les lettres," in *Oeuvres complètes*, p. 383.

60 Mallarmé, "Sur l'évolution littéraire," in *Oeuvres complètes*, p. 869.

61 Mallarmé, "Autobiographie," in *Oeuvres complètes*, p. 663.

62 Stéphane Mallarmé, "To Léo d'Orfer, June 27, 1884," in *Correspondance*, vol. 2, ed. Henri Mondor and Lloyd James Austin (Paris: Gallimard, 1965), p. 266.

63 Stéphane Mallarmé, "To Théodore Aubanel, July 28, 1866," in *Correspondance*, vol. 1, ed. Henri Mondor with Jean-Pierre Richard (Paris: Gallimard, 1959), pp. 224–25.

64 Gadamer, "On the Contribution of Poetry to the Search for Truth," in *The Relevance*, pp. 110, 110–11.

65 "The Relevance of the Beautiful," in *The Relevance*, pp. 34, 35.

66 Ibid., p. 37.

67 Ibid., p. 36.

68 Ibid., p. 37.

69 Ibid., p. 38.

70 Gadamer, "Aesthetics and Hermeneutics," in *Philosophical Hermeneutics*, p. 102.

71 See Gadamer's essays which form part 2 of *Dialogue and Deconstruction: The Gadamer-Derrida Encounter*, ed. Diane P. Michelfelder and Richard E. Palmer (Albany: State University of New York Press, 1989), pp. 75–125.

72 Fred Dallmayr, "Prelude: Hermeneutics and Deconstruction: Gadamer and Derrida in Dialogue," in *Dialogue and Deconstruction*, ed. Michelfelder and Palmer, p. 91.

73 Gadamer, "The Relevance of the Beautiful," in *The Relevance*, p. 28.

74 Roland Barthes, "The Death of the Author," in *Image-Music-Text*, trans. Stephen

Heath (New York: Hill and Wang, 1977), p. 148.

75 Barbara Johnson, intro. to Derrida, *Dissemination*, p. xiv.

76 Christopher Norris, *Derrida* (Cambridge, Mass.: Harvard University Press, 1987), pp. 53–54.

77 Derrida, *Dissemination*, p. 252.

78 Mallarmé, "Quant au livre," in *Oeuvres complètes*, p. 370.

79 Mallarmé, *Oeuvres complètes*, p. 74.

80 Lloyd Austin, "The mystery of a name," in *Poetic Principles and Practice: Occasional Papers on Baudelaire, Mallarmé and Valéry* (Cambridge: Cambridge University Press, 1987), p. 71.

81 Ibid., p. 72.

82 Mallarmé, "Le livre, instrument spirituel," in *Oeuvres complètes*, p. 378. See also p. 872.

83 Mallarmé, "Autobiographie," in *Oeuvres complètes*, p. 663.

84 Mallarmé, "Bibliographie de l'Édition de 1898," in *Oeuvres complètes*, p. 77.

85 Ludwig Wittgenstein, letter to Ludwig von Ficker; quoted in Janik and Toulmin, *Wittgenstein's Vienna*, p. 192.

86 Mallarmé, "Le mystère dans les lettres," *Oeuvres complètes*, pp. 386, 387.

87 For the French original and English translation, I quote from *French Symbolist Poetry*, trans. C. F. MacIntyre (Berkeley: University of California Press, 1958), pp. 56–63.

88 Robert Greer Cohn, *Toward the Poems of Mallarmé* (Berkeley: University of California Press, 1965), p. 17.

89 Lu Ji, preface to "Wen fu" [Rhymeprose on Literature], in *Wen xuan* [A Literary Anthology], ed. Xiao Tong, 1:239.

90 Qian Zhongshu, *Tan yi lu* [Discourses on Art], enlarged ed. (Beijing: Zhonghua shuju, 1984), pp. 88–93. For a discussion of Tao Qian in his literary milieu, see Kang-i Sun Chang, *Six Dynasties Poetry* (Princeton: Princeton University Press, 1986), pp. 3–46.

91 Jauss, *Toward an Aesthetic of Reception*, p. 35.

92 Yan Yanzhi, preface to "Tao zhengshi lei" [Eulogy on Tao Qian], in *Wen xuan* [A Literary Anthology], ed. Xiao Tong, 3:791.

93 Confucius, *Lunyu* [The Analects], xv.41, p. 349.

94 Zhong Rong, *Shi pin* [Ranking of Poetry], in *Lidai shihua* [Remarks on Poetry from Various Dynasties], ed. He Wenhuan, 1:13.

95 Chang, *Six Dynasties Poetry*, p. 13.

96 Du Fu, "Qianxing wu shou" [Five Poems Written as Discharge of Emotions], in *Du Shaoling ji xiangzhu* [Annotated Works of Du Fu], 10 vols, ed. Qiu Zhao-ao (Beijing: Wenxue guji, 1955), 4:21.

97 In the year of 405, Tao Qian was appointed magistrate of Pengze, a low-level office, but he was on the job for only eighty days when he quit, for he chose to resign rather than put on his official robe and call on the inspector sent by a higher office. This famous episode was first reported in the biography of Tao Yuanming in *juan* 93 of

Shen Yue's (441–513) *Song shu* [History of the Song Dynasty] (8 vols. [Beijing: Zhonghua shuju, 1974], 8:2287), and then copied in several other standard historical records as well as Tao's biography written by Xiao Tong (501–31), the Prince of Liang, compiler of the famous *Wen xuan* [A Literary Anthology], who also edited the first collection of Tao Qian's works.

98 Chang, *Six Dynasties Poetry*, p. 16.

99 Ibid., p. 12.

100 Ibid., p. 16.

101 Ibid., p. 25.

102 Ibid., p. 16.

103 Stephen Owen, "The Self's Perfect Mirror: Poetry as Autobiography," in *The Vitality of the Lyric Voice: Shih Poetry from the Late Han to the T'ang*, ed. Shuen-fu Lin and Stephen Owen (Princeton: Princeton University Press, 1986), p. 78.

104 Ibid., pp. 74, 75.

105 Ibid., p. 78.

106 Tao Qian, *Tao Yuanming ji* [Tao Yuanming's Works], ed. Lu Qinli (Beijing: Zhonghua shuju, 1979), p. 40.

107 Owen, "The Self's Perfect Mirror," in *The Vitality of the Lyric Voice*, ed. Lin and Owen, p. 77.

108 Ibid., p. 81.

109 Ibid., p. 79.

110 Ibid., p. 86.

111 Gadamer, "The Relevance of the Beautiful," in *The Relevance*, p. 26.

112 See James Hightower, "Allusion in the Poetry of T'ao Ch'ien," in *Studies in Chinese Literary Genres*, ed. Cyril Birch (Berkeley: University of California Press, 1974), pp. 108–32.

113 Tao Qian, *Tao Yuanming ji* [Works], p. 123.

114 Su Shi, "Comment on the Poetry of Han Yu and Liu Zhongyuan," *Su Shi wenji* [Collected Prose Works of Su Shi], 6 vols., ed. Kong Fanli (Beijing: Zhonghua shuju, 1986), 5:2110.

115 Lu Jiuyuan, *Lu Jiuyuan ji* [The Collected Works of Lu Jiuyuan], *juan* 34 (Beijing: Zhonghua shuju, 1980), p. 410.

116 Donald Holzman's review of Chang, *Six Dynasties Poetry*, in *Harvard Journal of Asiatic Studies* 48 (June 1988): 246.

117 Yim-tze Kwong, "Naturalness and Authenticity: The Poetry of Tao Qian," *Chinese Literature: Essays, Articles, Reviews* 11 (December 1989): 45–46.

118 Ibid., p. 76.

119 Shen Deqian, ed., *Gushi yuan* [A Sourcebook of Ancient Poetry] (Beijing: Zhonghua shuju, 1977), p. 204.

120 Fang Dongshu, *Zhao mei zhan yan* [Verbiage at Morn and Dusk], (Beijing: Renmin wenxue, 1961), 4.16, p. 101.

121 According to Gu Zhi's annotated edition, Tao Qian has forty-nine references to the

Zhuangzi, thirty-seven to the Confucian *Analects*, and twenty-one to another Taoist book, the *Liezi*. See Zhu Ziqing's (1898–1948) review of Gu Zhi's edition, "Tao shi de shendu" ["The Depth of Tao's Poetry"], in *Zhu Ziqing gudian wenxue zhuanji* [Zhu Ziqing's Writings on Classical Chinese Literature], 4 vols. (Shanghai: Shanghai guji, 1981), 1:568. By examining Tao's notions of truth (*zhen*) and purity (*chun*) with reference to Laozi and Zhuangzi, Zhu comes to the conclusion that "the main stream of thinking in Tao's poetry is indeed Taoist" (1:569).

122 Zhu Xi, *Zhuzi yulei* [Sayings of Zhuzi], 8 vols. (Taipei: Cheng Chung Book Co., 1982), 8:5207.

123 See Chen Yinke, "Tao Yuanming zhi sixiang yu qingtan zhi guanxi" [The Relation between Tao Yuanming's Thought and "Clear Talk"], in *Jinmingguan conggao chubian* [Chen's Essays, First Series] (Shanghai: Shanghai guji, 1980), pp. 180–205.

124 Ibid., p. 196.

125 Ibid., p. 205.

126 See Confucius, *Lunyu* [The Analects], xi.26, p. 257.

127 Tao Qian, *Tao Yuanming ji* [Works], p. 14.

128 Ibid., p. 96.

129 Ibid., p. 25.

130 Confucius, *Lunyu* [The Analects], xiii.4, p. 284.

131 Tao Qian, *Tao Yuanming ji* [Works], p. 89.

132 Ibid., p. 41.

133 *Zhuangzi*, xvi, p. 246.

134 Ibid., xxviii, p. 421.

135 See Zhu Ziqing, "Shi duoyi juli" [Examples of Poetic Polysemy], in *Zhu Ziqing gudian wenxue zhuanji* [Zhu Ziqing's Writings on Classical Chinese Literature], 1:67.

136 *Zhuangzi*, iv, pp. 67–68.

137 Ibid., xxvi, p. 407.

138 Ibid., xxii, p. 319.

139 Ibid., xxii, p. 326.

140 Yu-kung Kao, "The Aesthetics of the Regulated Verse," in *The Vitality of the Lyric Voice*, ed. Lin and Owen, p. 371.

141 In Tao's biography, Shen Yue notes that the *Biography of Mr. Five Willows* so closely resembles Tao's own life that "his contemporaries all took it as a factual account" (*Song shu* [History of the Song Dynasty], 8:2287).

142 Tao Qian, *Tao Yuanming ji* [Works], p. 175.

143 Qian Zhongshu, *Guan zhui bian* [Pipe-Awl Chapters], 4:1228.

144 Shen Yue, *Song shu* [History of the Song Dynasty], 8:2288.

145 *Laozi*, xli.91, p. 26.

146 *Zhuangzi*, xiv, p. 90.

147 Bai Juyi, "Pipa yin" [The Pipa Player's Song], in *Bai Juyi ji* [Works of Bai Juyi], ed. Gu Xuejie, 4 vols. (Beijing: Zhonghua shuju, 1985), 1:242.

4 Author, Text, Reader

1 *Shangshu zhengyi* [The Book of Documents], in *Shisan jing zhushu* [Thirteen Classics], ed. Ruan Yuan, 1:131.

2 *Mao shi zhengyi* [The Book of Poetry], in *Shisanjing Zhushu*, ed. Ruan Yuan, 1:269.

3 Mencius, *Mengzi zhengyi* [The Works of Mencius with Exegesis], ed. Jiao Xun, in vol. 1 of *Zhuzi jicheng*, 5a.4, p. 377.

4 Ibid., 5b.8, p. 428.

5 Liu, *Language-Paradox-Poetics*, pp. 96, 97.

6 Liu Xie, *Wenxin diaolong zhushi* [The Literary Mind or the Carving of Dragons], p. 518.

7 Ibid.

8 Lü Buwei (290–235 B.C.), *Lüshi chunqiu* [Lü's Spring and Autumn], ed. Gao You, in vol. 6 of *Zhuzi jicheng* [Collection of Classics], *juan* 14, p. 140.

9 Tao Qian, *Tao Yuanming ji* [Works], p. 123.

10 Qiu Zhao-ao, preface to Du Fu, *Du Shaoling ji* [The Works of Du Fu], 1:2.

11 E. D. Hirsch, *Validity in Interpretation* (New Haven: Yale University Press, 1967), p. 25.

12 Ibid., p. 8.

13 Ibid., pp. 143, 136.

14 Ibid., pp. 18, 38. Hirsch's italics.

15 Gerald Graff, "Determinacy/Indeterminacy," in *Critical Terms for Literary Study*, ed. Frank Lentricchia and Thomas McLaughlin (Chicago: University of Chicago Press, 1990), pp. 166, 167.

16 Hirsch, *Validity in Interpretation*, p. 124.

17 Qiu Zhao-ao, preface to Du Fu, *Du Shaoling ji* [The Works of Du Fu], 1:1.

18 Ibid., 1:2.

19 Hirsch, *Validity in Interpretation*, p. 236.

20 Ibid., p. 242.

21 See Dilthey, "Entwürfe zur Kritik der historischen Vernunft," *Gesammelte Schriften*, 7:225.

22 Dilthey, "The Rise of Hermeneutics," p. 243.

23 Hirsch, *Validity in Interpretation*, p. 242, n. 30.

24 Dilthey, "The Rise of Hermeneutics," p. 244.

25 Editors' introduction to Wilhelm Dilthey, *Selected Works*, vol. 5, *Poetry and Experience*, ed. Rudolf Makkreel and Frithjof Rodi (Princeton: Princeton University Press, 1985), pp. 19, 17.

26 Rudolf A. Makkreel, *Dilthey: Philosopher of the Human Studies* (Princeton: Princeton University Press, 1975), p. 417.

27 Ibid., p. 418.

28 Gadamer, *Truth and Method*, p. 293.

29 E. D. Hirsch, "Meaning and Significance Reinterpreted," *Critical Inquiry* 11 (Decem-

ber 1984): 216.

30 Barbara Herrnstein Smith, *On the Margins of Discourse: The Relation of Literature to Language* (Chicago: University of Chicago Press, 1978), p. 138.

31 Roman Ingarden, *The Literary Work of Art: An Investigation on the Borderlines of Ontology, Logic, and Theory of Literature*, trans. George G. Grabowicz (Evanston, Ill.: Northwestern University Press, 1973), pp. 246, 249.

32 Ibid., p. 249.

33 Graff, "Determinacy/Indeterminacy," in *Critical Terms for Literary Study*, ed. Lentricchia and McLaughlin, p. 165.

34 Hirsch, *Validity in Interpretation*, p. x.

35 Stephen Knapp and Walter Benn Michaels, "Against Theory," in *Against Theory: Literary Studies and the New Pragmatism*, ed. W. J. T. Mitchell (Chicago: University of Chicago Press, 1985), p. 17.

36 Ibid., p. 18.

37 Hershel Parker, "Lost Authority: Non-sense, Skewed Meanings, and Intentionless Meanings," in *Against Theory*, ed. Mitchell, pp. 76, 78.

38 Stanley Fish, "Interpreting the *Variorum*," in *Is There a Text in This Class?: The Authority of Interpretive Communities* (Cambridge, Mass.: Harvard University Press, 1980), p. 150.

39 Ibid., p. 163.

40 Fish, "What It's Like To Read *L'Allegro* and *Il Penseroso*," in *Is There a Text?* p. 116.

41 The original text is in Li Shangyin, *Li Shangyin xuanji* [Selected Works of Li Shangyin], ed. Zhou Zhenfu (Shanghai: Shanghai guji, 1986), p. 1.

42 *Zhuangzi*, i, pp. 53–54.

43 Jorge Luis Borges, *Twenty-Four Conversations with Borges, Including a Selection of Poems*, trans. Nicomedes Suárez Araúz et al. (Housatonic, Mass.: Lascaux, 1984), p. 39.

44 Hirsch, *Validity in Interpretation*, p. 76.

45 This and the other commentaries discussed below, unless otherwise indicated, are all quoted in Zhou Zhenfu's notes to the "Patterned Lute" in Li Shangyin, *Li Shangyin xuanji* [Selected Works of Li Shangyin], pp. 2–5.

46 Huang Tingjian, quoted in Cai Zhengsun (fl. 1279), *Shilin guangji* [In the Woods of Poetry] (Beijing: Zhonghua shuju, 1982), p. 100.

47 Jonathan Culler, *Structural Poetics: Structuralism, Linguistics and the Study of Literature* (London: Routledge & Kegan Paul, 1975), p. 177.

48 Qian Zhongshu, *Tan yi lu* [Discourses on Art], pp. 435–38. Also quoted in Zhou Zhenfu's notes; see Li Shangyin, *Li Shangyin xuanji* [Selected Works], pp. 2–4.

49 Paul Verlaine, "Art poétique," in *French Symbolist Poetry*, trans. MacIntyre, p. 34.

50 Dilthey, "The Rise of Hermeneutics," p. 243.

51 Schleiermacher, *Hermeneutics*, p. 110.

52 Ibid., p. 113.

53 Gadamer, *Truth and Method*, p. 297.

54 Ibid., p. 293.

55 Ibid., p. 299.

56 Ibid., p. 297.

57 Erich Auerbach, *Mimesis: The Representation of Reality in Western Literature*, trans. Willard R. Trask (Princeton: Princeton University Press, 1953), pp. 6–7.

58 Ibid., pp. 11–12.

59 Bernard Huppé, *Doctrine and Poetry: Augustine's Influence on Old English Poetry* (New York: State University of New York Press, 1959), p. 24.

60 St. Augustine, *On Christian Doctrine*, trans. D. W. Robertson, Jr. (Indianapolis: Bobbs-Merrill, 1958), 4.7.15, pp. 128–29. See also 2.6.8, p. 38: "No one doubts that things are perceived more readily through similitudes and that what is sought with difficulty is discovered with more pleasure."

61 Umberto Eco, *Art and Beauty in the Middle Ages*, trans. Hugh Bredin (New Haven: Yale University Press, 1986), p. 55.

62 Ibid., p. 56.

63 Huppé, *Doctrine and Poetry*, p. 30.

64 Paul Valéry, *The Collected Works of Paul Valéry*, 15 vols., ed. Jackson Mathews (Princeton: Princeton University Press, 1956–75), 14:505, 359.

65 Besides Old English poetry, Huppé also sees Isidore of Seville, Vergil of Toulouse, Bede, Alcuin, Rabanus, and Scotus Erigena as influenced by Augustine's theory of literature. See *Doctrine and Poetry*, pp. 28–63.

66 Renato Poggioli, *The Theory of the Avant-Garde*, trans. Gerald Fitzgerald (Cambridge, Mass.: Harvard University Press, 1968), p. 37.

67 See ibid., pp. 146–47.

68 Victor Shklovsky, "Art as Technique," in *Russian Formalist Criticism: Four Essays*, trans. L. T. Lemon and M. J. Reis (Lincoln: University of Nebraska Press, 1965), p. 12. Jan Mukařovský, "Standard Language and Poetic Language," in *A Prague School Reader on Esthetics, Literary Structure, and Style*, trans. Paul L. Garvin (Washington, D.C.: Georgetown University Press, 1964), p. 18.

69 Jurij Striedter, *Literary Structure, Evolution, and Value: Russian Formalism and Czech Structuralism Reconsidered* (Cambridge, Mass.: Harvard University Press, 1989), pp. 88, 89.

70 William Wordsworth, "Preface to *Lyrical Ballads* (1802)," in *The Oxford Authors: William Wordsworth*, ed. Stephen Gill (Oxford: Oxford University Press, 1984), p. 596.

71 Ibid., p. 597.

72 Shelley, *A Defence of Poetry*, in *Shelley's Critical Prose*, p. 12.

73 Striedter, *Literary Structure, Evolution, and Value*, p. 96.

74 Roland Barthes, *S/Z*, trans. Richard Miller (New York: Hill and Wang, 1974), p. 4; Roland Barthes, *The Pleasure of the Text*, trans. Richard Miller (New York: Hill and Wang, 1975), p. 22.

75 Ibid., pp. 9–10.

76 Auerbach, *Mimesis*, pp. 13–14.

77 For an insightful discussion on "Homer and Allegory," see Ernst Robert Curtius, *European Literature and the Latin Middle Ages*, trans. Willard R. Trask (Princeton: Princeton University Press, 1973), pp. 203–7.

78 Homer, *The Iliad*, trans. E. V. Rieu (Harmondsworth: Penguin, 1960), p. 68. Analogous to this are Christopher Marlowe's famous lines: "Was this the face that launch'd a thousand ships, / And burnt the topless towers of Ilium?" (*Doctor Faustus*, 5.1.97).

79 Hans Robert Jauss, *Aesthetic Experience and Literary Hermeneutics*, trans. Michael Shaw (Minneapolis: University of Minnesota Press, 1982), p. 9.

80 Shen Deqian, ed., *Gu shi yuan* [A Sourcebook of Ancient Poetry] (Beijing: Zhonghua shuju, 1977), p. 73.

81 Xin Qiji, "Chou nu-er" [in the tune of "The Ugly Maid"], in *Song ci xuan* [Selection of *Ci* Lyrics from the Song Dynasty], ed. Hu Yunyi (Shanghai: Shanghai guji, 1962), p. 278.

82 Wordsworth, "Lines Written a Few Miles above Tintern Abbey," 90–92, in *The Oxford Authors*, p. 134.

83 Keats, "Ode on a Grecian Urn," 11–12, in *Complete Poems*, p. 282.

84 Wang Wei, *Wang youcheng ji jianzhu* [Works of Wang Wei], 2 vols., ed. Zhao Diancheng (1683–1756) (Shanghai: Zhonghua shuju, 1961), 1:255.

85 Ibid., 1:120.

86 Qu Yuan, "Yu fu" [The Fisherman], in *Chu ci jizhu* [Annotated Edition of the Songs of Chu], ed. Zhu Xi (1130–1200) (Shanghai: Shanghai guji, 1979), p. 117.

87 The same noncommittal attitude, that "nothing can be suitable and nothing cannot be suitable," is also what Wang Wei recommends to a friend of his. See his "Yu Wei jushi shu" [Letter to Mr. Wei], in *Wang youcheng ji* [Works], 2:334.

88 For a discussion of Wang Wei in relation to traditional Chinese criticism as well as Western literary theory, especially phenomenological criticism and symbolist poetics, see Pauline Yu, *The Poetry of Wang Wei: New Translations and Commentary* (Bloomington: Indiana University Press, 1980), in particular her "Critical Introduction," pp. 1–42.

89 Zhong Rong, preface to *Shi pin* [Ranking of Poetry], in *Lidai shihua* [Remarks on Poetry from Various Dynasties], ed. He Wenhuan, 1:2.

90 See Sikong Tu, *Shipin jijie* [The Moods of Poetry with Annotations], ed. Guo Shaoyu (Hong Kong: Shangwu, 1965), pp. 5, 19, 35.

91 Ibid., p. 21.

92 *Zhuangzi*, ii, p. 27.

93 Sikong Tu, "Yu Lisheng lun shi shu" [Letter to Mr. Li on Poetry], and "Yu Jipu dan shi shu" [Letter to Jipu on Poetry], in *Shipin jijie* [The Moods of Poetry], pp. 47, 48, 52.

94 Liu Xizai, *Yi gai* [The Principles of Art] (Shanghai: Shanghai guji, 1978), p. 73.

95 Martin Heidegger, *Being and Time*, trans. John Macquarrie and Edward Robinson (London: SCM Press, 1962), p. 208.

96 See Qian Zhongshu, *Tan yi lu* [Discourses on Art], pp. 414–15.

97 See Yan Yu, *Canglang shihua jiaoshi* [Canglang's Remarks on Poetry], ed. Guo Shaoyu (Beijing: Renmin wenxue, 1983), p. 12.

98 Ibid., p. 26.

99 Mei Shengyu, quoted in Ouyang Xiu (1007–72), *Shihua* [Remarks on Poetry], in *Ouyang Xiu quanji* [The Complete Works of Ouyang Xiu], 2 vols. (Shanghai: Shijie shuju, 1936), 2:1037.

100 Jiang Kui, *Baishi daoren shishuo* [The White-Stone Taoist's Discourse on Poetry], in *Lidai shihua* [Remarks on Poetry from Various Dynasties], ed. He Wenhuan, 2:681.

101 Su Shi, "Song Shenliao shi" [To the Reverend Shenliao], in *Su Shi shiji* [Collected Poems of Su Shi], 8 vols., ed. Wang Wengao (Beijing: Zhonghua shuju, 1987), 3:906.

102 Jauss, *Aesthetic Experience*, p. 9.

103 Tang Xianzu, "Rulan yiji xu" [Preface to the Collection of Rulan's Works], in *Tang Xianzu shi wen ji* [Collected Poems and Prose of Tang Xianzu], 2 vols. (Shanghai: Shanghai guji, 1982) 2:1062.

104 Paul Valéry, "Leonardo and the Philosophers," in *Collected Works*, 8:118. Quoted in Jauss, *Aesthetic Experience*, p. 55.

105 Jauss, *Aesthetic Experience*, p. 56.

106 Ibid., p. 57.

107 Ibid., p. 59.

108 Culler, *Structural Poetics*, p. 175.

109 Ibid., p. 164.

110 Jauss, *Aesthetic Experience*, p. 87.

111 Ibid., p. 88.

112 Ibid., p. 87.

113 Gadamer, "The Speechless Image," in *The Relevance*, p. 83.

114 Gadamer, "The Relevance of the Beautiful," in *The Relevance*, p. 26.

115 Ibid., p. 28.

116 Ibid., p. 29; see also Gadamer, *Truth and Method*, pp. 117ff.

117 Eliot, "The Music of Poetry," in *Selected Prose*, p. 110.

118 Gadamer, "The Relevance of the Beautiful," in *The Relevance*, p. 37.

119 Eliot, "The Music of Poetry," in *Selected Prose*, p. 111.

120 Gadamer, "Aesthetics and Hermeneutics," in *Philosophical Hermeneutics*, pp. 101, 102.

121 Du Fu, "Ou ti" [Random Subject], in *Du Shaoling ji xiangzhu* [The Works of Du Fu], 7:96.

122 John Milton, *Paradise Lost*, 7.31, in *Complete Poems and Major Prose*, ed. Merritt Y. Hughes (Indianapolis: Bobbs-Merrill, 1957), p. 346.

123 Eliot, "The Music of Poetry," in *Selected Prose*, p. 111.

124 Valéry, "Commentaries on *Charmes*," in *Collected Works*, 7:155–56.

125 Ingarden, *The Literary Work of Art*, p. 252; see also p. 337.

126 Ibid., p. 340.

127 Felix Vodička, "The Concretization of the Literary Work: Problems of the Reception of Neruda's Works," trans. John Burbank, in *The Prague School: Selected Writings, 1929–1946*, ed. Peter Steiner (Austin: University of Texas Press, 1982), p. 110.

128 Striedter, *Literary Structure, Evolution, and Value*, p. 124.

129 Ingarden, *The Literary Work of Art*, p. 334.

130 Ouyang Xiu, "Tang Xue Ji shu" [The Calligraphy of Xue Ji of the Tang Dynasty], in *Ouyang Xiu quanji* [The Complete Works of Ouyang Xiu], 2:1155.

131 *Zhouyi zhengyi* [The Book of Changes], in *Shisan jing zhushu* [Thirteen Classics], ed. Ruan Yuan, 66a, 1:78.

132 Jin Shengtan, *Jin Shengtan piben xixiang ji* [*The West Chamber Romance* with Jin Shengtan's Notes and Commentaries], ed. Zhang Guoguang (Shanghai: Shanghai guji, 1986), p. 10.

133 Ibid., pp. 17, 21.

134 Xue Xue, *Yipiao shihua* [Yipiao's Remarks on Poetry], in *Qing shihua* [Remarks on Poetry from the Qing Dynasty], 2 vols., ed. Ding Fubao (1874–1952) (Beijing: Zhonghua shuju, 1963), 2:714.

135 Wolfgang Iser, *The Act of Reading: A Theory of Aesthetic Response* (Baltimore: Johns Hopkins University Press, 1978), p. 22.

136 Stanley Fish, "Why No One's Afraid of Wolfgang Iser," *Diacritics* 11, no. 1 (1981): 7.

137 Fish, introduction to *Is There a Text?* p. 11.

138 Fish, "How to Recognize a Poem When You See One," in *Is There a Text?* p. 335.

139 See Striedter, *Literary Structure, Evolution, and Value*, p. 165.

140 Ibid., pp. 126, 158–59.

141 See Stanley Fish, *Surprised by Sin: The Reader in Paradise Lost* (Berkeley: University of California Press, 1971).

142 Steven Mailloux, "Truth or Consequences: On Being Against Theory," in *Against Theory*, ed. Mitchell, p. 67.

Epilogue: Toward Interpretive Pluralism

1 Conner, *Postmodernist Culture*, pp. 9–10.

2 Fish, "Literature in the Reader: Affective Stylistics," in *Is There a Text?* p. 43.

3 Richard McKeon, "Pluralism of Interpretations and Pluralism of Objects, Actions, and Statements Interpreted," *Critical Inquiry* 12, a special issue on "Pluralism and Its Discontents" (Spring 1986): 596.

4 W. J. T. Mitchell, "Pluralism as Dogmatism," *Critical Inquiry* 12 (Spring 1986): 497, 499.

5 Bruce Erlich, "Amphibolies: On the Critical Self-Contradictions of 'Pluralism,'" *Critical Inquiry* 12 (Spring 1986): 523.

6 Ellen Rooney, "Who's Left Out? A Rose by Any Other Name Is Still Red; Or, The Politics of Pluralism," *Critical Inquiry* 12 (Spring 1986): 561.

7 Gadamer, "Text and Interpretation," in *Dialogue and Deconstruction*, ed. Michelfelder

and Palmer, p. 110.

8 Gadamer, *Truth and Method*, p. 385.

9 Ibid., p. 161.

10 Ibid., p. 95.

11 Annabel Patterson, "Intention," in *Critical Terms for Literary Study*, ed. Lentricchia and McLaughlin, p. 141.

12 Ibid., p. 143.

13 Ibid., p. 145.

14 Ibid., p. 144.

15 Mencius, *Mengzi zhengyi* [The Works of Mencius], 7b, p. 594.

16 *Zhouyi zhengyi* [The Book of Changes], in *Shisan jing zhushu* [Thirteen Classics], ed. Ruan Yuan, 77b, 1:89.

17 Dong Zhongshu, *Chunqiu fanlu* [The Luxuriant Gems of Spring and Autumn] (Shanghai: Shangwu, 1926), p. 6b.

18 Shen Deqian, *Tang shi biecai* [A Selection of Tang Poetry], 4 vols. (Beijing: Zhonghua shuju, 1964), 1:1.

19 Wang Fuzhi, *Jiangzhai shihua jianzhu* [Annotated Jiangzhai's Remarks on Poetry], ed. Dai Hongsen (Beijing: Renmin wenxue, 1981), pp. 4, 5.

20 Xie Zhen, *Siming shihua* [Siming's Remarks on Poetry], in *Lidai shihua xubian* [A Sequel to Remarks on Poetry from Various Dynasties], 3 vols., ed. Ding Fubao (Beijing: Zhonghua shuju, 1983), p. 1137.

Bibliography

Works in Western Languages

Abrams, M. H. *The Mirror and the Lamp: Romantic Theory and the Critical Tradition.* Oxford: Oxford Universtiy Press, 1953.

Aristotle. *"Poetics," with the "Tractatus Coislinianus," Reconstruction of "Poetics II," and the Fragments of the "On Poets."* Trans. Richard Janko. Indianapolis: Hackett, 1987.

Auerbach, Erich. *Mimesis: The Representation of Reality in Western Literature.* Trans. Willard R. Trask. Princeton: Princeton University Press, 1953.

Augustine, St. *Of Christian Doctrine.* Trans. D. W. Robertson, Jr. Indianapolis: Bobbs-Merrill, 1958.

Austin, Lloyd. *Poetic Principles and Practice: Occasional Papers on Baudelaire, Mallarmé and Valéry.* Cambridge: Cambridge University Press, 1987.

Baron, Frank, Ernst S. Dick, and Warren R. Maurer, eds. *Rilke: The Alchemy of Alienation.* Lawrence: Regents Press of Kansas, 1980.

Barthes, Roland. *Image-Music-Text.* Trans. Stephen Heath. New York: Hill and Wang, 1977.

———. *The Pleasure of the Text.* Trans. Richard Miller. New York: Hill and Wang, 1975.

———. *S/Z.* Trans. Richard Miller. New York: Hill and Wang, 1974.

Bell, Ian F. A., ed. *Ezra Pound: Tactics for Reading.* London: Vision, 1982.

Birch, Cyril, ed. *Studies in Chinese Literary Genres.* Berkeley: University of California Press, 1974.

Bloom, Harold, ed. *Modern Critical Views: T. S. Eliot.* New York: Chelsea, 1985.

Borges, Jorge Luis. *Twenty-Four Conversations with Borges, Including a Selection of Poems.* Interviewed by Roberto Alifano. Trans. Nicomedes Suárez Araúz et al. Housatonic, Mass.: Lascaux, 1984.

Buber, Martin. *Ecstatic Confessions.* Trans. Esther Cameron. New York: Harper & Row, 1985.

Burnshaw, Stanley. *Robert Frost Himself.* New York: George Braziller, 1986.

Cassirer, Ernst. *Language and Myth.* Trans. Susanne K. Langer. New York: Harper & Brothers, 1946.

Chang, Kang-i Sun. *Six Dynasties Poetry*. Princeton: Princeton University Press, 1986.

Chang, Kwang-chih. *Art, Myth, and Ritual: The Path to Political Authority in Ancient China*. Cambridge, Mass.: Harvard University Press, 1983.

Cohn, Robert Greer. *Toward the Poems of Mallarmé*. Berkeley: University of California Press, 1965.

Conner, Steven. *Postmodernist Culture: An Introduction to Theories of the Contemporary*. Oxford: Basil Blackwell, 1989.

Culler, Jonathan. *Structural Poetics: Structuralism, Linguistics and the Study of Literature*. London: Routledge & Kegan Paul, 1975.

Curtius, Ernst Robert. *European Literature and the Latin Middle Ages*. Trans. Willard R. Trask. Princeton: Princeton University Press, 1973.

Dante Alighieri. *Literary Criticism of Dante Alighieri*. Trans. Robert S. Haller. Lincoln: University of Nebraska Press, 1973.

De Man, Paul. *Allegories of Reading: Figural Language in Rousseau, Nietzsche, Rilke, and Proust*. New Haven: Yale University Press, 1979.

Derrida, Jacques. *Dissemination*. Trans. Barbara Johnson. Chicago: University of Chicago Press, 1981.

———. *Margins of Philosophy*. Trans. Alan Bass. Chicago: University of Chicago Press, 1982.

———. *Of Grammatology*. Trans. Gayatri Chakravorty Spivak. Baltimore: Johns Hopkins University Press, 1976.

———. *Positions*. Trans. Alan Bass. Chicago: University of Chicago Press, 1981.

Dilthey, Wilhelm. *Gesammelte Schriften*. 17 vols. Stuttgart: B. G. Teubner; Göttingen: Vandenhoeck & Ruprecht, 1914–74.

———. "The Rise of Hermeneutics." Trans. Fredric Jameson. *New Literary History* 3 (Winter 1972): 229–44.

———. *Selected Works*. Ed. Rudolf A. Makkreel and Frithjof Rodi. Vol. 5, *Poetry and Experience*. Princeton: Princeton University Press, 1985.

Eckhart. *Meister Eckhart: A Modern Translation*. Trans. Raymond Bernard Blakney. New York: Harper & Brothers, 1941.

Eco, Umberto. *Art and Beauty in the Middle Ages*. Trans. Hugh Bredin. New Haven: Yale University Press, 1986.

Eliot, T. S. *The Complete Poems and Plays: 1909–1950*. New York: Harcourt, Brace & World, 1971.

———. *Selected Prose of T. S. Eliot*. Ed. Frank Kermode. New York: Harcourt Brace Jovanovich, 1975.

Erlich, Bruce. "Amphibolies: On the Critical Self-Contradictions of 'Pluralism.'" *Critical Inquiry* 12 (Spring 1986): 521–49.

Fenollosa, Ernest. *The Chinese Written Character as a Medium for Poetry*. Ed. Ezra Pound. San Francisco: City Lights Books, 1969.

Fineman, Joel. *Shakespeare's Perjured Eye: The Invention of Poetic Subjectivity in the Sonnets*. Berkeley: University of California Press, 1986.

Fish, Stanley. *Is There a Text in This Class? The Authority of Interpretive Communities.* Cambridge, Mass.: Harvard University Press, 1980.

——. *Surprised by Sin: The Reader in Paradise Lost.* Berkeley: University of California Press, 1971.

——. "Why No One's Afraid of Wolfgang Iser." *Diacritics* 11, no.1 (1981): 2–13.

Foucault, Michel. *Language, Counter-Memory, Practice: Selected Essays and Interviews.* Ed. Donald F. Bouchard. Trans. Bouchard and Sherry Simon. Ithaca, N.Y.: Cornell University Press, 1977.

——. *The Order of Things: An Archaeology of the Human Sciences.* New York: Vintage, 1973.

Franklin, Ursula. "The Angel in Valéry and Rilke." *Comparative Literature* 35 (Summer 1983): 215–46.

Freud, Sigmund. *Collected Papers.* 5 vols. Authorized translation under the supervision of Joan Riviere. New York: Basic Books, 1959.

Frye, Northrop. *Anatomy of Criticism: Four Essays.* Princeton: Princeton University Press, 1957.

Gadamer, Hans-Georg. *Gesammelte Werke.* Vols. 1 and 2, *Hermeneutik.* Tübingen: J. C. B. Mohr (Paul Siebeck), 1986.

——. *Philosophical Hermeneutics.* Ed. and trans. David E. Linge. Berkeley: University of California Press, 1977.

——. *The Relevance of the Beautiful and Other Essays.* Ed. Robert Bernasconi. Trans. Nicholas Walker. Cambridge: Cambridge University Press, 1986.

——. *Truth and Method.* 2d rev. ed. English translation revised by Joel Weinsheimer and Donald G. Marshall. New York: Crossroad, 1991.

Gardner, Helen. *The Art of T. S. Eliot.* New York: E. P. Dutton, 1950.

Garvin, Paul L., trans. *A Prague School Reader on Esthetics, Literary Structure, and Style.* Washington, D. C.: Georgetown University Press, 1964.

Hegel, Georg Wilhelm Friedrich. *The Phenomenology of Mind.* 2d rev. ed. Trans. J. B. Baillie. London: George Allen & Unwin, 1949.

——. *The Philosophy of History.* Rev. ed. Trans. J. Sibree. New York: Willey, 1944.

——. *Science of Logic.* Trans. A. V. Miller. New York: Humanities Press, 1976.

Heidegger, Martin. *Being and Time.* Trans. John Macquarrie and Edward Robinson. London: SCM Press, 1962.

——. *Poetry, Language, Thought.* Trans. Albert Hofstadter. New York: Harper & Row, 1975.

Heraclitus. *The Art and Thought of Heraclitus: An Edition of the Fragments with Translation and Commentary.* Ed. and trans. Charles H. Kahn. Cambridge: Cambridge University Press, 1979.

Hernadi, Paul ed. *What Is Criticism?* Bloomington: Indiana University Press, 1981.

Hirsch, E. D. *The Aims of Interpretation.* Chicago: University of Chicago Press, 1976.

——. "Meaning and Significance Reinterpreted." *Critical Inquiry* 11 (December 1984): 202–25.

————. *Validity in Interpretation.* New Haven: Yale University Press, 1967.

Holthusen, Hans Egon. *Rainer Maria Rilke: A Study of His Later Poetry.* Trans. J. P. Stern. Cambridge: Bowes & Bowes, 1952.

Homer. *The Iliad.* Trans. E. V. Rieu. Harmondsworth: Penguin, 1960.

Huppé, Bernard F. *Doctrine and Poetry: Augustine's Influence on Old English Poetry.* New York: State University of New York Press, 1959.

Ingarden, Roman. *The Literary Work of Art: An Investigation on the Borderlines of Ontology, Logic, and Theory of Literature.* Trans. George G. Grabowicz. Evanston, Ill.: Northwestern University Press, 1973.

Iser, Wolfgang. *The Act of Reading: A Theory of Aesthetic Response.* Baltimore: Johns Hopkins University Press, 1978.

Janik, Allan, and Stephen Toulmin. *Wittgenstein's Vienna.* New York: Simon & Schuster, 1973.

Jauss, Hans Robert. *Aesthetic Experience and Literary Hermeneutics.* Trans. Michael Shaw. Minneapolis: University of Minnesota Press, 1982.

————. *Toward an Aesthetic of Reception.* Trans. Timothy Bahti. Minneapolis: University of Minnesota Press, 1982.

Kant, Immanuel. *Critique of Judgment.* Trans. Werner S. Pluhar. Indianapolis: Hackett, 1987.

Keats, John. *Complete Poems.* Ed. Jack Stillinger. Cambridge, Mass.: Harvard University Press, 1982.

Kennedy, George A. *Selected Works of George A. Kennedy.* Ed. Tien-yi Li. New Haven: Yale University Press, 1964.

Komar, Kathleen L. *Transcending Angels: Rainer Maria Rilke's Duino Elegies.* Lincoln: University of Nebraska Press, 1987.

Lemon, Lee T., and Marion J. Reis, trans. *Russian Formalist Criticism: Four Essays.* Lincoln: University of Nebraska Press, 1965.

Lentricchia, Frank, and Thomas McLaughlin, eds. *Critical Terms for Literary Study.* Chicago: University of Chicago Press, 1990.

Lin, Shuen-fu, and Stephen Owen, eds. *The Vitality of the Lyric Voice: Shih Poetry from the Late Han to the T'ang.* Princeton: Princeton University Press, 1986.

Liu, James J. Y. *Chinese Theories of Literature.* Chicago: University of Chicago Press, 1975.

————. *Language-Paradox-Poetics: A Chinese Perspective.* Ed. Richard John Lynn. Princeton: Princeton University Press, 1988.

Lyotard, Jean-François. *The Postmodern Condition: A Report on Knowledge.* Trans. Geoff Bennington and Brian Massumi. Minneapolis: University of Minnesota Press, 1984.

MacIntyre, C. F., trans. *French Symbolist Poetry.* Berkeley: University of California Press, 1958.

McKeon, Richard. "Pluralism of Interpretations and Pluralism of Objects, Actions, and Statements Interpreted." *Critical Inquiry* 12 (Spring 1986): 577–96.

Makkreel, Rudolf A. *Dilthey: Philosopher of the Human Studies.* Princeton: Princeton University Press, 1975.

Mallarmé, Stéphane. *Correspondance*. Vol. 1. Ed. Henri Mondor with Jean-Pierre Richard. Paris: Gallimard, 1959.

———. *Correspondance*. Vol. 2. Ed. Henri Mondor and Lloyd James Austin. Paris: Gallimard, 1965.

———. *Oeuvres complètes*. Ed. Henri Mondor and G. Jean-Aubry. Paris: Gallimard, 1945.

Mauthner, Fritz. *Der Atheismus und seine Geschichte im Abendlande*. 4 vols. Stuttgart: Deutsche Verlag-Anstalt, 1922–23.

———. *Beiträge zu einer Kritik der Sprache*. 3 vols. 3d ed. Leipzig: Felix Meiner, 1922–23.

———. *Wörterbuch der Philosophie: Neue Beiträge zu einer Kritik der Sprache*. 2 vols. Munich: Georg Müller, 1910.

Michaud, Guy. *Mallarmé*. Trans. Marie Collins and Bertha Humez. New York: New York University Press, 1965.

Michelfelder, Diane P., and Richard E. Palmer, eds. *Dialogue and Deconstruction: The Gadamer-Derrida Encounter*. Albany: State University of New York Press, 1989.

Milton, John. *Complete Poems and Major Prose*. Ed. Merritt Y. Hughes. Indianapolis: Bobbs-Merrill, 1957.

Mitchell, W. J. T. *Iconology: Image, Text, Ideology*. Chicago: University of Chicago Press, 1986.

———. "Pluralism as Dogmatism." *Critical Inquiry* 12 (Spring 1986): 494–502.

———, ed. *Against Theory: Literary Studies and the New Pragmatism*. Chicago: University of Chicago Press, 1985.

Montaigne, Michel de. *Essays*. Trans. J. M. Cohen. Harmondsworth: Penguin, 1958.

Mueller-Vollmer, Kurt, ed. *The Hermeneutics Reader: Texts of the German Tradition from the Enlightenment to the Present*. New York: Continuum, 1985.

Norris, Christopher. *Derrida*. Cambridge, Mass.: Harvard University Press, 1987.

Plato. *The Collected Dialogues, Including the Letters*. Ed. Edith Hamilton and Huntington Cairns. Princeton: Princeton University Press, 1963.

Poggioli, Renato. *The Theory of the Avant-Garde*. Trans. Gerald Fitzgerald. Cambridge, Mass.: Harvard University Press, 1968.

Pound, Ezra. *Selected Poems*. Ed. T. S. Eliot. London: Faber and Gwyer, 1928.

———, trans. *The Confucian Analects*. London: Peter Owen, 1956.

Ramanan, K. Venkata. *Nagarjuna's Philosophy as Presented in the Maha-Prajñaparamita-Sastra*. Rutland, Vt.: C. E. Tuttle, 1966.

Redeker, Martin. *Friedrich Schleiermacher: Leben und Werk*. Berlin: Walter de Gruyter, 1968.

Ricoeur, Paul. *Hermeneutics and the Human Sciences*. Ed. and trans. John B. Thompson. Cambridge: Cambridge University Press, 1981.

Rilke, Rainer Maria. *Sämtliche Werke*. 6 vols. Ed. Ernst Zinn. Wiesbaden: Insel, 1955–66.

———. *The Selected Poetry of Rainer Maria Rilke*. Ed. and trans. Stephen Mitchell. New York: Vintage, 1982.

———. *The Sonnets to Orpheus*. Trans. Stephen Mitchell. New York: Simon & Schuster, 1986.

Ritter, Joachim, and Karlfried Gründer, eds. *Historisches Wörterbuch der Philosophie.* Vol. 5. Basel: Schwabe, 1980.

Rooney, Ellen. "Who's Left Out? A Rose by Any Other Name Is Still Red; Or, The Politics of Pluralism." *Critical Inquiry* 12 (Spring 1986): 550–63.

Rorty, Richard. "Philosophy as a Kind of Writing: An Essay on Derrida." *New Literary History* 10 (Autumn 1978): 141–60.

Rose, William, and G. Craig Houston, eds. *Rainer Maria Rilke: Aspects of His Mind and Poetry.* London: Sidgwick & Jackson, 1938.

Saussure, Ferdinand de. *Course in General Linguistics.* Trans. Wade Baskin. New York: Philosophical Library, 1959.

Schiller, Friedrich. *Werke.* 6 vols. Ed. Alfred Brandstetter. Zürich: Stauffacher, 1967.

Schleiermacher, Friedrich. *Hermeneutics: The Handwritten Manuscripts.* Trans. James Duke and Jack Forstman. Missoula, Mont.: Scholars Press, 1977.

———. *Hermeneutik: Nach den Handschriften.* Ed. Heinz Kimmerle. Heidelberg: Carl Winter, 1974.

———. *Introductions to the Dialogues of Plato.* Trans. William Dobson. New York: Arno Press, 1973.

Schopenhauer, Arthur. *On the Fourfold Root of the Principle of Sufficient Reason.* Trans. E. F. J. Payne. La Salle, Ill.: Open Court, 1974.

———. *Werke.* 2 vols. Ed. Werner Brede. Munich: Carl Hanser, 1977.

Schwarz, Egon. *Poetry and Politics in the Works of Rainer Maria Rilke.* Trans. David E. Wellbery. New York: Frederick Ungar, 1981.

Shakespeare, William. *The Riverside Shakespeare.* Ed. G. Blakemore Evans et al. Boston: Houghton Mifflin, 1974.

Shelley, Percy Bysshe. *Shelley's Critical Prose.* Ed. Bruce R. McElderry. Lincoln: University of Nebraska Press, 1967.

Sidney, Sir Philip. *An Apology for Poetry.* Ed. Forrest G. Robinson. Indianapolis: Bobbs-Merrill, 1970.

Simpson, David, ed. *German Aesthetic and Literary Criticism: Kant, Fichte, Schelling, Schopenhauer, Hegel.* Cambridge: Cambridge University Press, 1984.

Smith, Barbara Herrnstein. *On the Margins of Discourse: The Relation of Literature to Language.* Chicago: University of Chicago Press, 1978.

———. *Poetic Closure: A Study of How Poems End.* Chicago: University of Chicago Press, 1968.

Smith, Hallett. *The Tension of the Lyre: Poetry in Shakespeare's Sonnets.* San Marino, Calif.: Huntington Library, 1981.

Spurr, David. *Conflicts in Consciousness: T. S. Eliot's Poetry and Criticism.* Urbana: University of Illinois Press, 1984.

Steiner, Peter, ed. *The Prague School: Selected Writings, 1929–1946.* Austin: University of Texas Press, 1982.

Storck, Joachim W. "Poesie und Schweigen: Zum Enigmatischen in Rilkes später Lyrik." *Blätter der Rilke-Gesellschaft,* no. 10 (1983): 107–21.

Striedter, Jurij. *Literary Structure, Evolution, and Value: Russian Formalism and Czech Structuralism Reconsidered.* Cambridge, Mass.: Harvard University Press, 1989.

Suzuki, D. T. *Essays in Zen Buddhism.* 1st series. London: Luzac, 1927.

Ullmann, Stephen. *Principles of Semantics.* Oxford: Basil Blackwell, 1963.

———. *Semantics: An Introduction to the Science of Meaning.* New York: Barnes & Noble, 1964.

Valéry, Paul. *The Collected Works of Paul Valéry.* 15 vols. Ed. Jackson Mathews. Princeton: Princeton University Press, 1956–75.

Vico, Giambattista. *The New Science.* Trans. Thomas G. Bergin and Max H. Fisch. Ithaca, N.Y. : Cornell University Press, 1976.

Vossler, Karl. *The Spirit of Language in Civilization.* Trans. Oscar Oeser. New York: Harcourt, Brace & Co., 1932.

Weiler, Gershon. *Mauthner's Critique of Language.* Cambridge: Cambridge Univeristy Press, 1970.

Wellek, René. *Concepts of Criticism.* Ed. Stephen G. Nichols, Jr. New Haven: Yale University Press, 1963.

———. *A History of Modern Criticism: 1750–1950.* New Haven: Yale University Press, 1955.

Wilson, A. Leslie, ed. *German Romantic Criticism.* New York: Continuum, 1982.

Wimsatt, William K. *The Verbal Icon.* Lexington: University of Kentucky Press, 1954.

Wittgenstein, Ludwig. *Philosophical Investigations.* 3d ed. Trans. G. E. M. Anscombe. Oxford: Basil Blackwell, 1968.

———. *Tractatus Logico-Philosophicus.* Trans. C. K. Ogden. London: Routledge & Kegan Paul, 1983.

Wordsworth, William. *The Oxford Authors: William Wordsworth.* Ed. Stephen Gill. Oxford: Oxford University Press, 1984.

Yeats, William Butler. *Collected Poems.* New York: Macmillan, 1956.

Yu, Pauline. *The Poetry of Wang Wei: New Translations and Commentary.* Bloomington: Indiana University Press, 1980.

Works in Chinese

All ancient Chinese texts are quoted from modern reprinted editions. Most Chinese classics are quoted from the 1954 edition of *Zhuzi jicheng* [Collection of Classics], 8 vols, Beijing: Zhonghua shuju, 1954; rpt. 1986. As this edition does not have a consistent pagination in each volume but has pages numbered separately for each work, I indicate the specific volume number of the *Zhuzi jicheng* edition when a work is cited, and the page number refers to the internal pagination of the work itself.

Cai Zhengsun (fl. 1279). *Shilin guangji* [In the Woods of Poetry]. Beijing: Zhonghua shuju, 1982.

Chen Yinke (1890–1969). *Jinmingguan conggao chubian* [Chen's Essays, First Series].

Shanghai: Shanghai guji, 1980.

Confucius (551–479 B.C.). *Lunyu zhengyi* [The Analects with Exegesis]. Ed. Liu Baonan (1791–1855). In vol. 1 of *Zhuzi jicheng*. (See Confucius, *The Analects*, trans. D. C. Lau, Harmondsworth: Penguin, 1979.)

Ding Fubao (1874–1952), ed. *Lidai shihua xubian* [A Sequel to Remarks on Poetry from Various Dynasties]. 3 vols. Beijing: Zhonghua shuju, 1983.

———, ed. *Qing shihua* [Remarks on Poetry from the Qing Dynasty]. 2 vols. Beijing: Zhonghua shuju, 1963.

Dong Zhongshu (179?–93 B.C.). *Chunqiu fanlu* [The Luxuriant Gems of Spring and Autumn]. Shanghai: Shangwu, 1926.

Du Fu (712–770). *Du Shaoling ji xiangzhu* [Annotated Works of Du Fu]. 10 vols. Ed. Qiu Zhao–ao (fl. 1685). Beijing: Wenxue guji, 1955.

Fang Dongshu (1772–1851). *Zhao mei zhan yan* [Verbiage at Morn and Dusk]. Beijing: Renmin wenxue, 1961.

Ge Hong (283?–343). *Baopuzi* [The Work of Baopuzi]. In vol. 8 of *Zhuzi jicheng.*

He Wenhuan (1732–1809), ed. *Lidai shihua* [Remarks on Poetry from Various Dynasties]. 2 vols. Beijing: Zhonghua shuju, 1981.

Hu Yunyi, ed. *Song ci xuan* [Selection of *Ci* Lyrics from the Song Dynasty]. Shanghai: Shanghai guji, 1962.

Jin Shengtan (1610?–1661). *Jin Shengtan piben xixiang ji* [*The West Chamber Romance* with Jin Shengtan's Notes and Commentaries]. Ed. Zhang Guoguang. Shanghai: Shanghai guji, 1986.

Laozi (571?–? B.C.). *Laozi zhu* [The Annotated Laozi]. Ed. Wang Bi (226–49). In vol. 3 of *Zhuzi jicheng.* (See Lao Tzu, *Tao Te Ching*, trans. D. C. Lau, Harmondsworth: Penguin, 1963.)

Li Shangyin (813?–58). *Li Shangyin xuanji* [Selected Works of Li Shangyin]. Ed. Zhou Zhenfu. Shanghai: Shanghai guji, 1986. (See James J. Y. Liu, *The Poetry of Li Shangyin: Ninth-Century Baroque Chinese Poet*, Chicago: University of Chicago Press, 1969.)

Liu An (178?–122 B.C.). *Huainanzi* [The Master of Huainan]. Ed. Gao You (fl. 205?–12). In vol. 7 of *Zhuzi jicheng.*

Liu Xie (465?–522). *Wenxin diaolong zhushi* [The Literary Mind or the Carving of Dragons]. Ed. Zhou Zhenfu. Beijing: Renmin wenxue, 1981.

Liu Xizai (1813–81). *Yi gai* [The Principles of Art]. Shanghai: Shanghai guji, 1978.

Lu Jiuyuan (1139–93). *Lu Jiuyuan ji* [The Collected Works of Lu Jiuyuan]. Beijing: Zhonghua shuju, 1980.

Lü Buwei (290–235 B.C.). *Lüshi chunqiu* [Lü's Spring and Autumn]. Ed. Gao You. In vol. 6 of *Zhuzi jicheng.*

Mencius (371?–289 B.C.). *Mengzi zhengyi* [The Works of Mencius with Exegesis]. Ed. Jiao Xun (1763–1820). In vol. 1 of *Zhuzi jicheng*. (See *Mencius*, trans. D. C. Lau, Harmondsworth: Penguin, 1970.)

Ouyang Xiu (1007–72). *Ouyang Xiu quanji* [The Complete Works of Ouyang Xiu]. 2 vols.

Shanghai: Shijie shuju, 1936.

Qian Zhongshu (1910–). *Guan zhui bian* [Pipe-Awl Chapters]. 4 vols. Beijing: Zhonghua shuju, 1979.

———. *Tan yi lu* [Discourses on Art]. Enlarged ed. Beijing: Zhonghua shuju, 1984.

Ruan Yuan (1764–1849), ed. *Shisan jing zhushu* [Thirteen Classics with Annotations]. 2 vols. Beijing: Zhonghua shuju, 1980. (See *The Chinese Classics*, trans. James Legge, 5 vols, 2d revised ed, Oxford: Oxford University Press, 1893–95.)

Shen Deqian (1673–1769), ed. *Gu shi yuan* [A Sourcebook of Ancient Poetry]. Beijing: Zhonghua shuju, 1977.

———, ed. *Tang shi biecai* [A Selection of Tang Poetry]. 4 vols. Beijing: Zhonghua shuju, 1964.

Shen Yue (441–513). *Song shu* [History of the Song Dynasty]. 8 vols. Beijing: Zhonghua shuju, 1974.

Sikong Tu (837–908). *Shipin jijie* [The Moods of Poetry with Annotations]. Ed. Guo Shaoyu. Hong Kong: Shangwu, 1965.

Su Shi (1037–1101). *Su Shi shiji* [Collected Poems of Su Shi]. 8 vols. Ed. Wang Wengao. Beijing: Zhonghua shuju, 1987.

———. *Su Shi wenji* [Collected Prose Works of Su Shi]. 6 vols. Ed. Kong Fanli. Beijing: Zhonghua shuju, 1986.

Tang Xianzu (1550–1616). *Tang Xianzu shi wen ji* [Collected Poems and Prose of Tang Xianzu]. 2 vols. Shanghai: Shanghai guji, 1982.

Tao Qian (365–427). *Tao Yuanming ji* [Tao Yuanming's Works]. Ed. Lu Qinli. Beijing: Zhonghua shuju, 1979. (See *The Poetry of T'ao Ch'ien*, trans. James R. Hightower, Oxford: Oxford University Press, 1970.)

Xiao Tong (501–31) ed. *Wen xuan* [A Literary Anthology]. 3 vols. Annotated by Li Shan (c. 630–89). Beijing: Zhonghua shuju, 1977. (See *Wen xuan or Selection of Refined Literature*, 2 vols, trans. David R. Knechtges, Princeton: Princeton University Press, 1982.)

Wang Fuzhi (1619–92). *Jiangzhai shihua jianzhu* [Annotated Jiangzhai's Remarks on Poetry]. Ed. Dai Hongsen. Beijing: Renmin wenxue, 1981.

Wang Wei (701–61). *Wang youcheng ji jianzhu* [Works of Wang Wei]. 2 vols. Ed. Zhao Diancheng (1683–1756). Shanghai: Zhonghua shuju, 1961. (See Pauline Yu, *The Poetry of Wang Wei: New Translations and Commentary*, Bloomington: Indiana University Press, 1980.)

Wei Yuan (1794–1857). *Laozi benyi* [The Original Meaning of the Laozi]. In vol. 3 of *Zhuzi jicheng*.

Yan Yu (1195?–1245). *Canglang shihua jiaoshi* [Canglang's Remarks on Poetry]. Ed. Guo Shaoyu. Beijing: Renmin wenxue, 1983.

Zhu Xi (1130–1200). *Zhuzi yulei* [Sayings of Zhuzi]. 8 vols. Taipei: Cheng Chung Book Co., 1982.

———, ed. *Chu ci jizhu* [Annotated Edition of the Songs of Chu]. Shanghai: Shanghai guji, 1979. (See *The Songs of the South: An Ancient Chinese Anthology of Poems by Qu*

Yuan and Other Poets, trans. David Hawkes, Harmondsworth: Penguin, 1985.)

Zhu Ziqing (1898–1948). *Zhu Ziqing gudian wenxue zhuanji* [Zhu Ziqing's Writings on Classical Chinese Literature]. 4 vols. Shanghai: Shanghai guji, 1981.

Zhuangzi (369?–286? B.C.). *Zhuangzi jishi* [Variorum Edition of the Zhuangzi]. Ed. Guo Qingfan (1844–95?). In vol. 3 of *Zhuzi jicheng*. (See *The Complete Works of Chuang Tzu*, trans. Burton Watson, New York: Columbia University Press, 1968.)

Index

About the Author

Zhang Longxi is Assistant Professor of Comparative Literature at the University of California, Riverside. His publications include *A Critical Introduction to Twentieth-Century Western Theories
of Literature* (in Chinese).

Library of Congress Cataloging-in-Publication
Data
Chang, Lung-hsi.
The Tao and the Logos : literary hermeneutics,
East and West / Zhang Longxi.
p.   cm. — (Post-contemporary
interventions.)
Includes bibliographical references and index.
ISBN 0-8223-1211-5 (cloth : alk. paper). —
ISBN 0-8223-1218-2 (paper : alk. paper)
1. Literature, Comparative.   2. Literature,
Comparative—Chinese and European.
3. Language and languages—Philosophy.
4. Hermeneutics.   5. Criticism, Textual.
I. Title.   II. Series.
PN871.C545   1992
809—dc20   91-37126 CIP